Topics and Issues in National Cinema

Volume 4

Aesthetics of Displacement:
Turkey and its Minorities on Screen

Topics and Issues in National Cinema

Other volumes in the series:

Aesthetics of Displacement: Turkey and its Minorities on Screen

Özlem Köksal

Bloomsbury Academic
An imprint of Bloomsbury Publishing Inc

B L O O M S B U R Y
NEW YORK · LONDON · OXFORD · NEW DELHI · SYDNEY

Bloomsbury Academic

An imprint of Bloomsbury Publishing Inc

1385 Broadway	50 Bedford Square
New York	London
NY 10018	WC1B 3DP
USA	UK

www.bloomsbury.com

**BLOOMSBURY and the Diana logo are trademarks of
Bloomsbury Publishing Plc**

First published 2016

Library of Congress Cataloging-in-Publication Data
Köksal, Özlem.
Aesthetics of displacement : Turkey and its minorities on screen / Ozlem Koksal.
pages cm. – (Topics and issues in national cinema ; volume 4)
Includes bibliographical references and index.
ISBN 978-1-5013-0646-4 (hardback)
1. Minorities in motion pictures. 2. Motion pictures–Turkey–History and criticism.
I. Title.
PN1995.9.M56K66 2016
791.43'6529009561–dc23
2015027498

ISBN:	HB:	9781501306464
	ePub:	9781501306495
	ePDF:	9781501306488

Series: Topics and Issues in National Cinema

Typeset by Fakenham Prepress Solutions, Fakenham, Norfolk NR21 8NN
Printed and bound in the United States of America

To Engin Köksal and Fabio Sartori

Contents

List of figures

Acknowledgments

Writing of this book spans to several years, which begun life as a PhD project at the London Consortium, Birkbeck College. I benefited a great deal from faculty, and my fellow students for creating an intellectually stimulating environment. I have learnt a lot from them. I am also extremely grateful for the financial support I received from the London Consortium during my PhD.

I am particularly indebted to my supervisor Prof. Laura Mulvey who, throughout the duration of my PhD, thought me a great deal. She not only encouraged me and guided me but also influenced my thinking greatly. I would also like to thank Prof. Deniz Kandiyoti, Prof. Asuman Suner and Prof. Chris Berry for their comments, criticisms and support at different stages of this project. Hamid Naficy and Daniela Berghahn, who examined the final thesis, have also provided encouragement and valuable comments, which I benefited while working on the manuscript.

In 2012 the thesis was awarded the best dissertation award written on Turkey by the London School of Economics' Turkish Chair. I thank the award committee Şevket Pamuk, Deniz Kandiyoti and Hakan Seçkinelgin for giving me the final push to turn the dissertation into a manuscript.

During the research and writing stages I have enjoyed the generosity of many people. I would particularly like to thank Canan Balan, Umut Tümay Arslan, Devrim Kılıçer, Ümit Ünal, Miraz Bezar, Hüseyin Karabey, Louise Spence and Mustafa Gündoğdu for their time, help and understanding. I also thank to the series editor Armida de la Garza for her suggestions.

Arguments in this book were presented at various occasions. I thank the participants of Modern Language Association Annual Convention, Philadelphia (December 2009); Amsterdam School of Cultural Analysis Workshop, (March 2010); Screen Conference University of Glasgow (July 2010) and Boğaziçi University ATA institute (2014). An earlier, and shorter, version of chapter 4 was published in *Cinema Journal* 54:1 (Fall, 2014). I thank the journal for permission to reproduce material here.

Finally, I would like to express my gratitude to my friends and family. I thank Armagan Uslu, Ozan Varışlı and Özgür Tuncay for their friendship, to Eylem

Atakav for listening what I had to (and didn't have to) say, to Gökçen Çamlıyurt for always being there and providing unconditional support and love, to Tuna Erdem and Seda Ergül for being who they are, and to Richard Martin and Benjamin Dawson for their intellect and for the joy they bring. I am grateful beyond words to Ipek A. Çelik for not only reading the entire manuscript and providing me with detailed comments but also for her encouragement, support and friendship.

I am also thankful to Nafi Mitrani for helping me keep my self together when it was the most difficult to do so and for reminding me of the possibility of changing someone's life without expecting anything in return. My final thanks go to my family, particularly to my sister Duygu for her support and to my cousin Sinem for her understanding and help, and to everyone else in my family who put up with me during my worst moments.

This book is dedicated to my mother Engin Köksal for teaching me to be compassionate and to Fabio Sartori for the years long support, understanding and love. Without them I could not have possibly finish this project.

Abbreviations/Acronyms

ASALA: Armenian Secret Army for the Liberation of Armenia

ASAM: Centre for Eurasian Strategic Studies [*Avrasya Stratejik Araştırmalar Merkezi*]

AKP: Adalet ve Kalkinma Partisi [Justice and Development Party]

AP: Adalet Partisi [Justice Party]

BDP: Peace and Democracy Party [*Barış ve Demokrasi Partisi*]

CUP: Committee of Union and Progress [*İttihat ve Terakki*]

CHP: Republican People's Party [*Cumhuriyet Halk Partisi*]

DEHAP: Democratic People's Party [*Demokratik Halk Partisi*]

DP: Democratic Party [*Demokrat Parti*]

EU: European Union

HADEP: People's Democratic Party [*Halkın Demokrasi Partisi*]

JITEM: Gendarmerie Intelligence and Counter-Terror Service [*Jandarma İstihbarat ve Terörle Mücadele*]

PKK: Kurdistan Worker's Party [*Partiya Karkeren Kurdistan*]

OYAK: Armed Forces Pension Fund [*Ordu Yardımlaşma Kurumu*]

TRT: Turkish Broadcasting Corporation [*Türkiye Radyo Televizyon Kurumu*]

ANAP: Motherland Party [*Anavatan Partisi*]

Introduction

I grew up in Turkey in the 1980s, and my knowledge of Turkish history was limited, predominantly, to the information disseminated by the education system, which provided a binding, unifying narrative. Although at times a contradictory piece of information would enter into my world, I was, nevertheless, equipped with the necessary unifying narrative to put those fragments into working pieces within that narrative. Hence, I was convinced that the girl with a non-Turkish name in high school was a "foreigner" who spoke perfect Turkish. At school we were also taught that Turkey was a "cultural mosaic." This usually meant the inclusion of different ways of life (which revealed itself in accents, culinary differences, folk dances, etc.), but never the stories behind what created those differences. I first encountered the stories behind those different cultures in my twenties, and that was predominantly through film and literature.

When Yeşim Ustaoğlu's film *Bulutları Beklerken/Waiting for the Clouds* (2003) was released, I was in London and saw the film as part of the London Turkish Film Festival. Narrating the story of a Greek survivor of the forced marches of the early twentieth century, part of the efforts to homogenize the populations of both Greece and Turkey, the film ended on a relatively sad note. After the screening, I overheard a conversation between two Turkish speakers. While one of them appeared touched by the story, the other said that he did not like such films because "they make us [Turks] appear bad in Western eyes and give Greece even more reasons to accuse us [of injustices]." It was a reaction to the powerful and challenging narrative, but also to his own lack of knowledge on the subject: caught off-guard by a version of history which does not comply with the momumental narrative most Turks are familiar with, his initial response was defensive. Being constantly "assured" at school that when the Greek army invaded Western Anatolia the Turks "dumped the Greeks [the enemy] into the sea from the shores of İzmir," it was perhaps confusing to see a character in the film who not only claimed to be of Greek origin, but also had to hide her identity in order to survive in Turkey.

Until the late 1990s, the general public remained largely uninformed about the different discourses on unresolved aspects of the past in Turkey; they were, by and large, bombarded with the official versions disseminated by the state. The social and economic changes that took place in Turkey during the 1990s, particularly the constitutional changes brought about by the ongoing process of applying to join the European Union (EU), in contrast to the restricted civil liberties of the military regime of the early 1980s, among other factors, created a discursive space that allowed previously unavailable perspectives on history to be discussed. Before going any further, I should add that the writing of this book spans several years and, although the films analyzed, particularly the ones originating in Turkey, emerged in a context that allowed such discursive space, the success and sincerity of the official efforts toward protecting freedom of speech and civil liberties can be contested. Yet, the growing interest in the past, and the contestation it creates, has become particularly visible in all areas of cultural life in contemporary Turkey, from literature to cinema, in the context of the post-1980s nation. The interest in the recent past, the ways of remembering and representing the past, either with the intention of affirming it, or in order to challenge it, as well as cinema's particular and peculiar relation to memory itself, is the point of departure for this work.

The objective of this book is to explore the relation between cinema and memory in Turkey from a transnational perspective, by paying close attention to the depiction of memory and language and the ways in which the geographies of minority experience affect both narrative and cinematic space. Focusing on films made from the late 1990s onward, I investigate how cinema has responded aesthetically to the issues created by the unresolved past. The analysis carried out locates what is often referred as the "new cinema of Turkey" within the specific context of Turkish history, particularly in relation to the troubled relationship between the concept of unified citizenship and Turkey's unassimilated minorities. Treating displacement as the structuring condition of the "now" of these films, this study focuses on those who bring the taboo issues of the repression of minorities into visibility, which result from a gradual ideological shift toward an acknowledgment of the political validity of minority identity and its subjectivities. I argue that the political and social contexts in which these films emerge influence, and to a certain extent *determine*, the aesthetics of the image.

A substantial number of the films examined here pay attention to the issues that are related to Turkey's troubled but unresolved past. Since the late 1990s, films begun to be produced about issues that continue to haunt present-day Turkey, bringing previously ignored subjects into the realm of the visible. The image, in the majority of the cases that are examined here, is not one that "*shows*, equating visibility with knowledge and self-evidence; it is an image that must be *read*" (Rodowick: 148). These films, with their narrative and aesthetic strategies, raise more questions than they answer, and play a significant role in putting these issues into the realm of the visible in Turkey.

Memory, displacement, and cinema

The main object of this study is to understand how particular events, ones that are highly contested, are remembered and represented in film. Memory determines who we are, but the reverse is also true, that our identities determine what and how we remember. Cultural texts not only help us remember, but also introduce accounts that fall outside of the dominant discourse. Whether called "collective memory," "social memory," or "cultural memory," these terms all have one thing in common: they refer to the ways a given group's shared memories shape their identity. By definition these terms point to the constructed nature of memory. As Andreas Huyssen writes: "The past is not simply there in memory, but it must be articulated to become memory" (Huyssen 1995: 4), and cinema has become a very important part of this, as well as serving to challenge the established articulations by offering new ones. Nevertheless, "to focus solely on memory's constructed side is to deny the past's significance as a model for coming to terms with the present" (Schwartz 2010: ix).

This book, rather than taking history as the truth and memory as constructed, acknowledges that history and memory are both constructed in the sense that they both involve narration. Hence, it aims to look at the conditions and the ways of such narration, examining films and treating them as texts effecting and affected by the social, historical, and political milieu they react to or reproduce. The book imagines these texts—the films analyzed—in conversation with, or even as participants in shaping, historical thinking. If by the latter "we mean coming to grips with the issues from the past that trouble and challenge the present" (Rosenstone 1996: 162), then it is inevitably shaped by historically informed texts, and film is increasingly the most dominant form.

Different accounts of the past inevitably result in contestation, which "evokes a struggle in the terrain of truth. If what is disputed is the course of events—what really happened—new answers, particularly by groups whose knowledge has been discounted, may challenge dominant or privileged narratives" (Hodgkin and Radstone 2003: 1). Contestation, like memory, has more to do with the present than it has with the past. The past itself does not change, but its meaning does and "contests over the meaning of the past are also contests over the meaning of the present and over ways of taking the past forward" (Hodgkin and Radstone 2003: 1). The dynamics involved in this struggle are complicated and change over time. This, of course, is not to deny that the state or the dominant groups are not involved in repressing and/or silencing memories; it is rather to acknowledge that memory itself is an ongoing construction and that "both 'memory' and 'truth' here are unstable and destabilising terms" (Hodgkin and Radstone 2003: 2).

Representing such unstable and destabilizing notions in cinema introduces further challenges, particularly with regard to traumatic pasts. Hayden White writes that what he calls "holocaustal events", that is, events that are devastating and traumatic, "cannot simply be remembered; which is to say, clearly and unambiguously identified as to their meaning and contextualized in the group memory in such a way as to reduce the shadow they cast over the group's capacities to go into its present and envision a future free of their debilitating effects" (White 1996: 20). Among those effects, he lists the "difficulty felt by present generations of arriving at some agreement as to their *meaning*. […] What is at issue here is not the facts of the matter regarding such events but the different possible meanings that such facts can be construed as bearing" (White 1996: 21).[1]

White points out that there is a certain threat posed by representing these traumatic events, by turning them into the subject matter of a narrative: Telling a story might provide "a kind of 'intellectual mastery' of the anxiety which memory of their occurrence may incite in an individual or a community. But precisely insofar as the story is identifiable *as a story*, it can provide no lasting 'psychic mastery' of such events" (White 1996: 32). That is to say, turning these events into stories that are providing clear and unambiguous context and meaning produces a temporary understanding, not a lasting psychic mastery of the events. However, this does not mean that they defy representation. They are as representable as "any other event in human history. It is only that its representation, whether history or in fiction, requires the kind of style, the modernist style, that was developed in order to represent the kind of experience which social modernism made possible" (White 1992: 52). This is an important point in relation to some of the films dealing with the past. It is in their refusal to make the event intelligible as a story that certain narratives are able to create an ongoing discussion about the event itself.

There have been a number of studies on the relation between memory, history, and cinema from different angles, particularly within the last few decades.[2] There are also several influential thinkers, such as Walter Benjamin and Gilles Deleuze, whose works continue to effect and shape our thinking with regard to cinema and memory. Unsurprisingly, there have also been a number of publications in film studies examining groups of films in relation to the memories of their makers, examining who they are, where they come from, what they remember, and how they want to represent what they remember. Hamid Naficy's *Accented Cinema* (2001) and Laura Marks' *Skin of the Film* (2000) are two prominent examples. Both books look at displacement as a modern condition and its aesthetic ramifications in film.

Naficy's *Accented Cinema* studies a wide range of directors who have one thing in common: they are all displaced, either voluntarily or otherwise. He argues that the memories of home and the conditions of the host country are what accentuate these films. According to Naficy, the accent "emanates not so much from the accented speech of diegetic characters as from the displacement of the filmmakers and their artisanal production modes" (Naficy: 4). In his book, Naficy provides a comprehensive analysis of filmmakers from diverse backgrounds, and their films, mapping out the common tropes, from production modes to stylistic features. "The components of the accented style […] include the film's visual style; narrative structure; character and character development; subject matter, theme, and plot; structures of feeling of exile; filmmaker's biographical and sociocultural location; and the film's mode of production, distribution, exhibition, and reception" (Naficy: 21).

Similarly, Marks' book, in which she introduces the concept of intercultural cinema, explores how embodied memories are represented in film, focusing specifically on senses and their relation to memory. Marks formulates intercultural cinema as "a movement insofar as it is the emerging expression of a group of people who share the political issues of displacement and hybridity, though their individual circumstances vary widely" (Marks 2000: 2). She also argues that "the disjunction in space and time that characterize diasporan experience—the physical effects of exile, immigration, and displacement—also […] cause a disjunction in notions of truth" (Marks 2000: 1). Intercultural films tackle these different notions of truth, representing the world in an alternative way, in which memories (of a place, of an event) play an important role. Her study explores the ways in which memory of the senses is represented in intercultural cinema, which uses "experimental means to arouse collective memories" (Marks: 62).

Both Naficy and Marks investigate a certain type of image that emerges as a result of voluntary of forced displacement. This image, while trying to translate the experience of displacement into the realm of visual, is shaped by its relation to memory. Be it memory of home/land or memory of traumatic pasts, continuities and differences emerge only when the films are historically contextualized and thought through in relation to the experience of displacement.

The rising academic interest in memory and its representation in cinema has manifested itself in Turkey in an increasing number of publications, both in English and in Turkish.[3] The earliest and still the most important text focusing on the relation between memory and film in Turkey is Asuman Suner's *New Turkish Cinema* (2010), an updated version of an earlier publication, published in Turkish in 2005, as *Hayalet Ev: Yeni Türkiye Sinemasında Aidiyet, Kimlik ve Bellek* (*Haunted House: Belonging, Identity and Memory in New Turkish Cinema*). Suner examines the cinema of Turkey since the 1990s, paying particular attention to the notions of identity and memory. Although my book shares a common interest with Suner's, it differs from it, and from the similar projects that followed its publication, as it focuses on the aesthetic and narrative continuities in films about Turkish history, looking at the representation of minority experiences and displacement from a transnational perspective. Hence, some of the key questions this book seeks to explore are directly related to the phenomenon of displacement: How does cinema represent displacement and its effects on groups and individuals? What impact does the knowledge and experience of displacement have on its visual language and other aesthetic strategies?

This book asserts that changing political and social conditions determine not only types of stories, but also how they are told; that is, they also demand different aesthetics. The main concern of these films appears to be "displacement," which the filmmakers are continuously scrutinizing. In this respect, what started as a project aiming to examine the relationship between past and present in film in the Turkish context, evolved into a study of displacement itself. The films, which initially seem to be about interpretations of the past that differ from the dominant discourse, in fact deal with displacement and with loss of home, which makes them predominantly films about the "now," rather than about the past. Hence, displacement becomes the structuring condition of the "now" of these films; in all its shapes and forms, displacement is the "structure of feeling" with regard to the stories told.

"Structure of feeling" is a concept developed by Raymond Williams, which helps us to understand the changing social and cultural practices that do not fit into, or are not properly explained by, the already established forms and institutions. Williams writes that when dealing with culture, the general tendency is to assume that "the social is always past, in the sense that it is always formed," which also leads to an assumption that "all that is present and moving, all that escapes or seems to escape from the fixed and the explicit and the known, is grasped and defined as the personal" (Williams 1977: 128). However, this constant change, Williams suggests, should be recognized as part of the social, rather than being limited to personal. According to Williams, this is particularly relevant to art works because "the making of art is never itself in the past tense. It is always a formative process, within a specific present" (Williams 1977: 128). Critical of the social being reduced to fixed forms, Williams suggests the concept of "structures of feeling" to understand the change that is social and emergent, and not (yet) formed. It is "not feeling against thought, but thought as felt and feeling as thought: practical consciousness of a present kind, in a living and inter-relating continuity, [...] a social experience which is still *in process*, often indeed not yet recognized as social but taken to be private" (Williams 1977: 131).

Displacement becomes an important concept, the structure of feeling of the "now" of these films, not only because it runs through the films as a theme, but also because it informs the aesthetic practice. These films, whether as a result of conscious decision or not, see the world through the lense of displacement. Thus, they see the world through what seems to be a very personal and private experience and, in doing so, show continuities between the social and the personal, making the very experience of being displaced the single most important element informing the aesthetic and narrative decisions made. Moreover, some of the filmmakers whose work is included in this book do not live in Turkey as a result of such displacement. For instance, the families of both Atom Egoyan (*Ararat*, 2002) and Tassos Boulmetis (*Politiki Kouzina/A Touch of Spice*, 2003) originate from, but no longer live in Turkey as a result of historical wrongdoings. Only by treating displacement as a structuring condition of the "now" of these films can they be included in a project such as this.

With displacement (both physical and narrative) as the main focus, three interrelated characteristics of transnational filmmaking practices become salient: the first is the displaced nature of production processes, which often makes it difficult to determine the country of origin of these films and to limit them to the cinema of Turkey. More often then not, these films are coproductions and, in some cases, include multinational casts. The second characteristic is historical displacement, i.e. the physical (forced or voluntary) migration of people, and its consequences, in relation to how "home" is imagined and how memory is formed. The third and final characteristic relates to the films' distinctive narrative and visual strategies: the ways in which displacement is narrated and rendered on screen.

Situating the new cinema of Turkey within a transnational framework

After the heyday of Turkish cinema (known as "Yeşilçam years"), which ended in the late 1970s, filmmaking in Turkey was limited to the individual efforts of a few directors. Not only was the number of films produced very low, but also exhibiting the films posed an additional problem. After a considerably unfruitful period in Turkish filmmaking, the film that kick-started what is now called "new Turkish cinema" (or alternatively "the new cinema of Turkey") was Yavuz Turgul's *Eşkıya/Bandit* (1997), about an old bandit, Baran, released into the world, after serving thirty-five years in prison. A Kurd, although this is not explicitly mentioned, Baran returns to find his village evacuated, as it was flooded after the construction of a dam nearby.[4] He discovers that his best friend was the one who turned him in, just so that he could marry Keje, the woman who Baran has loved all his life, and decides to go to Istanbul to find them. The film was a huge success in bringing audiences back to film theaters.

During the 1990s, a new generation of directors, such as Zeki Demirkubuz, Nuri Bilge Ceylan, Yeşim Ustaoğlu, Handan İpekçi, and Reha Erdem, to name but a few, emerged with their own particular styles, adding to the work of already established directors such as Yavuz Turgul, Ömer Kavur, Şerif Gören, and Zeki Ökten. These early exponents of the new cinema of Turkey, Asuman Suner argues, should be "analyzed within the context of Turkey's integration into the process of globalization over the last two decades, an experience of integration that has resulted in anxieties and yearnings built up around the notions of homeland, sense of belonging, and identity" (Suner 2002: 61). These "anxieties" have also been created by unresolved issues in recent Turkish history. Films about the military coup of 1980, the anxieties around the issues of identity and belonging, and about the problems relating to minorities all began to be made during the late 1990s.

According to Suner, many characteristics of these films intersect with Hamid Naficy's definition of accented/exilic films. Indeed, some of the characteristics of accented films, such as "memory of and nostalgia for childhood and homeland, slippage between identity and performance of identity" (Naficy: 290) are also characteristics that form the backbone of the new wave of films coming out of Turkey since the late 1990s. A considerable number of these films scrutinize aspects of the unresolved past and memory, which have also initiated a mainstream discussions of taboo subjects. These films deal with problems and questions about home and identity and mainly focus on the ethnic minorities in Turkey. Yeşim Ustaoğlu's *Güneşe Yolculuk/Journey to the Sun* (1999) and *Bulutları Beklerken/Waiting for the Clouds* (2003), Handan İpekçi's *Büyük Adam Küçük Aşk/Hejar* (2001), and Uğur Yücel's *Yazı Tura/Toss-Up* (2004) are early examples of films that deal with such issues. As the dates reveal, there is clearly a tendency and/or a space to discuss these subjects from the late 1990s onward—a matter, which, in my view, cannot be fully grasped outside of the context of changes that took place from the 1980s onward in Turkey.

As the number of films and the size of the audience increases, so does the number of studies on the subject. In addition to increasing numbers of edited collections published in English, featuring articles that look at various aspects of Turkish cinema,[5] there have also been a growing number of books, in recent years, on different aspects of the new cinema of Turkey, particularly in relation to identity and memory. As well as Asuman Suner's book, Gönül Dönmez-Colin's book *Turkish Cinema: Identity, Distance and Belonging* (2008) also explores various aspects of identity in Turkish cinema, examining themes such as gender and migration. While this book is more focused on thematic exploration, Dönmez-Colin's most recent study, the *Dictionary of Turkish Cinema* (2013), is a more ambitious project, consisting of short entries not only on the key films and directors, but also on noteworthy themes and subjects. Another comprehensive study is Savaş Arslan's *Cinema in Turkey: A New Critical History* (2011). Arslan examines a large body of films and provides a comprehensive and a critical history of Turkish cinema covering its decades-long story from its early years to more contemporary filmmaking. Finally, Eylem Atakav's *Women and Turkish Cinema: Gender Politics, Cultural Identity and Representation* focuses on women and Turkish cinema, and examines film culture in Turkey since the military coup from a feminist perspective.

The *Aesthetics of Displacement* is not, however, a book about "Turkish" cinema. Instead of employing a national cinema framework, and looking only at "Turkish" cinema, this study adopts a more diverse, transnational framework. Not only is the concept of a "national cinema" very difficult to resolve, but also what is defined as national cinema offers a very limited framework for the purposes of this book. As Andrew Higson has asserted, the definitions of national cinema vary and all definitions come with their own specific problems. Whatever the parameters are (production, consumption, text-based, or criticism-led), the concept of national cinema is very often "used prescriptively rather than descriptively" (Higson 1989: 37). Moreover, "to identify a national cinema is first of all to specify a coherence and a unity; it is to proclaim a unique identity and a stable set of meanings" and this process is inevitably "hegemonising" and "mythologizing" (Higson 1989: 37).

The concept of a national cinema is very slippery and is subject to change, as are the borders of nation-states themselves. Higson, in a later article, suggests that the concept of a national cinema is helpful as a "taxonomic labeling device, a conventional means of reference in the debates about cinema, but the process of labeling is always to some degree tautologous, fetishising the national rather than merely describing it" (Higson 2000: 64). Although we cannot treat "transnational" as a portmanteau concept, nor can we assume the influence of the national is no more, we also cannot ignore the transnational connections. This book, following Chris Berry and Mary Farquhar's definition, treats transnational "not as a higher order, but as a larger arena connecting differences, so that a variety of regional, national, and local specificities impact upon each other in various types of relationships ranging from synergy to contest" (Berry and Farquhar 5).

What is more, because this book is primarily concerned with displacement and memory, it is also difficult to locate these concepts strictly within the concept of nationality. Therefore, although the films analyzed here are selected in terms of their relation to Turkey and to Turkish national identity, they are relocated within a transnational framework. This also allows a comparison of films and their reception by audiences, which then enables us to explore the varying ways of remembering/forgetting the past, changing ways of constructing and contesting the national identity, as well as revealing the common tropes shared by these films. Memories, like stories, travel in both time and space, and the dialogic relation that exists between languages, communities, and ideas also exists between films. In addition to general interaction within the transnational context, there exists a specific dialogue between the films and the directors who are concerned with Turkey, who are questioning the various aspects of the same past. This dialogue crosses boundaries and borders, and creates its own aesthetic. These films might be parts of different puzzles when looked at from one angle, but they also form a unique picture when considered together.

Hence, while using a transnational framework to bring these films together, my interest is in what these works say about Turkey and Turkish history.

Accordingly, this book locates what is often referred to as the "new cinema of Turkey" not just within a transnational framework, but also within the specific context of Turkish history, paying particular attention to the difficult relationship between the concept of unified citizenship and minorities. The films analyzed here stem from a new form of understanding of (be)longing. Therefore, the directors' ethnic backgrounds are not treated as the major defining aspect of the image analyzed here, although they are mentioned when relevant. A considerable number of the films examined are made by filmmakers belonging to the ethnic "majority" in Turkey. Thus, they have not suffered directly from the events that their films often deal with. For instance, Handan İpekçi, Yeşim Ustaoğlu, Uğur Yücel, and Ümit Ünal do not themselves come from nor identify themselves as belonging to an ethnic, religious, or linguistic minority. As Daniela Berghahn and Claudia Sternberg assert in their analysis of the concept of migrant and diasporic cinema (2010), "it is not the filmmaker's nationality or ethnicity which determines the classification of a production as migrant or diasporic, […] it is the subject matter in the broadest sense" (Berghahn and Sternberg: 17). This is also valid for this book as it is not the filmmakers' nationality nor their ethnic origin, but an understanding of a specific type of belonging, and the subjects they choose to engage with, that inform the works of these directors.

* * *

Since one of my main arguments is that the social and political context is important and decisive when it comes to how these films deal with the past, I begin by providing a brief overview of the historical background to the establishment of the modern Turkish Republic in Chapter I, paying specific attention to the attempts at "Turkifying" the population, which has arguably caused most of the problems Turkey is facing today. Focusing predominantly on the assimilation policies of the first few decades of the newly established Republic, I also reveal the rupture created by these policies. Additionally, the chapter provides a brief overview of the history of cinema in Turkey, emphasizing those aspects that will become relevant in the chapters that follow, providing a background for the discussions to come.

Chapter 2 pays attention to the recurring themes and the stylistic continuities that occur in these films. Looking at displacement as the condition informing the ways in which these films deal with their subjects, the chapter will examine these recurring themes under five major and interrelated categories: the politics of language, silence, spatial relations, haunted narratives, and epistolary narratives. I argue that movement is not limited to people; ideas, aesthetics, and cultures are also on the move, and this migratory existence is creating (or perhaps demanding) its own language.

The chapters that follow focus on selected issues that are particularly important with regard to the way they influenced the make-up of the population in Turkey today, and are dealt with in the films analyzed. Each one of these chapters will provide historical background to the events examined, followed by a detailed discussion of selected films. Accordingly the third chapter of this book examines the representation of non-Muslim minorities in Turkey. Minorities in Turkey, according to the official definition, are formed by non-Muslim groups as defined by the Lausanne Treaty (1923), and were granted certain rights that were denied to other groups (Alevis[6] would be one example). However, this did not stop the attempts by the authorities to force assimiliation and to create a unified society. As a result, these communities faced a number of discriminatory actions over the decades. Resistance to assimilation enhanced the already existing feeling that these groups were "ungrateful infidels," or "guests" living in Turkey, allowed certain "privileges." While the first half of this chapter provides background to the experiences of non-Muslim minorities in Turkey and the representations of this experience in films in the post-1980 context, the second half will focus on a close reading of two films: *A Touch of Spice* (Tassos Boulmetis 2003) and *Waiting for the Clouds* (Yeşim Ustaoğlu 2003).

Chapter 4 focuses on the discussions surrounding the massacre of Ottoman Armenians in 1915 and its denial in Turkey, which is still a subject of major dispute. Although Armenians are part of the minority groups defined by the Lausanne Treaty, the weight and importance of the subject in Turkey requires a separate chapter. Referred to widely as a "genocide" outside of Turkey, the massacre of Armenians forms the center of one of the most important historical discussions in contemporary Turkey. This chapter focuses on the representations of the event, paying particular attention to Atom Egoyan's *Ararat* (2002) and its reception in Turkey. I argue that the film's ability to stir intense discussion (despite its unsatisfactory reception) was due not only to the complicated nature of the subject, but also to its treatment in the film.

The fifth and final chapter concentrates on the largest ethnic minority group in Turkey with some of the most pressing demands: the Kurds. Referred to as the "Kurdish Issue" in Turkey, the Kurdish population and their decades-long struggle are one of the most important issues that contemporary Turkey is dealing with. This chapter will provide a brief background to the events, concentrating on examples of assimilation and relocation policies aimed specifically at Kurds, and the position of the Kurds in Turkey today. This will then inform my analysis of the films in which these issues are dealt with. Looking at films by both Turkish and Kurdish directors, this chapter demonstrates that the representation of the issue has changed throughout the last two decades and that these films played an important role in shifting the perception of both Kurds and the Kurdish language in Turkey.

The book concludes with a brief examination of a film that is in many respects different to the cinema analyzed in earlier chapters: Nuri Bilge Ceylan's *Once Upon a Time in Anatolia* (2011). Although the film does not appear to be openly dealing with the past, starting with its title, it allows a reading that is informed by the history of the land it narrates. I will argue that the film implies what other films openly make their subjects and, in doing so, highlight the aesthetic continuity and the dialogic relation between this film and the ones that are explicitly about historical wrongdoings.

Memory, Identity: The Turkish Context

During the 1980s and 1990s, Turkey witnessed major social, economic, and cultural changes. The neo-liberal policies introduced after the 1980s, within a framework of a rapidly globalizing world, inevitably caused profound changes in the country. On the one hand, the process of joining the European Union (EU), and the constitutional changes required by the process known as the Copenhagen Criteria, brought more freedom of speech to the country, compared to the restricted civil liberties during the military regime of the early 1980s. This process, according to Ayşe Kadıoğlu, introduced "some of the most important parliamentary reforms toward the acknowledgment of different religious and ethnic identities in Turkey" (Kadıoğlu 2007: 292).[1] On the other hand, the neo-liberal economic transformation resulted, much like everywhere else in the world, in an uneven distribution of wealth, making the gap between rich and poor wider. The process of globalization, and the rapid change in economic and social life, arguably created a rupture in the belief in the promise of the future, and resulted in people enquiring about the past in order to redefine their relationship, not just to the past, but also to the present. Yet, as willingness to acknowledge past atrocities grows, so, too, do reactionary nationalist movements. Arjun Appadurai, who writes that the nation-state, "as a complex modern political form, is on its last legs" (Appadurai 1996: 19), claims that during the 1980s and 1990s many nation-states had to simultaneously negotiate two pressures:

> the pressure to open up their markets to foreign investment, commodities and images and the pressure to manage the capacity of their own minorities to use the globalised language of human rights to argue for their own claims for cultural dignity and recognition. This dual pressure was a distinctive feature of the 1990s

and produced a crisis in many countries for the sense of national boundaries, national sovereignty and the purity of the national ethos, and it is directly responsible for the growth of majoritarian racisms in societies (Appadurai 2004: 65).

In this, Turkey is no exception. However, the so-called "decline of the nation-state," according to Jeffrey Olick, gives rise to a growing interest in memory and a "politics of regret." According to Olick, "the discourse of universal human rights is tied directly to a politics of regret because its advocates believe that only gestures of reparation, apology, and acknowledgment can restore the dignity of history's victims" (Olick 2007: 126). The question motivating Olick's entire book is "why the wave of regret now?" and he offers an answer from a historical–sociological perspective: "one that sees regret as part of broad transformations tied up with the decline, rather than the triumph, of the nation-state" (Olick 2007: 137). For the author, the politics of regret is a "major characteristic of our age, an age of shattered time and shifting allegiances" (Olick 2007: 137). It is one of the ways in which societies deal with the at best unpleasant aspects of their past and although the sincerity, effectiveness, and substance of such a "wave of regret" is debatable, it is nevertheless visible in Turkey.

The change that media and communication technologies went through in a relatively short period is also important in relation to the complicated and interwoven nature of these developments, and the resulting emergence of new narrative(s) about the relation to the past and present in Turkey. Television and radio broadcasting until the 1990s were under the control of the state, and were used to create and maintain the idea of a unified nation.[2] The introduction of privately owned television channels in the 1990s both contributed to and benefited from the already changing face of Turkey. As a result of these important changes, although constantly policed, a discursive space emerged that allowed alternative voices to be heard on various unresolved issues in relation to past and present identities through newly available media outlets. One of the most controversial of these new media outlets, made possible by new technologies, was the Kurdish ROJ TV in 2004, which previously broadcasted from the UK under the name of MED TV.[3] Hence, what might be described as "post-national sensibilities"[4] began to generate a demand, from various groups within Turkey, for the country to face up to its history. This demand develops hand in hand with the changes in understanding of nation and citizenship.

Understanding of citizenship, which is normally imagined to have a natural connection to the nation-state, has arguably been undergoing an important transformation. Nation-states are, more and more, envisaged and articulated as dynamic institutions with multiple dimensions. This triggers a transformation from an understanding of a uniform citizenship to a citizenship informed and shaped by multiple dimensions, which, according to Saskia Sassen, is defined by two interconnected conditions: "the change in the position and institutional features of national states since the 1980s" that resulted in various forms of globalization, and "the emergence of multiple actors, groups and communities partly strengthened by these transformations in the state and increasingly unwilling to automatically identify with a nation as represented by the state" (Sassen 2002: 277). However, as in the case of Turkey, this new understanding of citizenship "may not necessarily be new," but rather the result of "long gestations or features that were there since the beginning of the formation of citizenship as a national institution, but are only now evident because enabled by current developments" (Sassen 2002: 277).

According to Sassen, there is a distinction to be made between "post-nationalism and denationalization as they represent two different trajectories", and the difference between the two is a "question of scope and institutional embeddedness" (Sassen 2002: 286). Although these two terms are not mutually exclusive, "denationalization" denotes transformation of the national and "tend[s] to instantiate inside the national" while "post-nationalism" is about new forms "located outside the national rather than out of the earlier institutional framework of the national" (Sassen 2002: 286). Taking this differentiation between the two terms, Ayşe Kadıoğlu looks at Turkey's case and, mainly focusing on constitutional changes, reaches the conclusion that Turkey is not post-national, but rather undergoing denationalization. However, when attention is focused on the experiences of individuals and groups a different picture emerges, one that does not fit into the frame provided by the nation-state. I argue that the films analyzed in the following text stem from a new form of understanding of belonging, what I would like to call "post-national sensibilities". Inevitably this newly emerging language also questions the language of the past and what that particular past failed to articulate.

Although, on a global scale, the increasing interest in the past, as well as the interest in preserving and representing it, started in the 1970s, it became almost an obsession after the 1980s. Until the 1980s, "modernist culture was energized by present futures," Andreas Huyssen writes, which is replaced by "present pasts" in the post-1980 context as a result of the radical shift in the way time and space is experienced. What Huyssen calls a "memory boom," paradoxically, goes hand in hand with the boom of forgetting. According to Huyssen, "we are trying to counteract this fear and danger of forgetting with survival strategies of public and private memorialisation" (Huyssen 2003: 17). The "informational and perceptual overload combined with a cultural acceleration that neither our psyche nor our senses are adequately equipped to handle," in return, creates a lack of confidence in the future, which causes us to "turn to memory for comfort" (Huyssen 2003: 25).

Similarly, Barry Schwartz argues that the recent explosion of research on collective memory is due to a perceived break between past and present. According to Schwartz, "since the past frames the present existence, the complete detachment of past and present is theoretically as well as empirically impossible; however, in some instances the rupture of the tissue of memory is so severe that it becomes an object of special inquiry" (Schwartz 2000: 13). Such rupture is very rarely as observable as in the case of the modern Turkish Republic and its specific decision to separate itself from the Ottoman Empire.

Although still strongly resisted by the official discourse, regret, empathy, and apology as part of post-conflict peace building have also emerged in Turkey, visibly affecting the cultural field. Within the last few decades, academic works, literature, cinema, and television have become increasing concerned with the unresolved issues of the past in Turkey. Since its establishment, the country has been focused on the future continuously, suggests oral historian Leyla Neyzi, and the sudden interest in the past has caused "history's Pandora's box" to open (Neyzi 2007: 24).[5] A symptomatic example of contemporary interest in the past in Turkey can be seen in the increased attention paid to the events that took place before, during, and after the 1980 military *coup d'état*. Because the post-coup constitution ruled out any possibility of legal action against the junta regime, there was a noticeable absence of critical discourse in the public sphere about the military regime. However, in the last decade, the military coup of 1980 has become one of the most dealt-with subjects in Turkish film. Although there were very few films about the military coup until the end of the 1990s, the numbers on the subject rose dramatically from the beginning of 2000. Between 2004 and 2008, six feature films were made and screened in cinemas nationwide on various aspects of the military coup.[6]

The transition from the Ottoman Empire to the republic of Turkey

The modern Turkish Republic was founded in 1923, after the overthrow of the Ottoman Empire, following World War I. Mustafa Kemal Atatürk, who is regarded as the founder of the Turkish Republic, then carried out a set of revolutionary changes in social, cultural, and political life, designed to create a modern unified nation-state. The newly formed republic was not intended to be a continuation of the Ottoman Empire, but was the antithesis of it in many respects, specifically in its dedication to laicism.[7] The Ottoman Empire was a multiethnic and multireligious society in which Armenians, Turks, Greeks, Jews, and many other groups had lived together. These communities coexisted under the protection of the Sultan and, to a large extent, organized their own social and cultural lives in what was called the "*millet* system". Although the Ottoman *millet* system is sometimes discussed, with a hint of nostalgia, as an exemplary system of multiculturalism, these different groups, living under the rule of the Sultan, often maintained separate cultures. According to Çağlar Keyder, "Muslims, Greeks, Jews, and Armenians lived side by side, almost never intermarrying; their religious and cultural lives compartmentalized into corporate entities in a collusion between the community elites and Ottoman authorities" (Keyder 1999: 4–5). With the rise and spread of nationalism as a result of the French Revolution, these ethnic groups began to demand independence in the early 19th century, and the ensuing struggles caused great suffering on all sides.[8] Beginning with the Serbs and the Greeks, the Ottoman Empire had to deal with nationalist struggles of its communities (Ahmad 2005: 24), and, according to Taner Akçam, it was this suffering that "formed a crucial component of each nation's collective memory" (Akçam 2007: ix).

Following the establishment of the modern Turkish Republic, in an attempt to create a unified nation, the constitution defined Turkish citizens as everyone living in Turkey, regardless of their ethnic and religious background. Nevertheless, hegemony belonged to the Sunni Turks. The Alevis and Kurds, as well as non-Muslims, had to either suppress their identity or come to terms with being seen as "outsiders." Such unity, under the category of "Turkishness," was seen as a necessary move in order to create a nation-state, which, in turn, necessitated the "Turkification" of the population. However, as Akçam reminds us, the word "Turk" connoted unintelligence and vulgarity within the Ottoman Empire, and

Ottomans did not like to be called "Turks," especially by the West (Akçam 2003: 54–5). Hence, during the construction of the modern Turkish Republic, Turkish identity was created in opposition to the contempt it had previously aroused, systematically constructed around a pride with highly nationalistic overtones to create social cohesion.[9] The First National Historical Congress, held in Ankara in 1932, was an attempt to create a much-needed historical narrative to be proud of, which would then provide a framework of national pride and cohesion as the basis for the school history curriculum and for other standard textbooks.[10]

Turkish modernization is usually explained as a top-down project carried out by the Republican elite, which also often meant Westernization. According to many scholars, Turkey was "made in the image of the Kemalist elite which won the national struggle against foreign invaders and the old regime" (Ahmad 2005: ix). Writing on the Turkish modernization project, Çağlar Keyder points out that "the agency behind the project was the modernizing elite, and what they sought to achieve was the imposition of institutions, beliefs, and behavior consonant with their understanding of modernity on the chosen object: the people of Turkey" (Keyder 1997: 39). Similarly, Reşat Kasaba argues that in Turkey the political elite viewed themselves as the most significant force for change in the Ottoman Empire and Turkey:

> To them, Ottoman–Turkish society was a project, and the people who live in Turkey could at most be the objects of their experiments. They freely used categories such as "old" and "new" or "traditional" and "western" in order to reduce the dimensions of their task to manageable proportions and represent themselves as the sole bearers of progress. They regarded reform strictly as a top down process (Kasaba: 23–4).

According to Kasaba, the political discourse in Turkey has been characterized by the forced choice between the old and new. While "old" connotes backwardness, "new" implies progress. Kasaba identifies two groups who found themselves in "fundamental conflict with the new nationalist ethos" that was being created in the early republican years: Islamists and non-Muslim minorities (Kasaba: 28). The ruling elite, distrustful of ideas outside their control, and constantly circulating the rhetoric of a country surrounded by enemies to justify the repression, created a state that was from the very beginning very wary of individual rights and personal freedoms.[11]

However, responding to the literature that puts emphasis on the constructed nature of Turkish modernization, Meltem Ahıska notes that most of these works argue that what was experienced in the West as a process became a project in Turkey. "Although such an approach aims to criticize the Republican elite and Kemalism,[12] its insistence on the constructedness can do nothing more than reversing the ideology it seeks to criticize," as it fails to acknowledge the historicity of Turkish nationalism and sees it "outside sociology" (Ahıska 2005: 37). Whether seen as a successful example of modernization or a failed project, inherent in both approaches is an assumption of a "model," that is the West, which then makes Turkish modernization inevitably a copy of the "original" (Ahıska 2005: 38). Ahıska proposes a new conceptualization that neither dissolves the specific differences in vague universalism nor isolates those differences in the process of explaining them (Ahıska 2005: 42). During this complicated process, Turkey attempted to break away from its past, the Ottoman Empire, and to reconstruct itself as Western; however "in Turkey imagining the nation is simultaneously imagining it to be both eastern and western" (Ahıska 2005: 45).

The process of modernizing Turkey required changes that were thought necessary for the country to "catch up" with the West and move away from the Ottoman past. Some of these changes were aimed at organizing cultural and social life, such as the reform of clothing, which intended to change the appearance of society, but some were more symbolic. In order to mark the "new" state, the capital city was relocated to Ankara from Istanbul, which had been the capital of the Ottoman Empire for more than four centuries, an act often viewed as a symbolic break from the Empire. According to Keyder, Ankara was a "place without significations," hence ideal as it was "a neutral space devoid of history and symbolic weight" (Keyder 2006: 50). Ahıska argues that the relocation of the capital should be understood within a broader and historically constructed context of East and West opposition. While Istanbul was almost identical with the West in this discourse, Ankara provided a space that was almost empty and that allowed the new Republic to start from scratch (Ahıska 2005: 29).

In its effort to break from its past and align itself with the West, the newly established republic also adopted the Gregorian calendar in 1926, as opposed to the lunar calendar, which had been used by the Ottoman Empire. However, this created a rupture, as there was no continuity between the two: since the lunar year is eleven days shorter than the solar year, locating events in history became difficult. The reform, which made it possible to move from "the Oriental flow of time" to the "occidental" for the new republic, also made historical events that predated 1926 "appear as if they belong to a different temporal zone" (Özyürek

2007: 5). Undoubtedly, these reforms formed the "zero point" for the republic, marking the beginning of a new nation-state, configuring it from the point of view of an imagined Western gaze.

The effort to create a "zero point" requires a policy that is based on forgetting and silencing memories that do not conform to the newly constructed ideology and image. Forgetting is necessary to mark a new beginning—to start from "zero," but, as Ahıska points out, the present is also "haunted by the beginnings" (Ahıska 2003: 356). The atrocities that took place at the end of World War I and at the beginning of the Turkish Republic may have been the result of rising nationalism throughout the world; however, Turkey, until very recently, has resisted facing up to its past, and one of its defenses has always been "it happened before 1923," that is *before* the zero point.

Creating a unified nation: Language policies

In its efforts to move from the multiethnic Ottoman Empire to a nation-state, Turkey took a number of steps to create and maintain a unified nation, one of which was the creation of a unified language. As İlker Aytürk writes, "the making of a national language was the core of the republican project of identity-building" (Aytürk 2004: 2). The country took a number of measures to make sure that the nation would speak and write in one universal language: Turkish. Accordingly, the Roman alphabet was introduced in 1928 to replace the Arabic alphabet. This was followed by a reform in language aimed at clearing Turkish of foreign words (mostly Arabic and Farsi) and replacing them by either "pure" Turkish words, where they existed, or, where not, by inventing new words. The project was led by the Institute of Turkish Language (*Türk Dil Kurumu*), founded in 1932 by Atatürk. The institute's primary aim was to oversee the "hygiene" of the language.[13]

In addition to reforming language, the newly established state also wanted its subjects to speak it. "According to the first population census of the Republic, conducted in 1927, Turkey's population of 13.6 million held around 2 million people for whom Turkish was not the native language" (Aslan 2007: 245). In order to create a society that spoke Turkish, in January 1928 the Students' Association of Istanbul University launched a campaign featuring the slogan "*Vatandaş Türkçe Konuş!*" ("Citizen Speak Turkish!"). It received considerable support from the public as well as the government. According to Rıfat Bali, the campaign was so popular that soon after its launch there were occasions when people seen reading non-Turkish newspapers or heard speaking foreign languages were harassed (Bali: 2000).[14]

The idea that a nation-state should have a unified identity and language is not specific to Turkey, but the assumed unification point, the category of "Turk," decidedly overlooked the different ethnic and linguistic communities. Similarly, as part of its efforts to create a unified identity, in the 1930s the Republic went so far as to come up with new theories of Turkish history, *Türk Tarih Tezi* (Turkish History Thesis), and Turkish language, *Güneş Dil Teorisi* (Sun Language Theory), in which pseudo-scientific methods were used to imagine a past that broke with the Ottoman–Islamic heritage, connecting Turks to Hittites.[15]

The idea of an "indivisible unity of the nation" that began in the late 1920s was revised and enhanced in the 1982 post-coup constitution. This suggests the indivisibility of the "nation," criminalizing all claims to belong to an ethnic minority or to suggest the existence of any other than the ones protected by the Lausanne Treaty. As Turkey limited the definition of minorities to non-Muslims in the Lausanne treaty, the limited and often violated rights given to minorities were not enjoyed by the other groups, such as the Kurds. Thus, those acknowledging the existence of religious and linguistic minorities could be prosecuted for supporting separatism (Oran 2006: 83). By the same token, until 2003, the establishment of any association based on race, religion, or language was forbidden by law. While the 1961 constitution used the phrase "official language," it was changed to "the language of the state" after 1980, predominantly to prohibit the use of Kurdish (Oran 2006: 85). This decision was largely influenced by the rising tension between the Kurds and the state, as well as by the armed struggle led by the Kurdistan Workers Party (PKK),[16] which became stronger after the 1980 coup.

The regulations and constitutional changes concerning the use of minority languages are very complex and are subject to constant change in Turkey. It is beyond the scope of this book to examine them in detail. However, it is important to remember that the use of minority languages has created problems since the beginning of the Turkish Republic and, in some cases, it even proved impossible to express an opinion publicly in a minority language. It should also be noted here that the reason for the preference of the phrase "minority language," as opposed to "foreign language," stems from the fact that the prohibition did not extend to any language other than Turkish. While the state television corporation TRT, for instance, broadcast news in French, English, and German for many years on its radio and TV channels, minority languages spoken in Turkey were ignored.[17] In 2002, in accordance with the European Union integration reforms, the ban on broadcasting in the previously forbidden languages was lifted. This was followed by the launch of TRT's Kurdish channel in 2009. Nevertheless, as a consequence of a ban that had been in force for decades, the mere act of speaking Kurdish became a sign of political resistance in Turkey.

As Bourdieu suggests, the illusion of a "unified" language comes in the form of a "legitimate" language. He writes:

> The official language is bound up with the state, both in its genesis and in its social uses. It is in the process of state formation that the conditions are created for the constitution of a unified linguistic market, dominated by the official language. […] In order for one mode of expression among others […] to impose itself as the only legitimate one, the linguistic market has to be unified (Bourdieu: 45).

Moreover, "linguistic exchanges are also relations of symbolic power in which the power relations between speakers or their respective groups are actualized" (Bourdieu: 37), and the banning of the use of a language is an indication of the extent of the repression that took place in Turkey. Arguably, then, that which has previously been repressed is now, with relatively more freedom, finding its way back to the public sphere, which includes cinema.

"Purifying" the population

The historical issues that significantly affected the minority populations in Turkey, many of which the country is still dealing with today, span through decades and date back to before the official "zero point" of 1923. One of the most important and contested issues in Turkey that is still to be faced up to in all its detail and consequences, is the massacre of the Ottoman Armenians between 1915 and 1918, widely referred as the Armenian genocide. When the Ottoman Empire allied with Germany during World War I, some of the Armenians living in Eastern Anatolia saw a chance to form an independent nation-state by allying with Russia. In order to solve the problem that Armenian revolutionaries had created for the Empire, it was decided to relocate the entire Armenian population of Anatolia to Syria, away from the war zone. However, under this pretext, the entire Armenian population was forced to move, including those living outside of the war zone. According to Zurcher, members of the governing party, the Committee of Union and Progress (CUP),[18] who were later instrumental in forming the modern Turkish Republic, "wanted to 'solve' the Eastern Question by the extermination of the Armenians" and "used the relocation as a cloak for this policy" (Zurcher: 116). Between 1915 and 1918, *Teşkilat-ı Mahsusa* (Special Organisation), a secret division operating within the governing CUP, planned the deportation of Armenians to Syria. Many either died on the journey due to lack of care or were massacred by soldiers and thugs, a fact to which the authorities turned a blind eye, or even, according to various accounts, actually accommodated.[19]

Zurcher asserts that although the massacres were not motivated by a bogus racial theory, unlike the Nazi war crimes against the Jews, biological materialism and social Darwinism did have an influence on the CUP's actions. "In this worldview," he writes, "the Ottoman Armenians and Greeks could easily be viewed as 'microbes' or 'tumours' endangering the health and survival of the Ottoman 'body' and it is significant that we encounter this kind of terminology in the statements of those involved in persecutions" (Zurcher: 117). The official discourse explaining the events up to and after the massacres of the Ottoman Armenians is inflexible and categorically rejects the use of the word "genocide." According to the official account, the events were shaped by World War I and were limited to relocating a section of the Armenian population in order to prevent its possible collaboration with the Russians. It also insists that the events took place before the foundation of Modern Turkey and, therefore, the Turkish Republic cannot be held responsible for the loss of lives during the relocation. However, according to Akçam, one of the reasons why any discourse on the subject is avoided in Turkey is that "there is a continuity of the ruling elite from the Ottoman Empire to the Turkish Republic, and so there is a strong relationship between the Armenian Genocide and the foundation of the Republic" since many of those who were involved in organizing the massacres were also involved with the Turkish resistance and later with the newly established government (Akçam 2004: 238). While the predominant discourse in Turkey today views the events as unfortunate, it refuses to accept accountability for what happened, rejecting specifically the accusations regarding genocidal intent—that is the intention to clear Anatolia of Armenians. Hence the word "genocide" is taboo in Turkey when used in relation to the Armenians, although the massacre of the Ottoman Armenians is referred to as the "Armenian genocide" outside of Turkey. Turkish authorities continue to maintain a position that denies the genocidal intent of the CUP government and points to the lack of conclusive archival evidence to prove that intent.

"Genocide," undoubtedly, is a highly charged word, not only because of the scale of the crime, but also because of its conditions. Initially a legal term, it requires evidence of the intention to wipe out a group partly or entirely. This, however, is in direct contradiction to the event itself as genocide aims at complete annihilation without witness or evidence. Thus it creates a further ethical problem, one that is often faced when talking about the events of 1915 in Turkey: if historians fail to find "enough" evidence to agree to call the event a genocide, does the event itself disappear? Marc Nichanian writes that "the controversial aspect in relation to the victim/survivor resides precisely in the fact that the injunction, 'Prove it, just prove it …' is precisely the injunction of the executioner" (Nichanian 2004: 151). This, in turn, produces a vicious circle: to be seen by others one is required to prove his/her own visibility, which the Armenian Secret Army for the Liberation of Armenia (ASALA) attempted to do violently. It targeted mainly Turkish diplomats, and was aimed at forcing the Turkish state to acknowledge its responsibility for the Armenian genocide. Although no longer active, ASALA was an armed organization which carried out a number of attacks during the 1970s and 1980s, killing and injuring many people.

Writing about the place that the Armenian genocide and ASALA occupy in Turkish political and social life, Taner Akçam argues:

> The real problem was that the subject referred as the "Armenian Problem" occupied such a perverse place in our mind. The subject was so foreign to our way of thinking and the way we viewed the world (our Weltanschauung) that to approach it seriously meant risking all the concepts or models we had used to explain our world and ourselves. Our entrenched belief systems constituted an obstacle to understanding the subject (Akçam 2004: ix).

Akçam refers to this as a "fear of confronting" the issue (2004: ix), which maintained its hold until very recently as there was a considerable lack of discourse on the subject in Turkey. However, within the last decade discussions concerning the Armenian question have begun to force themselves into the Turkish public sphere.[20] In recent times, the issue has started to attract more attention and alternative voices to that of the dominant discourse are beginning to being heard.

Although a much less contested area, the compulsory population exchange of the 1920s between Greece and Turkey also changed the ethnic make up of Anatolia and caused considerable suffering in both countries, as it meant relocating large numbers of people on both sides of the Aegean Sea—mostly involuntarily. Executed under the aegis of the Lausanne Treaty (1923), Greek Orthodox citizens were relocated from Turkey to Greece in exchange for those Muslims living in Greece. Writing on the population exchange between Greece and Turkey, Renée Hirschon notes that the forced displacement in the Aegean region had already affected millions of people even before it was given a legal framework by the Lausanne Treaty. The Balkan wars of 1913–14 had already destabilized the region and caused an influx of people, both Muslim and Christians. "In a wider setting, the Lausanne Convention was the legal framework for the culmination of 'unmixing peoples' [...] an ongoing process which was already underway a decade earlier" (Hirschon 2006: 4). However, relocation continued to be seen as a possible solution to ethnic problems.[21]

Turkish nationalism and the project of Turkifying the nation caused constant pressure, and at times this erupted into verbal and physical violence for those who were seen to be outside the project. It is important to note that one of the continuous policies of the newly established republic was also to "Turkify the financial and labour markets" (Aktar: 114) in order to create the Turkish bourgeoisie. Using World War II as justification, Turkey introduced the infamous *Varlık Vergisi*/Capital Tax (also known as the "Wealth Tax") in 1942. This special tax reportedly did not discriminate; yet, according to Ayhan Aktar, it was a result of Kemalist nationalist ideology and a further manifestation of the Turkification process (Aktar: 136). Faik Ökte, treasurer in Istanbul at the time, who was directly involved in the process, writes that the treasury received a document from the Ministry of Finance in 1942, stressing "the urgency of collecting data on individuals who had gained enormous wealth, singling out the Greek, Armenian and Jewish citizens in a separate list" (Ökte: 18). When Ökte asked how the figures, which included estimates of wartime fortunes, were calculated, he was told that it was done "simply by guesswork" (Ökte: 18). These lists later were used to collect the tax. Because of the already existing resentment toward minorities, and ongoing negative media coverage, it would not have been difficult to explain these policies to the general public.[22] While the tax was abolished in 1944, that which was taken from the individuals was never returned. Although it was a one-off tax, in most cases the required amount was so high that in order to pay it families had to sell off their belongings at less than their worth and the only people who could afford to buy them were the Turks, who, in practice, did not have to pay the tax. Those who could not pay were sent to a labor camp in eastern Turkey.

Non-Muslim minorities in Turkey faced further xenophobia in 1955. On September 6 and 7, public riots were triggered by the news that Atatürk's house in Thessalonica had been bombed. This is now widely believed to have been staged by interest groups in Turkey, specifically to provoke the public. Within hours, fuming crowds targeted the non-Muslim population, their businesses, and their houses in Istanbul. The government of Adnan Menderes' Democratic Party proved impotent and unwilling to stop the riots, which developed into a "pogrom against Greek businesses" (Zurcher: 231).[23] It should be noted that the events that took place in September 1955 were not an unexpected public outburst; on the contrary, they were a result of the policies that had been carried out since the establishment of the Republic.

In 1964, Prime Minister İsmet İnönü's cabinet made a controversial decision. Influenced by the rising crisis over Cyprus, İnönü decided to "punish" the Greeks still residing in Turkey who carried Greek passports. An enactment was passed which cancelled the treaty of 1930 signed between Greece and Turkey. The bill, in effect, revoked the legal status of any Greeks without a Turkish passport. Most had been living in Turkey for decades and had built up families over the years. The decision affected a large number of people, and was a last blow to the Greek population in Turkey.[24] The newspaper *Milliyet* announced the news on March 17 with its headline, "privileges are cancelled" (*imtiyaz iptal edildi*). As a result, many Greek citizens left the country. Decades-long hostility toward minorities caused the non-Muslim population in Turkey to drop dramatically. According to Çağlar Keyder, Istanbul's Christian population dropped from 450,000 in 1914 to 240,000 in 1927, and by 1980 it was 60,000 (Keyder 1999: 10–11).

Another act that legitimized relocation of the population was the "*Sevk ve İskan Kanunu*" (Settlement Legislation Law) of 1934. It was aimed particularly at the organized Kurds and was an attempt to spread them all over Turkey and, therefore, break the resistance by relocating Kurds to areas populated by Turks and Turks to areas populated by Kurds. According to Mesut Yeğen, the primary aim of the legislation was to "re-shuffle the demographic composition of Anatolia according to ethnic measurements" (Yeğen 2009: 92). In the 1990s, the policy of relocating people took the shape of village evacuations in Kurdish areas and resulted in a large population of internally displaced people in Turkey.

The same law was also used to resettle the Jewish population of Thrace following the pogrom of 1934. The attacks targeting Jewish businesses appear to have been triggered by a few racist opinion pieces in the press, and also by the growing anti-Semitic feelings toward Jews in the world at the time. Yet, the fact that they broke out in a number of cities at the same time indicates that they had some organized nature to them. What started as boycotting Jewish businesses soon grew into violence against the Jewish community at large. This was the defining moment for the Jewish population of contemporary Turkey as many had left in the aftermath of the violence. Corry Guttstadt writes that the Resettlement Law, "[which] had been passed only a week before the riots authorized the government to resettle parts of the population viewed as 'not belonging to Turkish culture'" (Guttstadt: 65). Having lost their businesses or having been forced to sell them at less than their worth, many of the Jews who had fled did not "return to their hometowns but remained in Istanbul or left Turkey" (Guttstadt: 69).

Undoubtedly, relocation policies directly affect people's memory of place, how place becomes a part of identity, and also a container of memories. Among many of its effects, displacement ruptures collective identity by cutting the blood that feeds it: collective memory. However, usually, rather than disappearing from the memory of later generations, it takes a different shape: the rupture itself becomes part of the new identity, rather than the new location. Leyla Neyzi, in her study of oral history and subjectivity in Turkey, provides a compelling example. Her interviewee, Gülümser, a twenty-nine-year-old Alevi–Kurd woman, when asked, begins her personal history in 1938. Neyzi writes, "at the beginning of our interview, in response to my first question concerning her life story, Gülümser referred not to the date of her birth, but to a date that turned out to be of greater significance to her life story: 1938" (Neyzi 1999: 9). The violent repression of the local population of Dersim in that year, which caused its inhabitants to leave the city as it was "shut down" for the next two years, is inscribed in Gülümser's personal history through the stories she heard from her elderly family members. The date, or the old name of the city, "Dersim" (the city was renamed "Tunceli" after 1938), which bore little significance for the general public in Turkey until recently, is the starting point for her narration of herself. The national narrations that are supposed to create a unified identity clearly bear no significance in how Gülümser imagines and narrates her past and her identity.

These atrocities are excluded from dominant memory; they are neither commemorated nor taught in the national curriculum. However, what a nation officially commemorates is as important as what it chooses to forget. In today's Turkey, some of the significant and decisive moments during the Independence War are officially commemorated and are public holidays.[25] Further more, both the personality and the legacy of Atatürk have been central to the national memory in Turkey.[26] November 10, the day that he died, is a day of national mourning and at the exact time of his death, 9.05 a.m., a one-minute silence is carried out throughout the country. Atatürk's grave, also known as *Anıtkabir* (memorial tomb), is a celebrated memorial site, with its location and grandiose size, visible from most parts of Ankara.[27] Although Atatürk has always been present in the national psyche, Nazlı Ökten claims that after the military coup of 1980 "admiration for Atatürk evolved to veneration and reached its peak in the 1990s as a reaction to the rise of political Islam" (Ökten 2007: 6).

Military coups and post-1980s Turkey

The Turkish military played an important role in Turkish politics and was very influential until the early 2000s.[28] Unlike in many democratic countries, the Turkish military saw itself as the defender of secularism and the bearer of Kemalist ideology and, hence, intervened wherever it saw fit. The Republic has seen three military interventions throughout its short history: the first in May 1960; the second in March 1971; and the third in September 1980.

The founders of the Turkish Republic and its first president, Kemal Atatürk, all had military backgrounds. However, in an attempt to keep military out of politics, it was required that military personnel who wished to engage in politics had to resign their commissions in the army. Nevertheless, there was a general consensus between the government and the army about the future of Turkey. At the end of the single-party period, Atatürk's Republican People's Party (CHP) lost its popularity, and Adnan Menderes' Democratic Party (DP) was elected in 1950. After remaining in power for ten years, in 1960 the military overthrew the government formed by the DP, justifying the coup as an act in defense of the constitution. The 1960 coup was followed by the introduction of a "liberal" constitution. "Trade unions were given the right to strike, and socialists (though not communists) were allowed to form a party and offer their critique of Turkish society" (Ahmad 2005: 11). After the takeover, the junta regime closed down the DP and sent many of its members to prison. The party's leader, Adnan Menderes, and two ministers, Fatin Rüştü Zorlu and Hasan Polatkan, were sentenced to death in 1961. In the years to come, "Menderes became a martyr and his memory was exploited for political ends by virtually every politician and party" (Ahmad 2005: 137).[29]

In the following years, a number of changes in the armed forces took place in order to create a more or less "autonomous institution" (Ahmad 2005: 12).[30] The second military intervention took place on March 12, 1971 against Süleyman Demirel's Justice Party (Adalet Partisi/AP), forcing him to resign since his government proved unable to deal with the chaos escalating in the country. Many anti-democratic measures were taken during this period. By 1980, the same picture reoccured: chaos, political murders, and the emergence of many revolutionary political organizations. The army took over again on September 12, 1980, this time installing "successful" measures to completely depoliticize the country. The military remained in power for the next three years, during which basic human rights were violated and democracy disrupted. According to Zurcher, the coup of 1980 aimed at such a break with the past that the suspended parties' archives, "including those of the Republican People's Party of the last 30 years (the earlier parts had already been confiscated by the Democratic Party government in the 1950s and their whereabouts are unknown) disappeared and were probably destroyed" (Zurcher: 279).

Although elections took place in 1983, this did not mean a complete return to the democratic process since the military still had a strong influence over politics. All former political parties were banned. Three newly established political parties were allowed to take part in the election: the Nationalist Democratic Party (Milliyetçi Demokrasi Partisi), which received the support of the military; The Populist Party (Halkçı Parti), a center-left party; and Turgut Özal's Motherland (Anavatan/ANAP). ANAP won the elections in 1983 with a "magic formula" that welcomed "all of the four main political ideologies (the extreme right, Islamist, center-right and social democrat) into Motherland's fold" (Özbek 1997: 220). Even though the army has always identified itself as the defender of the secular system, Özal's close relations with Islamic leaders, and his sympathy for "Turkish Islamic Synthesis," also appealed to the military. "The army had been conditioned to see socialism and communism as Turkey's most deadly foes and it saw indoctrination with a mixture of fierce nationalism and a version of Islam friendly to the state as an effective antidote" (Zurcher: 288). It was also Özal who introduced the concepts of privatization and the free global market to Turkey. As a result, the political, as well as the cultural, scene in Turkey has changed dramatically since 1980. "The reshuffled political scene in Turkey got a further jolt when Kurds, who constitute the largest non-Turkish ethnic group in the country, reclaimed and asserted their distinct cultural and ethnic identity and used it as a basis for organizing an armed struggle against the Turkish army" (Kasaba 1997: 16). Hence the Kurdistan Workers Party (PKK) entered into the stage as an armed organization.

The PKK carried out its first attack in 1984 and, according to many, the military coup of 1980 played a significant role in increasing the number of people it was able to recruit after that date. According to sociologist Mesut Yeğen, what is usually referred to as the "Kurdish issue" in Turkey is not simply a matter of ethnic conflict, but one of political struggle (Yeğen 2009b). He connects the emergence of the Kurdish problem directly to the process of modernizing Turkey, which consists of grand projects such as centralizing, nationalizing, and secularizing and spreads across the last two hundred years (Yeğen 2009a: 15). However, the situation following the 1980s became increasingly violent which, in turn, had ramifications on every aspect of life, specifically life in that region. The armed conflict, in addition to thousands of lost lives, produced somewhere around one million internally displaced people (Hacettepe Üniversitesi 2006: 61). The Turkish state's attitude to the problem in the 1990s is often referred to as the "dirty war," as number of Kurdish opinion leaders were assassinated by "unknown actors" (*faili meçhul*). Between 1990 and 1994, sixty-four people affiliated with the Kurdish political party HEP (Halkın Emek Partisi/People's Labour Party) were assassinated, and in 1993 alone, a total number of 510 murders were listed as "by unknown actors." According to Martin van Bruinessen many of these killings were carried out by "persons acting on the instructions of or in cooperation with the police, or in particular, the intelligence service of the gendarmerie, JİTEM" (van Bruinessen 1996: 20–1).[31]

Although the 1980s and 1990s were years of state violence and repression, according to Nurdan Gürbilek, they were also the period in which various groups, such as Kurds, homosexuals, and women, begun to search for their own voices. She explains that "if the street has its own voice, that was felt at its most during the 80s" (Gürbilek 2007: 102). Similarly, Kasaba writes that the change that started in the 1980s was also motivated by an accumulated cynicism and suspicion about "the latest incarnations of the promises of 'enlightened and prosperous tomorrows'. Instead of making further sacrifices for a future that kept eluding them, they were starting to enquire about the histories, institutions, beliefs, identities and cultures from which they had been forcefully separated" (Kasaba 1997: 16).

However, Meltem Ahıska suggests that although it is possible to analyze the emergence of multiple identities in post-1980 Turkey as a way of resisting the repressing unification policies, "it is also possible to think of it within a broader framework, within the framework of the new subject positions created by the political context adjacent to the global and neo-liberal economy" (Ahıska 2005: 314). Nevertheless the reaction was, as Gürbilek argues, "directly against the modern identity." For Gürbilek this was the "return of the provinces," indicating not only areas outside the city, but also "everything that society [excluded] in order to become modern" (Gürbilek 2007: 103–4). Since, in Turkey, modernity was identified with the West, becoming modern meant, to a large extent, the exclusion of anything that was considered to be non-Western. During the 1980s, various segments of society found different ways of expressing the "provincial," the most significant of all being *arabesque*[32] music. Initially the music of the peripheries, *arabesque* was rejected as it could "contaminate" the cultural scene.

The cinema of Turkey: A brief overview

Cinema itself arrived quite early to the Ottoman Empire, with screenings in palaces to the Ottoman elite. The first public screenings were organized by a Romanian Jew, Sigmund Weinberg, in 1897, in a beer house in the Beyoğlu (Pera) district of Istanbul (Scognamillo 2003: 15–16). Filmmaking, however, took longer to begin. Many sources identify the first Turkish film as *Ayastefanos'taki Rus Abidesinin Yıkılışı/ The Demolition of the Russian Monument at San Stefano* (1914), which reportedly shows, as the title indicates, the demolition of the monument in Istanbul erected by Russians on the Ottoman territory to commemorate their victory over the Ottoman Army in 1878. However, there is no document remaining to prove that the film ever existed. According to Dilek Kaya Mutlu, the first reference to the film appears in Rakım Çalapala's 1946 chronicle of Turkish cinema *Türkiye'de Filmcilik/ Filmmaking in Turkey*, crediting Fuat Uzkınay as its director. Mutlu notes that Çalapala mentions the film in a brief note, which was later transformed, "in the hands of the Turkish film historians, into a nationalist, heroic narrative of the beginning of Turkish cinema, with Uzkınay becoming 'the first Turkish film director' and his documentary footage, known today as *The Demolition of the Russian Monument at San Stefan*, the first Turkish film" (Mutlu 2007: 75). Despite the ambiguous story surrounding the film, it is still referred to as the first Turkish film in many sources. Mutlu, analyzing the narratives surrounding the film, writes that there is an apparent obsession with Uzkınay's Turkishness. The film's "history was written in the Republican period, which was marked with the creation of a new Turkish identity detached from that of Ottomans" and, hence, several documentaries made within the borders of the Empire, before Uzkınay's alleged film, were disregarded because the identity of the filmmaker did not conform with the national narrative that was in the making (Mutlu 2007: 82). One of the earliest surviving films made within the Ottoman Empire, the Manaki Brothers' footage of Sultan Mehmed V, was not considered as the first film because, although Ottoman citizens, the brothers were of Greek origin. There are two related points to be made in relation to the discussions regarding the first Turkish film: the first point is that they arose mainly in the 1940s, at least three decades after Uzkınay's alleged film was made, hence indicating the imagined make up of the society, i.e. Muslim–Turkish, which excluded the Manaki Brothers from the timeline; second, the puzzling and unresolved nature of the discussion is a reminder of the difficulty of identifying a national cinema, pointing out the importance of transnational perspectives.

The first films made within the first few decades of the newly established Turkish Republic "display both an effort to construct a national identity and the heavy influence of the West" (Erdoğan and Göktürk 2001: 534). The period between 1922 and 1939 was dominated by one man, Muhsin Ertuğrul. However, one film from this period appears to differ from the rest. The film was written and directed by the famous Turkish communist and poet Nazım Hikmet, who also wrote a number of screenplays under the pseudonym Mümtaz Osman. Hikmet spent his life in and out of prison during the time he lived in Turkey. In 1951, he escaped to Romania, then moved on to the USSR, because of his communist beliefs. His first and only experience as a director was a film called *Güneşe Doğru/ Toward the Sun* (1937), about a man who lost his memory during World War I, but for seventeen years still believed that he was living in that period. After surgery, he recovers and suddenly finds himself in the Turkish Republic (Scognamillo 2003: 82–3). Although there were many later films in the 1960s and 1970s dealing with people who lose their memories (or one of the senses—usually that of sight), Hikmet's appears to be the only one about the experience of war and also was the first of its kind in Turkey. Scognamillo's account of it suggests that the film was highly symbolic in that the rupture, the transition to the Republic, was embodied by the protagonist's loss of memory. Unfortunately, that film has been lost.

The most definitive and important period in the history of Turkish cinema was the "Yeşilçam years." The name of a street in Istanbul, Yeşilçam also refers to the Turkish film industry, specifically the period between the beginning of the 1960s until the end of 1970s.[33] Most films made during the Yeşilçam years were melodramas, which according to Mutlu "provide useful sources for unraveling the social contradictions and anxieties caused by the Turkish modernization/westernization process" (Mutlu 2010: 418). She asserts that the desire for modernity, and the anxieties it creates, are represented through female characters in these films. Women in these films have to acquire certain modern codes of conduct and manners:

> namely how to look, eat, walk, and talk like a "civilized" modern woman (the ideal image of women that the Republican modernization project aimed to create). The woman might undergo a similar process of self-transformation also in order to win the love of a man. Remarkably, a non-Muslim instructor— Armenian or Greek or Turkish—teaches the woman these modern manners. However, while modernity is thus attributed to the West (represented here by minorities), the process of self-transformation is encoded as cosmetic westerni- zation/modernization, and as imitative, artificial, ridiculous, and snobbish—like the non-Muslim instructors themselves (Mutlu 2010: 420).

Yeşilçam's success ended in the late 1970s, when people began to stay away from movie theaters, partly as a result of the political chaos in Turkey, and also due to the arrival and popularity of television in the country. A large section of the industry was forced out of business, and the remaining part survived by producing pornography until the 1980 military coup. Nevertheless, the Yeşilçam era produced some of the biggest stars in Turkey, perhaps the most important of which was Yılmaz Güney. A Kurd from Turkey, Güney started his career as an actor and turned to directing in the 1970s. His film *Yol/The Way* (1982),[34] which was set in Eastern Anatolia under the military regime, won the Palme d'Or for best film at the 1982 Cannes Film Festival. He wrote the script and directed the film by proxy while he was in prison, with the help of his assistant Şerif Gören, who carried out Güney's detailed instructions while making the film. *The Way* tells the story of five inmates on furlough, only to find out that the entire country has been turned into a prison under an oppressive military regime and strict curfews, in which "inside"[35] and "outside" are almost the same thing. Although his films were banned until recently, Güney has never lost his popularity, and remained very influential both as a director and as a political figure in Turkey. His legacy continues today, and he has influenced many up-and-coming Kurdish directors.[36]

One of the defining aspects of filmmaking in Turkey was the practice of censorship. From the beginning, censorship determined the types of films that were made, and many filmmakers had to censor themselves in order to stay in the business. Reasons for censoring a film were various, at times caused by downright paranoia. In his book, *History of Turkish Cinema* (*Türk Sinema Tarihi*), Giovanni Scognamillo notes that a film called *Efelerin Efesi/The Bravest of the Brave* (Şakir Sırmalı, 1952) faced problems because of its subject matter and could only be screened with an additional voiceover at the end, as it was perceived as degrading the memory of war veterans (Scognamillo 2003: 105). Similarly, Metin Erksan's *Susuz Yaz/Dry Summer* (1964), which won the Golden Bear in Berlin in that same year, was censored for featuring underdeveloped farming (wheat fields did not appear to contain the right size of crop), which connotes backwardness.

The arbitrary nature of the censorship practices resulted in self-imposed limits on the stories that could be told, and the way in which those stories were told (see Abisel 2005: 100–1). This inevitably affected the representations of different ethnic and religious groups as the Turkifying policies (and their effects) were continuously felt. When we come to the 1960s, the heyday of Yeşilçam years, the society in Turkey had already been through an independence war, witnessed massacres and displacements in the name of creating a unified nation, discriminatory taxes imposed on its minorities and, in 1955, a pogrom against non-Muslims in Istanbul. Both the representation of minorities, and the representation of these recent historical events, were highly problematic: if mentioned at all, references were never explicit. Similarly, with the uneasiness created by their experiences, the remaining non-Muslim populations were understandably very cautious. A telling example of how auto-censoring was used to avoid trouble can be seen in the number of non-Muslim actors and actresses who changed their names to Turkish ones for the screen. An example of this is Armenian actor Sami Hazinses, whose real name was Samuel Uluçyan. His ethnic identity only became public knowledge after his death in 2002, even though he was very well-known to Turkish audiences. Although such a decision to change one's name appears to be "voluntary," it cannot be thought independent of the actual social and political pressures non-Muslims had to endure at the time.

There is not yet an extensive study on how censorship practices might have affected the representation of minorities in Turkey, but it would not be wrong to assume that any "sensitive" subject was either avoided or mentioned subtly. There are references to minorities in films from the 1960s and 1970s, but these are insignificant and limited in terms of numbers. Writing on the creation of a national identity in relation to cinema, Umut Tümay Arslan, for example, mentions two films: *Üç Arkadaş/Three Friends* (Memduh Ün, 1958) and *Ah Güzel Istanbul/ Oh Beautiful Istanbul* (Atıf Yilmaz, 1966). Arslan notes that *Three Friends*, made only three years after the September 1955 pogrom against the non-Muslim population, includes an Armenian character named Artin Dartanyan in its effort to acknowledge the ethnic make up of Istanbul.[37] *Oh Beautiful Istanbul* on the other hand, made ten years after the pogrom, longs for the glorious years of the city, and its disappearing beauty, through a character called Haşmet, but in the process eliminates the city's non-Muslim past, imagining an Istanbul that has always been Turkish (Arslan 2010: 208–20). Similar references were made to minorities in a number of films of the time, but the political climate was never ripe enough to actually question the recent history, to allow explicit acknowledgment of the minorities, and more importantly to look the past in the face. Their existence in these stories is limited to their accents, names, and to subtle comments. It should also be noted that their involvement in the industry went beyond acting as many also worked behind the camera, as well as managing film theaters from early on in the Republic. In short, in the case of non-Muslims in Turkish cinema, the situation reflected the general attitude of the country toward its non-Muslim citizens: rather than being shaped by specifically spelled-out regulations regarding their representation, their existence was written out of the history and, hence, from the visual realm of the country.

However, it was a slightly different situation with regard to the Kurds. In addition to the general Turkification policies that included all ethnic and religious minorities, the Kurds had to endure an additional pressure during the 1980s and 1990s, with regulations that were explicitly aimed to prohibit the use of the Kurdish language (see Chapters 2 and 5). This resulted in representations that could only "imply" Kurdishness, without explicitly making the Kurdish question the core of the narrative. But even such careful auto-censoring could not guarantee a trouble-free release, or any form of release at all, as was the case for Yılmaz Güney's films, particularly *The Way*.[38]

The list of films being censored since the 1930s is long, and the reasons for their "unsuitability" are various. Although the details of the matter are beyond this project, it is important to note that what seems to be one of the defining elements of the practice throughout the decades is what Ahıska defines as "occidentalist fantasy", which combines "the desire to be(come) western with the resistance to it" (Ahıska 2005: 327). This perception of the self from the perspective of an assumed Western gaze continues to exist and has always been in dialogue with the West, as the West, being "the 'true' owners of the 'original'," continued to redefine the limits of both the East and the West (Ahıska 2005: 47). What is more this "occidentalist fantasy" informs not only the practice of censorship, but also the Turkish cinema itself, as new ventures in the country often positioned themselves in relation to Western cinema by either producing copies of Western films or by defining themselves entirely against it.

The tension around the question of identity along with the social, economical, and political changes inevitably affected this process and the films produced. The period after the 1990s, which saw the revival of the Turkish cinema, represents an important break with this heritage. While the films made during the period between 1940 and 1970 tried, predominantly, to find the cinematic voice of the "nation," in other words making films that attempt to answer the question of "who we are," the period after the 1990s witnessed a body of films *asking* the question: "who are we?". Even though there is a danger of reducing a period of thirty years to a few groups of filmmakers, after the 1990s the search for a unique voice for already existing and defined local cultural practices is displaced by the need to understand the complexities that exist in Turkey. Instead of finding a voice for an existing image, filmmakers started questioning the legitimacy of the image itself, which marked the beginning of the "new cinema of Turkey."

2

Recurring Themes and Motifs

In a political and social climate marked by complex and rapid change, identity (both past and present) becomes a focal point, a site to observe cultural change but also a site where resistance to that change takes place. The political milieu inevitably reproduces itself, or its critique, in films, as is the case in Turkey. This is visible in the range of films produced in, and about, Turkey within the last two decades. The timing and the subject matter of these films, therefore, are not coincidental. As will become evident in the following chapters, the films examined as part of this book all deal with issues that are debated intensely and have been influential in shaping political and cultural life in Turkey. However, while there is a common concern running through these films, i.e. an interest in history, memory, and identity, there is also continuity in style. Although the films examined were chosen solely on the basis of their subject matter and their relation to the issues contested in contemporary Turkey, and not based on a predetermined, forced unity between them, a closer look reveals that they share certain aesthetic qualities, as well as a number of recurring themes. Furthermore, these shared aesthetic qualities are not adjacent to the themes they deal with, but are determined by those very themes, the lived experiences created by those events the films scrutinize. Hence, before examining the films and the conditions in which they are produced in detail, this chapter looks at the recurring themes and motifs in the films, which I examine under five categories: the politics of language, silence, spatial relations, haunted narratives, and epistolary narratives. These categories, however, are not mutually exclusive, but rather often intersect with one another. They intersect because each category relates to an aspect of memory and history, and how film deals with the past and present.

As the previous chapter has outlined, the social and economic changes taking place both in Turkey and in the world made an impact on cultural production, and opened a discursive space for certain matters to be argued more openly. This, however, should not, as it often is, be seen as "the return of the repressed," but perhaps the return of the suppressed/ignored/forgotten. The historical events with which these films deal (such as the Armenian genocide and the Kurdish question) have never completely disappeared from the public sphere, yet they have not necessarily been a part of the popular discourse in the past in the way, and to the extent, that they are at present.

Memory, although by definition about the past, is formed and shaped in the present. It is this aspect of memory, its affiliation with the present although it appears to belong to the past, that in these films becomes interesting and revealing about anxieties related to identity and memory in contemporary Turkey. Most of the films analyzed here are made by filmmakers who are not only aware of their ambiguous relation to history and memory, but who have also developed strategies to question the notion of truth as well as the medium's participation within the process of "truthmaking." This is not to say that truth does not/cannot exist and that it is constructed, but more often than not the narration of it leaves certain discourses out, while privileging others, and these films do not refrain from admitting it, sometimes with their self-reflexive qualities, sometimes by including the less represented discourses in their narration, but often by the simple act of acknowledging the existing lack of discourse and recognition of the subject matter.

Displacement, physical or otherwise, is an important element in the films examined here, one that binds together the five recurring elements discussed below. It also forms the kernel of this book, not only as a concept, but also as an analytical tool through which I attempt to read this emerging image and its aesthetic qualities. The rupture created displaces not only the body, but also the understanding of the self, causing a liminal existence that is neither here nor there. The involuntary/forced migrations in recent Turkish history resulted in many displaced communities both inside and outside Turkey. The lack of official recognition of the effects on the people who were forced to leave what they called "home" is a recurring concern of, if not the driving force behind, these films. It is not a coincidence that toward the end of 1990s, the time the films in question started being made, the reality and the scale of the Kurdish forced migration made itself known to the larger public. Between 1985 and 2005, the displaced Kurdish population was somewhere between 500,000 and a million people.

There were, however, other displacements and migrations in addition to that of the Kurds, as outlined in the previous chapter. As more silences were broken and more research carried out, more about the past came to the attention of the general public. The painful realities of the population exchange between Greece and Turkey, as well as the gloomy facts of the once there, but no longer existing Armenian population of Anatolia, and the absence of discourse on the subject until very recently, have demanded reconsideration of the past and its representation in the present.

Displacement in Turkey, however, is not limited to the physical removal/relocation of populations. In addition to those displaced in the name of creating ethnic purity and national unity, in its early years the Republic itself was imagined through displaced geography, from Anatolia to Central Asia. According to Keyder, Turkish nationalism not only constructed an unbroken ethnic history, much like all other nationalist movements wanting to break away from the Ottoman Empire, but also imagined the nation as originating "not in the new heartland of Anatolia but in a mythical geography" (Keyder 2006: 49).

> The foundation myth chosen for nationalist discourse posited a territorial origin in a distant land, "Orta Asya" or "Central Asya", which furthermore was supposed to have undergone major environmental transformation, causing the Turks to migrate. Consequently the land of origin could not be imagined: it was irreclaimable not only because it was distant but also because it was irreversibly altered. Significantly, this imagined land held a greater reality than the conquered and currently occupied Anatolia. National history in the republic was devoid of spatial reference (Keyder 2006: 49).

In other words, in an attempt to locate the republican project in a "neutral" space, the "Turkish History Thesis" displaced the history of people. This was seen as necessary in order to be able to overlook the non-Turkish history of Anatolia.

The struggle over space and its history/memory has been the determining factor in shaping the nationalist discourse in Turkey. The decision to relocate the capital from the former seat of the Ottoman Empire, Istanbul, to a small, rural city in the center of the country, Ankara, can be seen as part of this effort. Similarly the changing of the names of villages and towns from their Greek, Armenian, and Kurdish origins to Turkish, is one of the many results of the nationalist discourse producing space. It is, therefore, not entirely arbitrary that the spatial relations and the largely untold stories of particular peoples/locations become significant in the films made within the last twenty years as they coincide with renewed interest in the history and memory of Asia Minor.

Inevitably, with displacement as a driving force, certain themes come to the fore that are in close relation to various aspects of memory, practices, and technologies of remembering. In what follows, bearing in mind the issues and connections addressed, I will reflect on some of the recurring themes and motifs in these films, while thinking about the political and social conditions that allowed/caused this image to emerge. Although examined under five separate categories, these themes and motifs are interconnected not only in the ways they appear in films, but also in the ways in which they create meaning.

The politics of language and film

In a 2010 exhibition called *My Dear Brother*, curator Osman Köker brought together postcards sent by Ottoman Armenians 100 years ago, based on his book *Armenians in Turkey 100 Years Ago* (2005). One of the postcards exhibited captured a street in Kadıköy, a district of Istanbul. The caption pointed out the shop in the background whose signboard included writing in four different languages, reminding the visitors of a past that was there not so long ago, but that no longer exists. In contemporary Turkey, neither the practice of having multi-languaged signposts, nor the languages themselves that were once heard on the streets of Istanbul, still exist. However, what is noteworthy here is not the multilingual nature of daily encounters, but the curator's need to highlight the practice. The curator's decision to call attention to this particular aspect of the photograph not only informs *today's* audiences, but also reflects present-day sensibilities: the renewed interest in the assumed multicultural life in the Ottoman Empire and the disappearing sonic variety in both Istanbul and the rest of Turkey.

After the overthrow of the Ottoman Empire, creating a unified nation was a priority for the newly established Republic. One of the most important steps toward this aim was to create a unified language among its citizens, for which the Turkish Republic had a number of different strategies. The establishment of the Institute of Turkish Language (*Türk Dil Kurumu*) in 1932, to oversee the "verbal hygiene"[1] of Turkish, and the changing definitions of the "official language" (the "language of the state," according to the 1982 constitution), are among the strategies that created Turkey's problematic relationship with language. If nothing else, the language policies destroyed the multilinguistic heritage of the country, and created resentment among some of its citizens. The recently renewed interest in this aspect of the past is reflected in contemporary cinema. From the mid-1990s onward, the use of minority languages in films, languages that were once spoken widely in Istanbul as well as in Anatolia, have become significantly more frequent. Films such as *Bulutları Beklerken/Waiting for the Clouds* (Yeşim Ustaoğlu, 2003), *Büyük Adam Küçük Aşk/Hejar* (2001), *Autumn* (Özcan Alper, 2008), *İki Dil Bir Bavul/On the Way to School* (Orhan Eskiköy and Özgür Doğan, 2009), *Gitmek/My Marlon and Brando* (Hüseyin Karabey, 2008), and *Min Dit* (Miraz Bezar, 2009), among others all use more than one language, sometimes as a political statement (*Hejar, Autumn, On the Way to School*), sometimes as an element that haunts the narrative (*Waiting for the Clouds*), and at other times for no other reason other than realist concerns. The issue becomes visible in these films in various ways, all of which question and challenge the idea (or the myth) of a unified language.

Both Mikhail Bakhtin and Pierre Bourdieu write on the subject of unified language and the power relations that are interwoven with it. Although Bakhtin's and Bourdieu's views of popular culture differ (Bakhtin sees subversive potentialities in popular culture, whereas Bourdieu is more pessimistic about it), there are striking similarities between the two in their views on language and society. According to Bakhtin, not only are there different languages or dialects spoken within a given community, that is "polyglossia," but there are also different "social" languages which he calls "heteroglossia," a term that refers to socio-ideological languages used by different classes, different professions, and so on. For Bakhtin "language is heteroglot from top to bottom" at any given moment of its historical existence (Bakhtin 2008: 291), because "the meaning of a word is determined entirely by its context" (Bakhtin 1986: 79). Both polyglossia and heteroglossia are important in relation to Turkey's history, although polyglossia becomes more significant to the extent that it challenges the idea of the unified language, which is central to the official ideology of the Republic. In other words, there is, in most instances, no legal restriction or regulation on how heteroglossia functions, whereas the use of languages spoken by non-Turkish communities in Turkey was regulated and restricted by the state. Nevertheless, both polyglossia and heteroglossia challenge the notion of unitary language, which, Bakhtin writes, "is not something given but is always in essence posited—and at every moment of its linguistic life it is opposed to the realities of heteroglossia" (Bakhtin 2008: 270).

Bourdieu also sees language in its social context and rejects the possibility that language could be homogenous in any given community at any given time. Homogenous language is a creation, which requires certain conditions and the complicity of its subjects. Creating a homogenous language demands symbolic domination and "all symbolic domination presupposes, on the part of those who submit to it, a form of complicity which is neither passive submission to external constraints nor free adherence to values" (Bourdieu 2005: 51). Similar to Bakhtin's concept of heteroglossia, Bourdieu also acknowledges that the use of language "depends on the social position of its speaker, which governs the access he can have to the language of the institution that is, to the official, orthodox and legitimate speech" (Bourdieu 2005: 109). In his writings on language and power, Bourdieu mentions "legitimate" language, which more often than not is the same as the official language. According to him "the official language is bound up with the state, both in its genesis and in its social uses. It is in the process of state formation that the conditions are created for the constitution of a unified linguistic market, dominated by the official language" (Bourdieu 2005: 45). The myth of unified language in Bakhtin's writings, then, is the (mis)recognition of legitimacy in the language of the dominant in Bourdieu.

Hence, the coexistence of different languages in these films, the juxtapositions of them in the diegetic space, necessarily undermines the myth/notion of a unified language. However, when more than one language is spoken by one individual, switching between languages, it also functions as a reminder of the bilingual communities that, although forgotten, existed and still exist throughout Turkey. These language switches in turn help de-hierarchize the languages themselves, as the power relations between them are challenged.

Although an aspect of many films, specifically those that deal with displacement, diaspora and minority experiences, films about the Kurds give special importance to the question of language. Unlike the non-Muslim minorities, whose legal rights were secured to an extent by the treaty of Lausanne, Kurdish subjects did not enjoy such rights. Despite the League of Nations' definition of minorities based on religious, linguistic, and ethnic origins, in Lausanne, Turkey "did not accept the full criterion as applicable [...]; it recognized only 'non-Muslims' as constituting a minority" (Oran 2007: 35).[2] This, in turn, resulted in limiting the applicability of the rights articulated in the treaty, such as using their languages "in the press, or in publications of any kind or at public meetings" (article 39; see Oran 2006: 66–80), which had an impact on various Muslim minority groups in Turkey, most notably on the Kurds. One of the most important demands of the Kurdish population in Turkey has been the right to be educated in their native language. However, aware of the important role education plays "in the process which leads to the construction, legitimation and imposition of an official language" (Bourdieu 2005: 48), Turkey did the opposite and prioritized the teaching of Turkish to Kurdish children with government-funded boarding schools in Kurdish-populated areas, a policy that was particularly designed for the Kurds as part of the assimilation project. Although the ban on Kurdish is now lifted, the right to be educated in Kurdish is still seen as a threat by the state apparatus.

The 2009 documentary *On the Way to School* (Orhan Eskiköy and Özgür Doğan) deals directly with the issue of language from the perspective of education. The film follows a young Turkish teacher who is appointed to a primary school in a small Kurdish village in eastern Turkey, and documents a school year as he tries to teach the curriculum to his pupils, most of whom speak only Kurdish, a language that the teacher himself cannot speak. However, since Kurdish is the only language the pupils can speak, school becomes a place where communication itself is banned, unless and until they learn Turkish. This establishes the power structures, making sure the pupils learn not only the language itself but also the assumed hierarchy among languages. The film, successfully capturing the absurdity of the situation, caused heated debates in Turkey as discussions on education in Kurdish increasingly took the film as a reference point.

A few years later, Orhan Eskiköy collaborated with Zeynel Doğan on another project, *Babamın Sesi/My Father's Voice* (2012), this time subtly dealing with the issue of language, along with the realities of being a Kurd in the 1980s and 1990s, and with the generation of parents whose sons and daughters left to join the Kurdish guerrilla force. Although not the main concern of the film, the issue of education in one's native language crops up in the background; in addition the majority of the dialogue takes place in Kurdish. The most notable of those moments is when the film reminds its audience of the words of then Prime Minister Erdoğan, demanding that the Turks in Germany should have the right to be educated in Turkish if they choose to. However, Erdoğan had been refusing to discuss the same right for the Kurdish citizens of Turkey. The film brings Erdoğan's words to the narrative through the news, which is playing on the television in the background, without having the characters respond to it. It is a subtle insertion of the "now" in the film to its diegetic space via television, evoking the unjust nature of the situation through the words of the country's own prime minister, who is asking for just treatment for Germany's Turkish–German population, yet denying the same right to the Kurdish citizens of Turkey.

One of the first films to deal directly with the relation of power and language was Handan İpekçi's *Hejar*, in which a little Kurdish girl and a patriotic, retired Turkish judge are stuck in a flat together without a common language between them. At the time the film made a considerable impact, as it questioned the legitimacy of such a ban on the use of language. However, *Hejar's* most interesting aspect, with regard to language, is not the use of Kurdish, but rather the filmmaker's decision not to provide subtitles for the brief exchanges between the little girl, Hejar, and the retired judge, Rıfat. By doing this, the director creates a space for the audience to comprehend the situation without assigning power to either of the languages. Such conscious and instrumental use of subtitles inevitably gestures toward the politics of language, and, more specifically, toward the politics of subtitles: an area that is largely neglected in film studies, but which determines the filmic experience of the majority of the world.

Subtitles became part of foreign-language film viewing after the introduction of sound, as the "foreignness" of a film (with the introduction of sound film) became a problem when distributing these films. Many countries practiced dubbing along with subtitling when films in foreign languages were screened. However, as Danan points out, there is a relation between the preferred method of translation in film (dubbing over subtitling) and the language policies in a given country.[3] When a country seeks to standardize national language "for the sake of national unity, and [forbids] minority groups to speak their own dialects or languages," the preferred method is usually dubbing (Danan 612). Not surprisingly Turkey too sought to regulate the film industry with similar methods. Dubbing was used along with subtitling in the early decades of sound film and the Turkish market attracted films not only from Europe and the United States, but also from India and Egypt. Ahmet Gürata, looking at different modes of cultural adaptations in film in Turkey, considers dubbing as one of the tools that made familiarization with otherwise foreign texts possible. Gürata writes:

> Although most of the Egyptian films were dubbed and their soundtracks replaced by Turkish ones, a few were exhibited with subtitles and original soundtracks [...]. In 1942, the secretariat of the Republican People's Party, which

ruled throughout the one-party period, sent an official letter to the Interior Ministry pleading for a ban on such screenings in Adana and Mersin—cities with a significant Arab–Turkish population—, as these films were "damaging people's feeling toward the Turkish language". After this complaint, in June 1943 the Interior Ministry wrote to the Censorship Committee in Istanbul suggesting a ban on Egyptian films in Kurdish or Arab-populated areas in eastern Turkey: "We believe no films in Arabic—whether dubbed or in the original language— should be screened in Bitlis, Diyarbakır, Gaziantep, Hatay, İçel, Adana, Siirt or Mardin (Tikveş 1968: 97–8)" (Gürata: 87).[4]

However, the use of subtitling also has its own politics. In addition to the general difficulties of translation, there are medium-specific issues as well.[5] Subtitles are usually considered as an additional component, simply an aid to help the spectator follow the film, an addition to the image, meant to be overlooked. It is usually assumed that the text, that is the film, would have an audience who could access it without the aid of subtitles. Although this is true for many cases, there exists a specific kind of filmmaking in which questions of language play a key role. These films break the established rules of subtitling and in that subversion are able to achieve not only a critical stance on the use of language in film (hence the assumed hierarchy among languages), but also use subtitles as part of the frame. Similarly, by not providing subtitles during a "foreign" conversation, language and translation issues are made visible.

One of the most important aspects of the use of subtitles in the films analyzed here is that these films are "foreign"—to a degree—to all their viewers, as they deny full access to the text without the aid of subtitles. In the context of Turkey, positioning the "target audience" as "foreign" is an important political statement, considering the language policies that were in effect for a long time in the country. The decision not to provide subtitles for the conversations between the Kurdish girl and the Turkish judge in *Hejar*, for example, cannot be considered independently of the language policies about the use of Kurdish in Turkey, neither can the continuous appearance of bilingual characters.

Subtitles are also an important component of the image in Hüseyin Karabey's *My Marlon and Brando* (2008). Based on the true story of a young Turkish woman, Ayça Damgacı, who fell in love with an Iraqi Kurd, Hama Ali, the film follows her attempt to travel to northern Iraq in order to see Hama Ali. As she journeys, various languages (Turkish, Kurdish, English, and Farsi) are spoken. As a result, the film permits very few people to view it without needing the aid of subtitles, thereby stripping away the power any one language might have over another.

The use of Kurdish in both films (or any language in any film other than the dominant language) functions to challenge the notion of "legitimate language" and what it stands for, what it represents, and what it disseminates. The Kurdish language, which was banned or supposed to be forgotten in order to create a unified nation, reappears to haunt the narrative space, and disrupts the idea of a unified language. Nevertheless, neither the political and social conditions, nor the representations of those conditions remain the same. Looking at the films, it is possible to detect the changes in how the issue is perceived and represented. While *Hejar* emphasizes the anguish that the ban on language—and assimilation policies—caused, *My Marlon and Brando* is more concerned with acknowledging the existence of polyglossia, as well as heteroglossia, *despite* the efforts of assimilation.

Attention paid to the languages spoken in Turkey is a recurring element in the films made in the last two decades, not only in Kurdish, but also in other minority languages. *Waiting for the Clouds*, for example, includes Greek, as it specifically deals with a Turkish–Greek woman's loss of language, and with it her loss of part of her identity. It is, first through her rejection of Turkish, and later through her use of Greek, that the audience develops a sense of the rupture she has suffered. Moreover, the issue of language makes itself visible in many films, even when they are not explicitly dealing with language itself. In *Güz Sancısı/ Pains of Autumn* (2008), a film set in 1950s Istanbul, we see characters speaking both Greek and Turkish fluently, and continuously switching between them, with each other. Differing from *Waiting for the Clouds*, here the switches are more casual, highlighting the bilingual nature of the characters' lives.

Finally in *Autumn* (Özcan Alper, 2008), Hemshin/Homshetsma, a neglected language, the existence of which is forgotten by many, takes center stage. Hemshin is a dialect of western Armenian and is spoken in parts of the Black Sea region. The director had previously used Hemshin in his short film *Grandma/Momi* (2001), which takes place in the same region. *Momi* was not only Alper's first film, but also the first film to be made in this highly neglected language. A Hemshin (*Hemşinli*) himself, Alper refers to his experiences within the education system in an interview, outlining a story similar to that of the children in *On the Way to School*. He notes that Hemshin was the first language he learned and it remained the only one until he started school (Alper, *Bianet*). However, concerned that efforts to keep the language alive have been diminishing in recent years, Alper decided to make a film using his native language.

Autumn is Alper's first feature film and deals with a recent and devastating event. In 2000, in order to take control of the protestors in an Istanbul prison, Turkish troops were ordered into the prison. As a result of the operation, which was ironically called "Operation Back to Life" (*Hayata Dönüş Operasyonu*), twenty-six people died and many more were injured. The film focuses on an inmate, Yusuf (Onur Saylak), who was in prison at the time and witnessed some horrific scenes. After becoming terminally ill, he is released and the film chronicles the last few months of his life, which he spends in his hometown. Even though *Autumn* is an explicitly political film, according to the director its most political side is not its subject matter, but the fact that the Hemshin language is used in the film. Alper states that "we live in a place where the existence of other languages is ignored, where Turkification is forced" (Alper, *Birgün*), and it is for this reason that using Hemshin was a highly political gesture on his part. As both Bakhtin and Bourdieu, among others, remind us, words mean different things and acquire different powers depending on who utters those words and in what context. It is in the context of Turkey that the gesture of speaking in one's native language becomes a political statement.

The interest in the languages spoken in Anatolia is clearly an important element in these films. These languages are represented in these films as a result of a conscious decision on the part of their creators as they attempt to make the forced "nature" of the Turkish language as a unification point visible. The interest, however, is not limited to films but can be encountered in various realms of cultural production, since these films are ultimately reflecting an ongoing and renewed interest in the country's past.

Silence

Silence is an ambiguous concept that is a recurring narrative element in many films that deal with oppression and/or trauma. It can be a means of forgetting, a sign of denial, an act of commemoration (for instance in minute silences), or it can become an instrument for resistance, as well as for torture. Silence, depending on who is using it and in what context, can indicate consent and/or can be a tool for both the victims and the perpetrators. It can occur as a result of violence (symbolic or otherwise), as well as being an instrument of such violence. Although silence might seem to be the opposite of speech, the two work very much together. In sound film, silence has an effect on the viewer that is reminiscent of the still moments in film: it is in relation to sound that silence becomes "visible." As Lacan puts it, "crying does not stand out against a background of silence but on the contrary makes the silence emerge as silence" (Lacan 1977: 26). It is in connection with sound that silence becomes an articulation in itself.

While characters who reject speech form a recurring trope in most of the films analyzed here, their silences serve different purposes depending on the context. However, silence, in these films, is never used as opposite of speech. It is never an absence of meaning or a lack of communication. Its meaning also depends heavily on the listener, whether s/he exists to acknowledge the silence. The three-fold relation between film, cultural memory, and silence becomes more evident here because film, by definition, puts its audience in the position of listeners. It is, therefore, also crucial to consider what silence communicates to the audience as well as to the diegetic characters.

Silence, whether narrative or collective, is an inevitable element of stories that deal with history, forgetting, and remembering. In the establishment of the Turkish Republic, and in the act of nation-building, certain events were silenced, brushed under the carpet, in order to maintain a monumental history. Such silence does not necessarily always occur in the form of a ban on the freedom of speech, but sometimes as a mere exclusion of certain parts of the history from the dominant discourse: silencing memories through absence of discourse. This is most relevant regarding the discourse on the Armenian genocide in Turkey, as the subject "disappeared" from the public sphere within a decade of its occurrence.

Although silence, and silent characters, in general, occur often in these films, the depiction of women's silences is particularly important, not because it "means" more when women are silenced, but because it creates a bigger, "quieter" silence. If the ultimate method of silencing is to annihilate the person, then the instances of so called "honor killings" are testimonies to such silencing being exercised on women. Such was the story of Yılmaz Güney's acclaimed *Yol* (1982), as well as of a more recent film by Handan İpekçi, *Saklı Yüzler/Hidden Faces* (2007). Similarly, Zeki Demirkubuz, one of the most celebrated directors of the new cinema of Turkey, has portrayed silent female characters who have lost their ability to hear, and, hence, to speak, due to domestic violence. One of the most popular films in the history of Turkish cinema (and the film that for some initiated the revival of the Turkish cinema), *Eşkıya*/Bandit (Yavuz Turgul, 1997) includes a female character who is forced into an unhappy marriage and subsequently refuses to utter a single word. Finally, Ayşe/Eleni, in *Waiting for the Clouds*, and Nusret, in *Pandora'nın Kutusu/Pandora's Box* (2008), both films by Yeşim Ustaoğlu, are both characters whose lives are shaped by their own—as well as others'—silences.

The portrayed silence of women in recent films is meaningful in the context of Turkish history. In the forced migrations of certain minorities, many young girls were left behind with Turkish families because it was safer than the journey itself. In most cases, they were adopted, converted to Islam, and kept quiet about their pasts. It was not until the late 1990s that their stories came to be known by a larger public. Two noteworthy examples are Fethiye Çetin's book *Anneannem/ My Grandmother*, and Yeşim Ustaoğlu's film *Waiting for the Clouds*, also stories told by women. While Ustaoğlu's film is based on a book by Yorgo Andreadis, *Tamama: Pontus' Lost Child*, Çetin's book is based on her grandmother's personal experiences. Although she spent most of her childhood living with her grandparents in Maden, a small village in the southeast of Turkey, Çetin did not know about her grandmother's Armenian roots until she was twenty-five years old. In her book, she tells her grandmother's story and her silence regarding the atrocities that she had to witness. A large part of her family were killed or forced to leave their village, while her grandmother and some other girls were adopted by a Turkish family. Most of these girls converted to Islam and changed their names to blend in. Their past was never mentioned, although almost everyone in the village knew the truth. However, the silence that existed was not an absolute silence. In order to maintain the ambiguous status of these women (or any victim of oppression come to that) a degree of "whispering" was also needed to keep them at bay, since the very act of including these girls in the society worked against the initial attempt of purifying the society. Not surprisingly, the anecdotes in Çetin's book confirm that some families, fearing that they would "contaminate" their blood, rejected these women as potential brides.

Writing on the book and its, to a certain degree, unexpectedly warm and emotional reception in Turkey, Ayşe Gül Altınay observes that the book "by remembering a silenced history [...] opens up a new space for sharing" (Altınay 2006: 130). The book has been, in more ways than one, instrumental in triggering an important discussion by breaking the decades-long silence of one woman. Coincidently, and as a testimony to the interest in such stories, Ustaoğlu's film *Waiting for the Clouds* was released a year before the book's

publication. However, in comparison to the book, *Waiting for the Clouds* did
not receive a similar emotional response from audiences, perhaps due, in part to
the way that the character and her silence are narrated. In *My Grandmother*, the
woman hides her story from even her family members, and dies with her secret.
As she did not hold anyone accountable, her silence appears as an acceptance
of the situation, devoid of anger. In *Waiting for the Clouds*, on the other hand,
the director portrays Ayşe/Eleni's anger as she holds those who were responsible
for her forced silence accountable for her suffering. She does not hide her anger
and disappointment and it is Ayşe/Eleni herself who articulates it. Rather than
portraying it as an event that happened in the past for which today's society
cannot be held accountable, the film brings the issue close to home, and thus
requires an ethical position rather than an emotional response to an individual
(story). The film reflects the larger silence of the society in Ayşe's/Eleni's silence.

Wendy Brown writes that "the work of breaking silence can metamorphose
into new techniques of domination, how our truths can become our rulers
rather than our emancipators, how our confessions become the norms by
which we are regulated" (Brown: 91). Yet, the use of silence in film can potentially function in such a way that it "gestures" toward both aspects of silence. It
can simultaneously function to signify the subject's silence, as well as breaking
it without "metamorphos[ing] into new techniques of domination." Film, in
this sense, can offer the possibility of both acknowledging the silence, and at
the same time breaking it, particularly because film allows space for silence
to appear for what it is: as just silence. Its use in cinema, which is surprisingly
often in films dealing with displacement and migration, becomes a device that
articulates a certain type of experience. Such a silence is remarkably the kernel
of two of the films dealt with here, namely the previously mentioned *Waiting for
the Clouds* and Atom Egoyan's *Ararat*.

Waiting for the Clouds includes a character who, in order to survive, has had
to take up a forged identity and remain silent about her past for most of her
adult life. This silence, which connotes a symbolic violence, is later turned into
a liberating and chosen silence during which she goes through a liminal phase.
The language that is forced upon her, which is supposed to be unifying, is a
mechanism of oppression. In her reclamation of her lost identity, her silence
articulates more than speech. In *Ararat*, however, the silence occupies a larger
space and is used in a more ambiguous way. In addition to silence that is used to
deny knowledge to certain characters (i.e. Ani's refusal to provide Celia with the
answers that she is after), silence is also used when representing Arshile Gorky,

who occupies a pivotal space within Armenian history with his landmark painting *Artist and His Mother* (discussed in detail in Chapter 4), in addition to his importance in Egoyan's film.

Egoyan, throughout his career, made use of silence in his films in various ways. In a lengthy interview with Hamid Naficy, responding to a question regarding the silent characters in his films (who are mostly Armenians), Egoyan mentions the notion of the "silent witness":

> That is, someone who has information, a key that would give the viewers some access to what is going on. [...] These [characters] are all people who have secrets but cannot actually express them because they've been traumatised into silence. I think that the whole notion of persecution, of speech being a potential weapon, and of being silenced are obviously things that are part of my history (Egoyan 1997: 222).

In *Ararat* Egoyan depicts Gorky in his studio working on *Artist and His Mother*. Egoyan's awareness of the problems of both discourse and historical truth forces him to create a liminal character out of Gorky, who exists, as a character, in between the world of many discourses. And, by making him utter not a single word, while going through a pain that is beyond imagination, Egoyan asks his audience to recognize the sound of the tree that fell in the forest, even though there was nobody to hear it when it fell. Silence becomes not only a condition of survival, but also the possibility to overcome what created it in the first place.

Egoyan's silences, and the notion of the silent witness, appear more subtle when compared to the 2014 film on the Armenian genocide, *The Cut*, by the Turkish–German director Fatih Akın. In Akın's film, he places a silent—or silenced—character, Nazaret (Tahar Rahim), at the center of the story. Nazaret becomes mute as a result of not only what he has endured, but also what he has had to witness and what he has had to carry within himself as a result of it. He receives a cut to his throat, a cut that was meant to slit his throat and kill him, but which instead leaves him silent. However, Nazaret's condition is not physical; it is his psyche that is lacerated and that leaves him unable to speak about what he has endured, unable to bring what he witnessed to the level of language.

Although silence occurs often as a narrative element, some of these films choose to acknowledge the silence without using it as a narrative element embodied by a character. In these films, although they do not necessarily feature a character who refuses, or is unable to speak, silence created by untold, unacknowledged pasts still casts a shadow over the narrative. Such pregnant silences, charged with the knowledge of what has been written out by the official history, enable the narrative to acknowledge what has been left unsaid, without explicitly articulating it. This, in other words, is a narrative silence, which refers to itself, making the processes of silencing occur intelligible, revealing the foundations of its own construction. Hence, by acknowledging its own silence, the text is able to refer to a larger silence. In *Waiting for the Clouds*, for instance, we are given an example of both a silent character and a historical silence that has affected the character's life. Although the protagonist, Ayse/Eleni, stops talking in the second half of the film and decides to embody the historical silence imposed upon her—and in that very act subverts it—the film, in fact, opens with another type of silence, charged with the felt presence of the unacknowledged. When Ayse's/Eleni's real background, her real parents' name, and her real ethnic origin, are all concealed, the silence is no longer the mere absence of words, but the absence of truth. Similarly, Serdar Akar's film *Dar Alanda Kısa Paslaşmalar/Offside* (2000) includes a character whose silence is revealed only at the end, after his death. He is unveiled as an Armenian who remained quiet about his identity, and the moment his silence becomes visible is also the moment that society's silence is exposed. Here the film does not use silence as a narrative element, but acknowledges its existence within the society. As Suner points out, the silence that existed in the community made the community "function." However, "beneath the appearance of a harmonious community life lies the silencing of cultural difference" (Suner 2009: 76).

The existence, or the forced nature, of such harmony is questioned in the portrayal of another silent woman, in Ümit Ünal's 2001 film, 9. It focuses on the murder of a homeless Jewish woman, Kirpi, and its investigation, during which the people in the neighborhood are interrogated. During the course of these interrogations, not only does Kirpi's story surface, but we also see how the idea of harmony, the idea of harmonious community, is maintained; how, to be in this "happy family" picture, each individual is required to remain silent about who they are. Yet Kirpi is not even invited into the picture because her presence alters it radically: she is seen as "dirt," not just metaphorically, but also literally as, reminding us of Mary Douglas' famous definition of dirt, is a "matter out of place."

Finally, Ustaoğlu's *Pandora's Box*, similar to her previously mentioned *Waiting for the Clouds*, also follows an aging woman and her family. In the film, what is left unsaid between the family members is also never revealed in detail to the audience. It is only through fragmented accounts of the past, mentioned here and there, that the audience develops a sense that "something" has happened. What starts out seemingly as the struggle of an elderly woman turns out to be a struggle against the unspoken past, and ends when she decides to "walk" to "her mountain." In her fragmented and unexplained accented speech (reminiscent of the accent of non-Muslims in Turkey), she says she is being told to walk. This in itself, or within the context of the film, does not communicate anything significant. It is only within the larger context of Turkish history that what she says becomes meaningful and this knowledge is evoked "silently."

When mentioning Primo Levi's metaphor of drowning to explain the experience of the concentration camp, Wendy Brown writes that "this is a drowning in a world of unfamiliar as well as terrifying words and noise, a world of no civil structure yet so crowded with humanity that one's own humanness becomes a question" (Brown: 93). If cultural home includes also the acoustic environment then perhaps one can make the claim that displacement creates an acoustic environment that is overcrowded with too many different sounds, which in turn might turn into a deafening experience, resulting in the subject's complete silence. In these films, silence finds its place as a narrative element that goes beyond the binary opposition between sound and silence. It has as much to say as the words and images.

Space/spatial relations

Space and time are inseparable: one constantly marks the other, and cinema is arguably one of the most elaborated ways of dealing simultaneously with both space and time, together with their social and political implications. In film, reproduction of spatial configurations reveals certain particularities about the social and cultural dynamics as well as certain aesthetic preferences due to these particularities. Hence, in order to reveal the "now" of these films, it is important to look at how they deal with space itself. As displacement is a theme running through the films, their relation to and representation of space becomes particularly important, especially in relation to national identity, and how space comes to represent the relation between individuals and their identity. In this regard, with displacement and space at the center of attention, the notions of the threshold as a marker of space (and with it the concept of liminality), journeying, the relation to home, as well as the concept of the chronotope, become significant and recurring notions when dealing with (and representing) space in film.

When space itself is the subject of a crisis, it becomes a topic of enquiry. Hence, the reality of forced and voluntary migrations, combined with the reality of the internally, and involuntarily, displaced Kurds are constantly scrutinized by directors. The events that marked communities and caused painful departures will be individually examined in detail in the relevant chapters. However, for the purposes of this chapter suffice it to say that the condition of displacement is not only the subject matter of these films, but it also informs them in their search for an appropriate visual language. This is not limited to film and is evident in other areas of cultural production. A powerful example of this is the artist and filmmaker Kutluğ Ataman's 2004 exhibition *Küba*, in which he fashioned a space that "embodied" the situation created by displacement. Küba is an off-the-map neighborhood in Istanbul consisting predominantly of Kurds who migrated to Istanbul in the 1980s and 1990s, either due to economic conditions, or in order to escape the armed conflict between the guerrilla force PKK and the Turkish army. The exhibition comprised forty randomly scattered television screens, each displaying an inhabitant of Küba as he/she talked about who he/she was, explaining his/her experiences in the neighborhood and about his/her life, in general.

Küba, as a neighborhood, is not a fixed and planned entity with clearly defined borders. Ataman's exhibition, in conversation with the neighborhood, took place in an abandoned building: an old Royal Mail sorting office in London. It later travelled on to similarly liminal and temporary locations in the UK, rather than established and permanent exhibition spaces. The exhibition was a remarkably good example of how representation of space can become a manifestation of, and respond to, the geographical and social space it seeks to represent, thus resembling the Küba community in many respects.[6] Both the community and the spaces that the exhibition occupied fit into the definition of "liminal" in Victor Turner's sense of the word.

The concept of "liminality" was first introduced by the anthropologist Arnold Van Gennep, in his 1909 book *Rites of Passage*. Van Gennep described *rites de passage* as having three different phases: separation, margin (or *limen* signifying "threshold" in Latin), and aggregation. Turner later expanded the concept in his studies on tribes, rituals, and symbols. According to Turner, the condition of liminality or of liminal persons generally eludes or slips through the network of classifications that normally locate states and positions in cultural space.

Liminal entities are neither here nor there; they are betwixt and between the positions assigned and arrayed by law, custom, convention and ceremonial. [...] Thus, liminality is frequently likened to death, to being in the womb, to invisibility, to darkness, to bisexuality, to the wilderness and to an eclipse of the sun or moon (Turner 2008: 95).

Although Turner used the term to describe a temporary phase, he recognized that liminality can both be a "phase and a state" (Turner 2008: 167). Groups or individuals may be outside the social norms for diverse reasons and share nothing or very little in common apart from the characteristic that "they are persons or principles that (1) fall in the interstices of social structure, (2) are on its margins or (3) occupy it lowest rungs" (Turner 2008: 125). Because the social structure is not yet established in liminal societies, Turner calls them *communitas* that "emerges where social structure is not" (Turner 2008: 126). In *communitas*, as the hierarchy of the previously existing social structure is lost, the liminal condition experienced by people has become the main binding force. In this respect, the concept of liminality is also related to conditions created by migration and displacement.[7]

These liminal spaces formed by displaced communities are represented in many films made over the last few years, in which Istanbul occupies an important role. Istanbul has always been the most represented city in films about Turkey; however, its representation in the films made within the last few decades, particularly in films seeking to capture the experiences of the migrant and/ or displacement, the city appears much less attractive when compared to films from the 1950s and 1960s that were also looking at the migrants' experiences. This change in representation can be read against the background of the rapid change that the city has gone through. During the 1980s, Istanbul, with urban regeneration projects everywhere, was already becoming a global city "designed for cultural consumption" (Keyder 1999: 17). Keyder states that, with the rapid economic changes and the flow of people to the city, Istanbul became a "divided city," rather than a "dual city," mainly because while one part was participating in the global financial flow, the other part lived on the peripheries and remained, by and large, outside the global flow (Keyder 1999: 25). Together with the city itself, its representation in film also changed: in the recent films Istanbul is no longer the mesmerizing city that it once was but, instead, represents emotional displacement.

An early example to this changing image of the city can be seen in Derviş Zaim's critically acclaimed *Tabutta Rövaşata/Somersault in a Coffin* (1996). As

Asuman Suner points out, the image of Istanbul in the film is twofold: the first is Istanbul as experienced by the main character, who is a homeless man, and the second is Istanbul as a rising global city (Suner 2010: 142), which is largely inaccessible to the main character. The city, in the film, is "divided," rather than "dual," to reiterate Keyder's formulation. This juxtaposition of two different and opposing images of the city is repeated often in recent films made in Turkey. Moreover, Suner indicates that the main character's relation to the city itself in *Somersault in a Coffin* can be described as a "condition of confinement to open space" (Suner 2010: 147). This condition reoccurs in many films looked at here. In both *Hejar* and *Journey to the Sun*, the characters' relation to Istanbul can be read as "confinement to open space," not only because "home" is somewhere else, but also because this new space ("the big city") denies them the tools to make it their own. The little girl and her family in *Hejar*, as well as Berzan and Mehmet in *Journey to the Sun*, are characters who appear confined even in open spaces. Director Reha Erdem, who has made a number of critically acclaimed films, also represents Istanbul in a similar manner. Erdem's *Kaç Para Kaç/Run for Money* (1999) includes scenes on a boat on the Bosphorus; usually the most unenclosed space in Istanbul, it becomes suffocatingly small in the film. In *Hayat Var/My Only Sunshine* (2009), Erdem depicts Istanbul in a similar vein. He continually uses the Bosphorus as a background and yet the space continuously connotes entrapment.[8]

Stripping away the image of significant, easily recognizable reference points of the city also serves to represent the emotional as well as physical displacement of these communities. Istanbul, as immigrants experience it, does not correspond to the image of the city in circulation, and the films evoke this subjective point of view. Istanbul, for them, is not only a giant city beyond comprehension, but it also lacks any memory. In this respect, liminality in these films is not just limited to the geographical displacement of these people, but is also about a mental and emotional state.

When the subject matter is displacement, the journey inevitably becomes central to the narrative and its structure. As each chapter will demonstrate in detail, these films not only include journeys, but also include characters that exist in in-between places, or phases of life, and journey between them. *Waiting for the Clouds* is about a character going through a journey both psychological and physical, while *My Marlon and Brando* depicts a journey from Turkey to North Kurdistan. In fact, all the films examined as part of the "Kurdish issue" in Turkey have liminal conditions or persons, as well as continuous border crossings. Finally, *Ararat*, a film about the legacy of the massacre of Ottoman Armenians, includes not only liminal characters (most noticeable of all being the prominent Armenian painter Arshile Gorky), but also uses liminal places such as airports, borders, and a film set. In short, the majority of the films examined as part of this study at some point visit a transitional space. The theme of journeying is, furthermore, particularly significant in relation to specific conditions and contexts in which these films have been produced. Journeying can thus correspond to something literal: the reality of displaced communities. The idea of "home" and the concept of "identity" are both shaken and reaffirmed in these journeys.

Naficy considers journeying in film as an example of Mikhail Bakhtin's chronotope, "since each journey has both direction and duration, journeys transform space into time" (Naficy 2001: 223). Bakhtin defines the chronotope, literally "time–space," as the artistic expression of the "connectedness of temporal and spatial relationships" (Bakhtin 2008: 84). He borrows the term from Einstein's Theory of Relativity and uses it in literary criticism "almost as a metaphor—but not entirely," because in effect the term "expresses the inseparability of space and time" (Bakhtin 2008: 84). In the chronotope, time "thickens, takes on flesh, becomes artistically visible; likewise space becomes charged and responsive to the movements of time, plot and history" he writes (Bakhtin 2008: 84)—and although Bakhtin was writing about the chronotope as a constitutive category in literature, it is perfectly appropriate to use the term for cinema as well. As Robert Stam asserts, the chronotope "allows us to historicize the question of space and time in the cinema," reminding us of "the existence of a life/world independent of the text and its representation" (Stam 1989: 41). Hence, thinking about these films with Bakhtin and his concept of the chronotope reveals as much about the films themselves as it does about the conditions from which they emerged.

In his essay "Forms of Time and of the Chronotope in the Novel," Bakhtin specifically mentions a type of chronotope that is reminiscent of Turner's argument of the concept of liminality: the chronotope of *threshold*. The chronotope of threshold, writes Bakhtin, is "highly charged with emotion and value" and "can be combined with the motif of encounter" (Bakhtin 2008: 248), which is intertwined with the chronotope of the road.

[I]ts most fundamental instance is as the chronotope of *crisis and break* in a life. The word "threshold" itself already has a metaphorical meaning in everyday usage (together with its literal meaning) and is connected with the breaking point of a life, the moment of crisis, the decision that changes a life (or indecisiveness that fails to change a life, the fear to step over the threshold). [...] The chronotope of the threshold is always metaphorical and symbolic, sometimes openly but more often implicitly. [...] In this chronotope, time is essentially instantaneous; it is as if it has no duration and falls out of the normal course of biological time (Bakhtin 2008: 248).

Crisis occurs on a threshold, and a threshold is experienced because of a crisis: airports, cliffs, and borders gain metaphorical meanings. This also relates to the repeated activity of border crossing in these films, which is important on two levels: geographical, as in national borders (hence, the theme of journeying), and formal border crossings, as in journeys between documentary and fiction in the space of the same film. *Waiting for the Clouds*, for instance, starts with old footage taken from a newsreel, which the director found in an archive, showing a mass migration of people. *My Marlon and Brando*, on the other hand, crosses the formal borders between fiction and documentary, moving back and forth until the distinction itself becomes meaningless. For instance, in the scene where the protagonist, Ayça, wants to cross the border to Iraq, but is unable to as the border is closed temporarily due to security concerns, Karabey blurs the distinction between documentary and fiction. As Ayça tries to find out how to cross the border, or whether it will be open anytime soon, a policeman appears in the frame and tells people not to wait. When, in an interview, I asked him about how he convinced the policeman to act in the film, Karabey told me that he did not. Because a prior permission is needed to film there, and concerned that the knowledge of a film being made would change the "natural" behavior of the police, and others around him, he instead decided to employ a documentary technique and filmed the scene as it happened. With no prior script, he ordered Ayça (the only actor in the scene) to try and find out how to cross the border and filmed it until he was noticed and stopped. Karabey, in fact, confesses to often waiting for a scripted event to take place "naturally," rather than recreating the event for the camera.

In relation to the often-repeated theme of journeying in accented cinema, Naficy writes that, "in accented films, the westering journey dominates because it reflects the trajectory of the movement of a majority of the filmmakers and displaced populations" (Naficy 2001: 225). However, the majority of films analyzed here are dominated by journeys toward the east rather than the west. There are two intertwined reasons for this. The first is that the initial journey of leaving home is not always from east to west. The second reason is that the journey back home is as important as the departure from it. From German–Turkish directors such as Fatih Akın, to Armenian–Canadian directors such as Atom Egoyan and Karin Torossian, the journey back home is what is continuously scrutinized. Home in these films usually functions as a "structuring absence."[9] In the case of diasporic filmmakers it is also important to note that, because they are usually of a later generation, their problematic relation is as much with the "host" country as it is with the "home" country, which is constitutive of their identity, but remains an imaginary place in the psyche. When journeys are taken back "home," expectations do not always correspond to reality.

However, even when journeys are not toward an imaginary or real home, journeying always brings with it the idea of home: it is either the point of departure or the desired destination. It is during the journey itself that the relation to home is understood, home being an imagined concept emblematic of warmth and security and connoting belonging. In this sense most of the characters are "homeless" in these films, as their relationship to a place called "home" is ruptured. When "home" is represented, it usually accentuates the complicated relations it involves, but more importantly always includes a character who cannot call that specific place home, hence pointing to convoluted relations. In *Hejar*, the little girl, who is literally homeless, takes refuge in the judge's home. In *Ararat*, although there is the maternal home, it is clear that Raffi does not call it home anymore, looking for answers in a place that he has never been to and from where his ancestors came. The Armenian survivors who no longer live in the land of their ancestors, the forced migration of Pontus Greeks, the reality of the evacuated villages, and the internally displaced people, all find expression in the absence—or challenging presence—of home itself. Perhaps the most significant and haunting utterance of this grim fact is the literal representation of an evacuated village on the screen with its empty houses and streets. Although the knowledge of evacuated villages may haunt a narrative through the presence of displaced people, its materialization on screen, as in *Journey to the Sun*, makes a powerful statement. A sight that is normally associated with archaeological ruins appears on screen in immediate relation to the present rather than the past. When writing about ruins and nostalgia, Andreas Huyssen points out that "in the body of the ruin the past is both present in its residues and yet no longer accessible, making the ruin an especially powerful trigger for nostalgia" (Huyssen 2006: 7). Yet, the image of an evacuated village is haunting because it is both present and accessible.

The idea of home, the ways in which it is imagined, relates to the treatment of space in two important ways: how "home" is imagined and remembered, and how home is separated from the "outside" world. The first directly relates to the concept of nostalgia, while the second relates to the dialectic relations between inside and outside. Nostalgia is "longing for a home that no longer exists or has never existed," writes Svetlana Boym; it is "a sentiment of loss and displacement, but it is also a romance with one's own fantasy" (Boym 2001: xiii). Modern nostalgia, for Boym, "is a mourning for the impossibility of mythical return, for the loss of an enchanted world with clear borders and values" (Boym 2001: 8) and its rise had to do not only with displaced people, but also with the changing conception of time. Similarly, Andreea Deciu Ritivoi writes that nostalgia causes an important shift between temporal and spatial dimensions. "It becomes less important that the nostalgic suffers from being separated from her familiar environment and much more significant that she suffers from being cut off from her past" (Ritivoi: 20).

Contrary to the general conception of nostalgia as longing for a specific place, it is in fact a yearning for a specific time, or perhaps a specific type of existence in that specific time, which is the result of, according to Boym, "a new understanding of time and space" (Boym 2001: 11). With the idea of progress, which Benjamin famously called the storm in Klee's *Angelus Novus*, time acquired a new meaning: differing from task-oriented time,[10] the new under-standing of time was standardized, and objectified, turning it into a commodity. "What mattered in the idea of progress was improvement in the future, not reflection on the past" (Boym 2001: 10). This is also the paradox of nostalgia: its object is somewhere in the past, or a lost opportunity in the future, but in either case not achievable. It depends, like progress, on "the modern conception of unrepeatable and irreversible time" (Boym 2001: 13), which makes nostalgia a product of the modern conception of time, but at the same time allows resistance to the very process that created it.

Boym identifies two kinds of nostalgia: restorative and reflective. Restorative nostalgia "puts emphasis on *nostos* and proposes to rebuild the lost home and patch up the memory gaps. Reflective nostalgia dwells in *algia*, in longing and loss, the imperfect process of remembrance" (Boym 2001: 41). While restorative nostalgia "manifests itself in total reconstructions of monuments of the past" and characterizes "national and nationalist revivals," reflective nostalgia "lingers on ruins, the patina of time" (Boym 2001: 41), and is more concerned with "the irrevocability of the past and human finitude" (Boym 2001: 49). Although the type of nostalgia exemplified in these films is usually reflective nostalgia (home is a place in the past), most are not nostalgic themselves as texts, but reflect on the existing nostalgia, while maintaining a critical distance. Such reflection works on two levels: through nostalgic characters within the story, and/or through nostalgia that exists outside the narrative. When a character is nostalgic about his or her home (for example, Berzan about his village in *Journey to the Sun*, Raffi about an idealized land of his ancestors in *Ararat*, or Ayşe/Eleni about the life she had with her family in her village in *Waiting for the Clouds*), we are given an account of how these characters imagine and long for their homes. This, however, is not supported as a general sentiment within the narrative, as in each case the idea of home is contrasted with the reality of the imagined land/place: Berzan's village is gone, Raffi's journey to his ancestors' land brings disappointment, and Ayşe/Eleni finds a brother who does not remember her. Yet, the nostalgia reflected on in these stories also corresponds to a restorative nostalgia that exists in the collective imagination outside the narrative. Hence, although they themselves are not necessarily nostalgic, these films are in constant conversation with nostalgia and more often than not respond to it critically.

The idea of "home" brings another challenge in these films: the tension between inside and outside. Rather than being binary opposites, inside and outside at times form a dialectical relation, one extending into the other. The intimacy assigned to inside renders the hostility attached to outside and vice versa. In Gaston Bachelard's words, "outside and inside are both intimate—they are always ready to be reversed, to exchange their hostility" (Bachelard 1994: 217–18). Perhaps the most manifest occurrence of such merging between inside and outside is exemplified in Hiner Saleem's *Dol* (2007), in which interior moves outside. What is more, question of identity, experience of displacement and the problem of denial cannot possibly be thought independent of what constitutes inside and who decides where inside ends and outside starts, an issue any filmmaker dealing with historical injustice and displacement cannot shy away from and has to find a visual language to go about it. Hence, the ambiguous condition generated by displacement is explored in these films through representations of space. However, with the ambiguity of space, "the mind also loses its geometrical homeland and the spirit [starts] drifting" (Bachelard 1994: 218). Undoubtedly, a drifting spirit is nothing but a specter whose "presence" haunts space as well as time.

Haunting

Appearing in a film about ghosts, Jacques Derrida defines cinema as "the art of ghosts," the art of "allowing ghosts to come back" (*Ghost Dance*, Ken McMullen, 1983). Although Derrida's appearance on screen, and in particular talking about ghosts, is already a haunting experience, since his death, cinema, in many respects, is the art of ghosts, evoking haunting experiences. The coexistence of past, present, and future in the cinematic now creates a space for apparitions, and it is this possibility that is used repeatedly in the films dealing with contemporary Turkey and the country's peculiar relation to its history. As they attempt to tell untold stories from the past, stories that are excluded from the official narration of the nation, they invite the ghosts of the past (or the future) into the present. Ghosts/specters serve as metaphors for unresolved past events and unjust treatments and recur repeatedly in films that question the past: with their uninvited presence and their "significant absence," they defy definitions and boundaries. If "to write stories concerning exclusions and invisibilities is to write ghost stories," as Avery Gordon says (Gordon 2008: 17), then the films dealt with here are, in effect, ghost stories.

In her book *Ghostly Matters*, Avery F. Gordon tackles the question of "how to understand modern forms of dispossession, exploitation, repression and their concrete impacts on the people most affected by them" (Gordon 2008: xv). Haunting, she suggests, is not the same as being traumatized or being exploited, although they are not entirely separate. However, "what's distinctive about haunting is that it is an animated state in which a repressed or unresolved social violence is making itself known, sometimes very directly, sometimes more obliquely" (Gordon 2008: xvi). Haunting "occurs when home becomes unfamiliar, when your bearings on the world lose direction, when the over-and-done-with comes alive, when what's been in your blind spot comes into view. [...] It has a real presence and demands its dues, your attention" (Gordon 2008: xvi).

Although haunting, and the allegorical representation of past wrongdoings in the figure of a ghost, is mostly used in the horror genre, haunting and being haunted is not specific to horror films. The horror that the unjust/unresolved past creates is often explored in many other films, which do not use the generic conventions of the horror genre. Because haunting is not only about what happened but also what could have happened, about the "historical alternatives," stories that deal with the past often haunt our understanding of present. Ghosts come back to demand justice and in Derrida's words "to talk about ghosts [...], about certain others who are not present" is to talk in the name of justice (Derrida: xviii: 1994).

In this sense, there are many examples of ghost films made in Turkey from the late 1990s onwards, where past wrongdoings haunt the narrative space. In *Toss Up* the stone houses in Rıdvan's village are referred to as "haunted houses." In the same film, his friend, Cevher, is called "Cevher the Ghost" for he is a character of whom people are afraid, but, most importantly, he embodies the trauma of the war, as during a clash with the PKK guerrillas he lost his hearing in one ear, which is replaced by an, at times, unbearable hissing sound. Similarly, in Ünal's *9*, the homeless character Kirpi's presence evokes that of a ghost. Not only does nobody know where she came from, hence her ability to make people uneasy just by her presence, but also the entire film is about an investigation of her violent murder, told predominantly from the point of view of the police camera in the inter-rogation room. As "witnesses" talk, the complicated past of the neighborhood comes to light, under the shadow of Kirpi's ghost who metaphorically lingers over each one of them. Moreover, although the film remains ambiguous as to who killed Kirpi and why, this produces its own knowledge rather than creating suspense: she was violated and made invisible long before her murder. The decision to show her wearing the Star of David, as well as singing an "unknown song" (an old Yiddish song) can—and should—be read as Ünal's gesture toward acknowledging Turkey's past and its non-Muslim population.

Ghostly presences and the haunting past is a recurring theme in many other films, some of which are examined in detail in the following chapters. In *Waiting for the Clouds*, for example, the main character is haunted by her own past. This was also director Ustaoğlu's narrative strategy in her previous film *Journey to the Sun*, in which the protagonist's (Mehmet's) body becomes the body of a ghost as he "becomes" his dead friend Berzan. However, the most haunting image of the film comes at the end when Mehmet literally lets go of his friend's coffin, which he has carried with him with the intention of burying him in his "home." Yet, the village is evacuated and under water, and there is no burial ground to speak of. As the empty houses of this ghost village haunt the image, so does the recent past with regard to the Kurdish citizens. According to Asuman Suner these houses are "like mute witnesses to violence, war and the forced deportation that Kurdish people have experienced in south-eastern Turkey over the last two decades" (Suner 2010: 59). A different version of this image, the image of a ghost town, also recurs in *Işıklar Sönmesin/Let There Be Light* (Reis Çelik, 1996) and Hüseyin Karabey's *My Marlon and Brando* (2008). *Hiçbiryerde/Innowhereland*

(Tayfun Pirselimoğlu, 2002), another film that also deals with the effects of the armed conflict between the Turkish security forces and the Kurdish guerrilla, also uses the motif of ghost. As the main character Şükran (Zuhal Olcay) leaves Istanbul and goes to eastern Turkey to find her son who has vanished (and possibly joined the guerrilla force), she ends up chasing her son's ghost for days in a town where she knows no one. The son appears to his mother like a ghost, in a form that only she can see.

Perhaps the most ironic sequence regarding haunting experiences takes place in *Anlat İstanbul/Istanbul Tales* (Ömür Atay, Selim Demirdelen, Kudret Sabancı, Yücel Yolcu, Ümit Ünal, 2005). Directed by five different filmmakers as five short films, together they form a feature-length film, as each film includes references to the others. *Istanbul Tales* is a modern, and somehow pessimistic, take on five well-known fairytales, including "Little Red Riding Hood" and "Sleeping Beauty." In the segment forming the modern day "Sleeping Beauty," Saliha, the sleeping beauty in this case (played by Nurgül Yeşilçay), lives in a deteriorating haunted house that had belonged to her family for generations, and she claims she receives visitors from the past. When a Kurdish man, who recently arrived in Istanbul in the hope of finding a job, breaks into the house to find something to eat, Saliha immediately thinks he is the ghost of her grandfather. Since neither speaks the language of the other, the exchange between them proves non-productive. While Saliha insists on speaking Turkish in the hope that he will eventually understand, he desperately tries to make her understand that he cannot. Unable to comprehend why he (her grandfather in her eyes) cannot speak in a language she can understand, Saliha comes to the conclusion that it is because he is speaking the "language of dead people." This comment goes beyond the simple exchange between them and evokes Kurdish history, specifically the repression of the Kurdish language. In a short sequence the film is able simultaneously to play with language, space, and the haunting: the space is haunted by ghosts, and it is the unexpected entry of the Kurdish language to the narrative space that brings the ghosts back.

As these examples illustrate, although none are ghost films per se, in each one of these films there is a ghostly presence lingering over the narrative. Asuman Suner, in her book titled *Hayalet Ev/Haunted House* (2005), suggests that "at the heart of the New Turkish Cinema, there is the figure of the haunted house" (Suner 2005: 15).

A ghost is an ambiguous, in between figure: an image with no concrete existence; a living dead; a soul without a body. The word is associated with being uncanny, eerie and disturbing. In most cases, narrations that centre around a figure of a ghost, the dead comes back to the world of the living and takes revenge of an unjust act that s/he suffered. From this perspective, a ghost is the one who refuses to be forgotten, the one that reminds others of itself by force, the one that carries the past to present, the mark that resists being erased, or the "return of the repressed." [...] The New Turkish Cinema that talks about the stories of haunted houses puts forward a cultural backdrop that the tensions on the issue of belonging become visible (Suner 2005: 15–16).

Bearing in mind that "minorities" are usually the social bodies that remind the "majorities" of the fragility of their position, the recurring concept of "haunted" places in these films becomes more significant.

As time and space are never separate, or in Bachelard's words "space contains compressed time" (Bachelard 1994: 8), what is haunted by specters is never only space itself. Ghosts haunt not only space but also time. Because they move in time (both backward and forward) they disrupt the idea of linear progress. Examining Wong Kar-Wai's *In the Mood for Love* (2000), Chris Berry and Mary Farquhar read the film as a haunted text in which the "co-presence of past and future in the cinematic now [...] destabilizes the very idea of clearly demarcated present, which is the cornerstone of modern linear time" (Bachelard 1994: 39). Thus, the film haunts both past and future. A similar comment can be made about the films analyzed here. Addressing the audience's knowledge and memory (or the knowledge of lack of memory), films such as *Waiting for the Clouds*, *9*, and *Journey to the Sun* become haunted narratives in the way that they deal with the recent past. Similarly, a film such as *Ararat*, which is not a "Turkish" film, but rather a film that deals with the recent history of Turkey, is also haunted in more ways than one. The film not only includes characters haunted by the past but its use of time, the "co-present of past and future," makes it a haunted text.

"Being haunted draws us affectively, sometimes against our will always a bit magically, into the structure of feeling of a reality we come to experience, not as cold knowledge, but as a transformative recognition," writes Avery F. Gordon (Gordon: 8). It is haunting that makes transformative recognition possible, which then makes the ghost a social figure. This figure is free floating, knows no boundaries. Its function is to make us see differently and force us to recognize what has been forgotten unjustly. These films are not only haunted, but they haunt their audiences in unexpected ways. They aim to bring your blind spot into view, making it present, demanding its dues, and demanding your attention.

Epistolarity: Photographs and other media

Physical and emotional displacement as a result of forced or voluntary migration necessarily create a rupture that is temporal as well as spatial. The distance that is created as a result of separation is not only from family, friends, language, and home, but also from continuity with the past, from the environment that embodies that continuity. This inevitably results in nostalgic yearning for a time that is gone, or was never even there. In these films, in which displacement forms the kernel, there is an unavoidable time-lag, a dialogue with loss, with an idea, with a specter. Epistolary narrative challenges the language of progressive time with a time that is dislocated. It allows communication with an absentee, whether by means of writing or by other means of communication, including photographs and video recordings.

Jane G. Altman defines "epistolarity" as "the use of letter's formal properties to create meaning" (Altman 1982: 4), similar to the definition in the *Oxford English Dictionary*, in which the entry for "epistle" reads: "a communication made to an absent person in writing." Hamid Naficy lists epistolarity as one of the characteristics through which he defines accented films, dividing epistolary films into three different types: film-letters, telephonic epistles, and letter-films, admitting that the "differences are not clear-cut in all cases, and many epistolary films contain more than one epistolic medium and narrative system" (Naficy 2001: 101).

In his discussion of epistolary films, Naficy mentions the "enunciative properties" of free indirect speech. "One of the key contributions of this style," writes Naficy, "is to force dominant language [...] to speak with a minoritarian voice" (Naficy 2001: 102). Free indirect discourse, originating from literature, frees the characters' speech from quotation marks, making it less clear who the narrator is. In an article exploring the possibilities free indirect speech offers in cinema, Pasolini argues that the form allows the author to penetrate "entirely into the spirit of his character of whom he thus adopts not only the psychology but also the language" (Pasolini 1976: 549). In cinema, free indirect discourse produces a free indirect subject that goes "beyond the two elements of the traditional story, the objective, indirect story from the camera's point of view and the subjective, direct story from the character's point of view" (Deleuze 2000: 148). The camera does not dictate the story but becomes what/who it narrates. In a similar vein, Naficy argues that the indirect style includes:

reflection of the characters and objects, by means of mirror shots and eyeline matches; and projection of character's mental processes. [...] Reflection, projection, and introjection subjectivize the films and their characters and may create ambiguities about what is happening on the screen and who exactly are the subjects—that is, the owners or the objects of the gaze, thought, voice, and epistles. Such narrative ambiguity re-creates and expresses the ambivalent subjectivity and hybridized identity of exilic and diasporic conditions (Naficy 2001: 102).

According to Naficy, because the question of address and addressee is inherent in them, accented films "juxtapose direct, indirect and free indirect discourses in novel and varied ways to produce a bewildering array of address forms" (Naficy 2001: 103). In the process, the epistle's addressee becomes multiple/ambiguous through the narration. But perhaps the most important of all, epistolary texts are "driven by epistephilia, which often involves a burning desire to know and to tell about causes, experiences and consequences of disrupted personal and national histories" (Naficy 2001: 105).

Although the traditional letter itself is an obvious epistle, I argue that photographs, video recordings, and even television news, also occur in these films as different ways of communicating with absent persons. This is undoubtedly related to the technological advances that make it possible to capture a moment in life and send it in ways other than writing. While not mutually exclusive, their use and function in film can be split into two, regarding their mnemonic attributes. The first one, use of photographs and personal video recordings, often highlights the tension between past and present with regard to the individual memory. The second utilization, using old television footage within the narrative, is frequently used to trigger a collective memory of a certain time as the images primarily relate to a collective knowledge of an event, while also functioning as a means of communication within the diegetic space. They all disrupt the flow of the story, make the time-lag that is inherent in epistolary communication visible, and ask the audiences to engage with the image differently.

Photographs might not immediately be considered as epistles, although one of their purposes in the early twentieth century was to let loved ones know about the well-being of family members who were far away. This, however, rather than signaling a transformation in form, allows a modern way of communication, one that goes hand in hand with the space–time shift. Writing can inevitably articulate life in detail and in ways no other mechanical reproduction can. However, analogue photographs can, to quote Roland Barthes, create "an awareness of *having-been-there*" (Barthes 1977: 44) which no letter can. According to Barthes this newly developed awareness creates a "new space–time category: spatial immediacy and temporal anteriority, the photograph being an illogical conjunction between the *here-now* and *there-then*" (Barthes 1977: 44). It is precisely for this reason that Arshile Gorky acquired the photograph of himself and his mother taken in Van. The photograph, on which he later based his most famous painting, was sent to his father, who was in America at the time trying to find a better life. Atom Egoyan, in return, pays exclusive attention to the photograph, as well as to the painting, in *Ararat*.

Photographs, while creating personal archives, also disrupt the flow of time momentarily by capturing a slice of it. Laura Mulvey, reading Barthes and Bazin together on photography and the medium's relation to death, comments that their shared perspective diverges when it comes to how this relation functions. "For Bazin, it is to transcend death, part of the process of mourning; for Barthes, it is 'the dive into death', an acceptance of mortality" (Mulvey 2006: 60). This uncanny quality of photography, the ability to transcend death while reminding us of it, is used very often in the films analyzed in the chapters to follow. In these films, when a photograph appears on screen, more often than not it is of someone who is no longer among the living. The only way their presence could have a foot in the film, and in life, is through photographs.

Photography reproduces a moment in time, and in it something else: a detail that flashes out to arrest the spectator. However, as both Bazin and Benjamin wrote, it (the effect) does not last. It "does not create eternity, as art does, it embalms time, rescuing it simply its proper corruption" writes Bazin (Bazin 1967: 14). For Benjamin, on the other hand, photography "is like food for the hungry or drink for the thirsty," whereas with painting the eyes will "never have their fill" (Benjamin 2007: 183). Hence a photograph appearing in a film, arresting the time of the narrative for a moment is a different kind of experience than the stillness of a painting. In *Ararat*, when Arshile Gorky decides to paint his (dead) mother from a photograph, and when Egoyan in return decides to represent the act of the painting, destruction (death) and reconstruction (giving her back an aura, an eternal existence) take place at the same time in the same cinematic space.[11]

The tension between stillness and movement, and in it tensions between life and death, past and present, exists because in essence a photograph is a frozen moment in time. When inserted into the moving images photographs create tension, a contestation. Peter Wollen likens the relation between film and photograph to the relation between fire and ice. "Film is like fire, photography is like ice. [...] Photography is motionless and frozen, it has the cryogenic power to preserve objects through time without decay. Fire will melt ice, but then the melted ice will put out the fire" (Wollen 2007: 110). This is a metaphor that comes to life in Hollis Frampton's 1971 (*nostalgia*), which also brings to mind Benjamin's dialectical image.[12]

> Every present is determined by those images that are synchronic with it: every now is the now of a specific recognition. In it, truth is loaded to the bursting point with time. (This bursting point is nothing other than the death of *intentio*, which accordingly coincides with the birth of authentic historical time, the time of truth.) It is not that what is past casts its light on what is present, or what is present its light on what is past; rather, image is that wherein what has been comes together in a flash with the now to form a constellation. In other words, image is dialectics at a standstill. For while the relation of the present to the past is a purely temporal, continuous one, the relation of what-has-been to the now is dialectical: not temporal in nature but figural (Benjamin 2002: 463).

The knowledge of the past that the belated nature of the image brings with it, the knowledge of history and/or memory, then, can create a dialectical image: an image that embodies the tension between the past and the present. These conflicting moments in film also allow for cultural and political meanings to arise within the narrative. In his article "The Pensive Spectator" (1984), Raymond Bellour discusses the presence of still photographs in film, concluding that the presence of a photograph "has the effect of uncoupling the spectator from the image," creating what he calls the "pensive spectator" (Bellour 2007: 122). He acknowledges that the use of photographs is not the only way to uncouple the spectator from the image in cinema, however it is the most visible. His argument is, in many ways, very similar to the way Benjamin talks about history, as he constantly underlines the dialectical relations. According to Benjamin, while historicism "gives the 'eternal' image of the past, historical materialism supplies a unique experience with the past" (Benjamin 2007: 262). The type of thinking historical materialism requires involves "not only the *flow* of thoughts, but their *arrest* as well. Where thinking suddenly stops in a configuration pregnant with tensions, it gives that configuration a shock, by which it crystallizes into monad. A historical materialist approaches a historical subject only where he encounters it as a *monad*" (Benjamin 2007: 262–3, emphasis mine). As the arrest of thoughts in the flow of thinking gives way to a shock, it displaces the idea of homogenous empty time. A similar disruption in film is possible: at the moment of that "halt," where the flow is disrupted by bringing forth the tension between stillness and movement, the pensive spectator becomes possible. A striking example of this occurs in *Waiting for the Clouds*.

Waiting for the Clouds opens with archive footage of the population exchange between Greece and Turkey, which took place between the late 1910s and early 1920s. The footage shows a large group of people walking with their belongings and boarding boats. Among a number of close ups, there is one of a little girl and a boy, which is the last image before the director shifts into the narrative's present time. It is only at the very end of the film that this image is revisited, and the film ends with a freeze frame with the same image. However, with the knowledge of Ayşe/Eleni's personal story, her loss of her brother during the march, this fragment now tells a very different story. Freezing the image on the screen allows the spectator to contemplate its meaning. Stillness, in this respect, is the news of something extraordinary; it uncouples the spectator and requires investigation. What stillness primarily achieves is an unexpected moment in the flow of the film that "uncouples" the audience from the image and makes time visible. Nevertheless, this is not the only way to create crystals of time, to use Deleuze's concept. These films also use other media to trigger the notion of time outside the narrative. The use of television news, together with sending personal news, by way of other means of communication, including video letters, are some of the most used strategies in order to arrest narrative time.

In films that deal with contested pasts, television news often brings documentary qualities to the narrative space; furthermore, what is "news" to the diegetic characters is often no "news" for its audience. Usually the images shown are known to the film's audience—such as news of the invasion of Iraq in *My Marlon and Brando*—and they trigger a collective memory of an event, allowing the audience to make the connection themselves. To bring the familiar into the sphere of the unfamiliar, i.e. the story being told, the audience is forced to reconsider the image that already existed in memory in a new context. When, for instance, news of the clash between the police and the protesters is shown on television in *Journey to the Sun*, it not only functions to bring news of Berzan to Mehmet (as he appears to be among the protestors being arrested) but also puts a human face to the images that existed for the primary audience of the film, those that live in Turkey, as, in reality, these protests and the hunger strikes occupied the media for a long time. Similarly, in *My Marlon and Brando*, when Karabey decides to bring the news of the invasion of Iraq in 2003 to its protagonist through television, the (now iconic) images of the bombardment of Baghdad are part of, and directly impact on, real life as Ayça worries about a loved one. Thus, while these news clips bring news of the loved ones to the diegeteic characters, they also simultaneously function to trigger the collective memory of the audience.

Another strategy uses video recordings to serve as personal letters. Rather than uncoupling the audience from an already established meaning, they make the time-lag, which is inherent to, but mostly invisible in, the process of film viewing itself, manifest. This is used extensively in two of the films analyzed in the following chapters: Egoyan's *Ararat* and Karabey's *My Marlon and Brando*, both of which use video as an epistle. Because epistolary cinema "is both fictional and documentary and [...] simultaneously personal and social" (Naficy 2001: 105), the journeys between fictional and documentary, between social and personal, in both *Ararat* and *My Marlon and Brando*, are created though intimate video letters: to a mother and to a lover respectively. However, the time-lags addressed in these films are different.

In *My Marlon and Brando*, Hama Ali's video letters come as joyful letters informing Ayça about his well-being, in addition to events in his hometown. They are amusing, humorous, and loving letters, in stark contrast with the war that is taking place not so far away from where he is. He not only records these letters, but also includes scenes from low-budget films that he has acted in. Because Hama Ali is playing himself in the film and does work as an actor, these films do exist in real life, thus making the boundaries between reality and fiction blur once again. What is more, Hama Ali dies while recording one of these letters, leaving it unfinished and unsent. In *Ararat*, however, the video letters work differently as both Raffi (the protagonist) and the audience are aware of the ambiguities of the past, as Raffi, addressing his mother, looks for his own place in history with imagery captured in his ancestors' land. Hence, while *My Marlon and Brando* haunts its audience, *Ararat* itself is haunted.

"The epistolary situation, in which both time-lag and absence play a large role, lends itself to the temporal ambiguity whereby past is taken for present" (Altman 1982: 132). It is in Raffi's video diaries in *Ararat*, seemingly addressed to his mother, yet revealed at the airport under inspection before they reached the addressee, that the audience experiences a temporal ambiguity that exists throughout the film. Similarly it is due to this temporal ambiguity, inherent in the time-lag, that the last letter to arrive in *My Marlon and Brando* is haunting.

Watching Hama Ali's last video-letter, in which we find out the reason why he could not meet Ayça at the Iranian border with Iraq, is in itself a haunting experience. Hama Ali, whose existence in the diegetic space is only through these video-letters, records another letter as he tries to cross the border. However, this turns out to be his last letter: as he is recording his letter a shot is fired, which kills him. His letter becomes a recording of his own death. What is more, for the first time in the film the audience receives the letter before Ayça. Since throughout the film the audience read/watched these letters together with Ayça, the narrative time developed in parallel to Ayça's biographic time. By shifting this alignment and "delivering" the letter to the audience before Ayça, the film creates an even more complicated relation to the narrative time than achieved by epistolary form. In fact, it is never revealed to the audience whether Ayça was able to see this last letter.

Similarly, in *My Father's Voice*, Zeynel Doğan and Orhan Eskiköy use tape recordings as part of their narration. These recordings are from the past, apparently used as letters, since the father had to go abroad to work leaving his wife and his two children behind. These recorded letters function in a similar fashion as the video letters do in *My Marlon and Brando*. Although we do not see the characters actively inserting these tapes into cassette players, the voice of the father and the letters sent in response consisting of the mother's and boys' voices are played in conversation with the dialogues that take place at the diegetic present between the mother and the younger son, who is the only one left behind. The older son, we are told, has left and joined the guerrilla force and the father has died in a work-related accident.

The epistolary form functions in these films in other ways as well. The distance and absence inherent in the epistolary narrative inevitably form an important part of these narratives. In *Waiting for the Clouds*, for example, Ayşe/Eleni receives the news that changes her life and that sets her out on a journey to Greece through an unexpected letter. However, regardless of the way it functions in each film, epistolarity, in these films, becomes a narrative device that both questions and embodies the complicated nature of displacement. Because epistolary communication brings with it the concepts of separation and time-lag simultaneously, it is often used in these films to comment on their characters' subjective point of view, life as experienced by them. In the process, most of these films turn, at least in part, into epistles themselves.

* * *

This chapter has outlined the recurring themes and motifs in the films that are discussed in detail in the following chapters. While each film deals with various aspects of history, memory, and identity, they all deal with the contested history of Turkey. However, a closer look revealed that the "now" of these films not only influences their subject matter, but it also determines a certain narrative and aesthetic style that creates a continuity running through them. With displacement being the shared concern of each text, I have identified five main recurring themes and motifs running through the films analyzed here: politics of language, silence, spatial relations, haunted narratives and epistolary narratives. These categories are not necessarily independent of each other, but are interwoven and dialogic as they stem from the same question: how to deal with the atrocities of the past in film, without merely reproducing them? They are all connected to each other in how film deals with past and present.

As displacement creates an existence on the margins, liminality becomes an important concept that connects the motifs often used, which affects the aesthetics of the image in three major areas: narrative as liminal, topographic liminality, and liminal characters. Narrative space treated as liminal allows a certain treatment of time, one that focuses on the idea of time-lag. This is emphasized by use of epistolary narrative as well as ghosts, both of which have peculiar relation to the idea of progressive heterogeneous time, creating a "corridor of time" between different temporal zones. Topographic liminality, on the other hand, concerns itself with space: neighborhoods on the margins of the city and transitional spaces, such as borders, are often used in these films. These spaces, in return, provide an appropriate setting for the representation of liminal characters. These characters, whether because they are pushed to the margins of society (Mehmet in *Journey to the Sun*, Kirpi in *9*), or because they are going through a transitional period (Ayşe/Eleni in *Waiting for the Clouds*, Raffi in *Ararat*), make use of silence and language in various ways: broken, fragmented sentences, and/or language switches, often used in these films along with pregnant silences.

3

Covering and Discovering: Non-Muslim Minorities and Film

"All ideas of nation and peoplehood rely on some idea of ethnic purity or singularity and the suppression of the memories of plurality" writes Appadurai (1996: 45). Whether ethnic, religious or otherwise, minorities function as a reminder of "social uncertainties" that cause hostility, and in some cases violence, against the minorities. This is due to the idea of purity and totality inherent in the idea of nation-state, or any other form of social identity put forward by an institution. However, the idea of the totality of a nation is as constructed as the concept of minority. What is more, not only are the nation and national unity constructed but their perception and performance depend on various factors, such as social and economic background. Although Europe, and much of the world, has been dealing with rising nationalisms, and the ascent of the far right, there is also a growing desire to recognize and under-stand the other. The films about minorities in Turkey appear to be a response to this process, as well as being the products of the country's own internal dynamics, which arguably created a discursive space for the unresolved issues of the past to be discussed.

Within the last two decades, there have been a considerable number of films dealing with non-Muslim minorities, specifically with the events that are left outside the official narrative of history yet shaped the population of Turkey. These films either deal directly with traumatic historical events, such as the population exchanges of the 1920s, and the pogroms against non-Muslims (*Bulutları Beklerken/Waiting for the Clouds, Güz Sancısı/Pains of Autumn*) or take a minority identity as an implicit aspect of the narrative (*Dar Alanda Kısa Paslaşmalar/Offside, 9*), making the silence that existed on various aspects of history concerning minorities visible.

This chapter looks at films that are either about non-Muslim minorities in Turkey or about events that concern these communities. In what follows, I will first give a brief account of the various historical moments that affected the non-Muslim population of Turkey, providing an overview of the films made within the last two decades on some of these issues discussed here. The second half will then provide a close examination of two films: *Politiki Kouzina/A Touch of Spice* (2003), the story of the last Greek exodus from Istanbul, the 1964 deportation of Greek residents, made by an Istanbullite Greek director Tassos Boulmetis, and *Waiting for the Clouds*, a film that deals with a Greek women who lost her family as a result of the forced migrations.

There have been a number of events and regulations in the last century affecting the non-Muslim population of Turkey. Starting from the war years leading up to the establishment of the modern Turkish Republic, and continuing in the following years and decades, these events caused the number of non-Muslims in Turkey to drastically reduce. One of those events was the great fire of Smyrna (İzmir Yangını), in 1922. The fire started toward the end of the Greek–Turkish war, when the Turkish army gained control of the city of İzmir. Starting near the Greek and Armenian quarters of the city, it destroyed a large part of İzmir, causing many of its inhabitants to evacuate the city. While Turks maintained that Greeks "burned down the city before evacuating," Greeks claimed that it was Turkish forces who started the fire. What is telling about the narrative developed around the fire is that, despite the complex nature of the event, its depiction allows there to be no ambiguity for the Turks and the Greeks. While the event is mourned in Greece as a disaster, the Turkish side sees it as the liberation of the city. According to Biray Kolluoğlu-Kırlı the fire was written out of local history by means of recreating the city, and to "mark a beginning, a point-zero," the space became the embodiment of the newly created nation-state. Hence, the fire "can be interpreted as both an immense act of destruction and an act of creation: creation of national spatialities" (Kolluoğlu-Kırlı 2002: 2).

Such erasure of the memory of the place should be thought of in relation to erasure of the people, and the attempts to purify the nation on both sides of the Aegean Sea. The compulsory population exchange was one of the most important attempts toward this direction, which was based on an agreement between the two states—Greece and Turkey—(1923). The agreement provided a legal framework for finishing touches to be made for the "unmixing of people," which in fact started a decade earlier (Hirschon 2006; Keyder 2006; Aktar 2008).

The compulsory exchange involved Turkish nationals of the Greek Orthodox religion living in Turkey and the Muslims living in Greece. The Orthodox population of Istanbul and the Muslims living in Western Thrace were exempt from the exchange. The policy inevitably had long-term effects, as well as the immediate human suffering that it caused. Keyder writes that "the Turkish nation [...] was itself formed through this process of ethnic unmixing" and, therefore, "it is difficult to isolate the impact of the exchange on Turkish society from the wider process of nation-state formation" (Keyder 2006: 43–4). What is more, although both the Great Fire of Smyrna and the compulsory population exchange redefined the ethnic composition of the region, there is hardly any mention of them in textbooks in Turkey.[1] Although silences exist in every nation's history, Turkey presents a particular case in considering "the enormity of the effort to negate the previous existence of non-Turkish populations in the land that eventually became Turkey" (Keyder 2006: 48).

In a study analyzing a large number of novels and short stories written in Turkish, Hercules Millas points to the silence with regard to the population exchange. According to Millas, between 1923 and 1980 the references to the population exchange in Turkish literature "are very few and mostly indirect" (Millas 2006: 221), whereas in Greek literature many novels and short stories were written during the same period about the experiences of Christians (Millas 2006: 224). Only after the 1980s did the situation start to change and the interest in the subject became evident. In cinema, director Yeşim Ustaoğlu's *Waiting for the Clouds* was one of the first films to deal directly with the effects of the population exchange. While it is about a Christian woman whose family left their land as a result of the exchange (and it is examined in detail below), there are also films dealing with Muslim subjects who were forced to leave their homes and came to Turkey as result of the exchange, one of which is *Dedemin İnsanları/My Grandfather's People* (Çağan Irmak, 2011). Recently a small museum was opened in their memory in a small town near Istanbul.[2]

Although the population exchange was the defining event in terms of reshaping the population of Anatolia (along with the massacres and deportations of Armenians), the general attitude toward minorities did not improve a great deal in the following years either. The *Varlık Vergisi* (Capital Tax, also known as the Wealth Tax, 1942), the Pogrom of September 6 and 7, 1955, as well as the 1934 pogroms against Jews in Thrace are among those defining moments in Turkish history that shaped the country's relationship with its non-Muslim citizens. These events, all part of the attempt to Turkify the nation that began in the first few decades of the Republic, continued to affect societies long after they took place.

In recent years, both the historical moments regarding minorities and the country's relation to its minorities have become the center of attention in film as well as in other areas of cultural life.[3] These memories, suppressed for a long time, swept under the carpet of "common sense" of national sensibilities and not known to younger generations, started reemerging. Although at times these texts function only to wash the society's conscience clear, they nevertheless point to a newly awakened concern. Intriguingly, their remembrance and reemergence have remarkable similarities to the place ghosts occupy in culture, haunting the national psyche.

Non-Muslims on screen

Emerging in the late 1990s and early 2000s, the majority of the films concerning minorities are made by later generations, whose memories and identities are shaped by the conditions created after the 1980s. Similarly, the majority of their audiences also do not have direct memories of these events. Before briefly introducing these films, it should be pointed out that among the historically unjust moments that affected non-Muslim minorities, and often driving them out their own country, one event that still awaits attention is the pogrom in Thrace against the Jews in 1934. Known as the "Thrace events," these pogroms are still to be addressed in the popular media and in film. In fact, among the films examined here, there is only one film that deals with a Jewish character. It is not my intention to speculate on the reasons why there is a lack of discourse in the popular media on the subject, although a number of reasons come to mind, one of which is the latent anti-Semitism that continues to exist in Turkey. However, for the purposes of this chapter suffice it to say that there is a lack of discourse on the subject outside of academia.

It should also be pointed out that the mere existence of a discourse on a painful episode of the past is in itself *not* a sign of transitional justice, but perhaps rather an indication that the long existed silence is forced to be broken. Among the narratives that break those silences, Tomris Giritlioğlu's film *Salkım Hanımın Taneleri/Mrs Salkım's Diamonds* (1999) was one of the most popular. The film tells the story of the notorious Capital Tax that was imposed mostly on the non-Muslim minorities in 1942, and focuses on Halit Bey (Kamran

Usluer), a rich Turkish businessman in Istanbul, and his non-Muslim wife Nora. However, as a result of being subjected to the same heavy tax as non-Muslims, Halit finds out that his father was a *"dönme"* (a term that is used for people who converted to Islam). Unable to pay the tax entirely, the men are sent to a labor camp in Aşkale to pay off their debts, while Turks acquire their possessions for much less than their worth. Most of what Halit and others own is subjected to the tax. Their possessions are bought by Durmuş (Zafer Alagöz), a man who has recently arrived in Istanbul to "change his destiny." Although he worked for Halit's business as a carrier for a while, his ambition to become rich makes him take advantage of the situation ruthlessly. As people desperately liquidate their properties to pay the tax, he buys the properties and businesses. Durmuş, in this respect, is a symbolic character representing the aim of the tax, which according to scholars was introduced to facilitate wealth to change hands, to create a Turkish bourgeoisie.[4]

Halit's wife, Nora, is portrayed as a silent character, who stopped talking long ago, after she was raped by her father-in-law. Traumatized by her past, Nora is portrayed as a temporally displaced character. Although silent most of the time, when she does speak, her speech belongs to a different temporality, revealing her displaced psyche, which is haunted by her past. Her husband, Halit, also haunted by the past, later confesses to Levon that "the door was open," and that he saw everything, referring to the rape without explicitly mentioning it. Failing to prevent what his father did to his wife, he never talked about it to anyone else. Hence silence, in different forms, dominates both their lives: Nora's silence is a retreat to her imagined world by refusing to communicate with the world around her, whereas Halit's is more in the hope that it will all be forgotten, although it is not clear whether he wishes to forget what he knows. Nevertheless, a strong desire to forget the past coming before the need and necessity of recognition of that particular past makes reconciliation impossible, which the film fails to/refrains from critically commenting on.

Mrs. Salkım's Diamonds also subtly comments on the changing ethnic make up of the society. In a conversation with Nora's brother Levon, Durmuş's wife Nimet (Derya Alabora), who disapproves of Durmuş's ambitions, mentions how her hometown, Niğde, a small town in southern Turkey, has changed and that "people left." Later, on a different occasion, she mentions that they used to have "non-Muslim neighbors," but not any longer. These conversations are followed by silences, pregnant with unsaid words. Although the film simplifies its characters into pure good and pure evil, it is nevertheless one of the earliest films to deal with the subject of the Capital Tax, hence creating discussions about both the film and the tax itself, as well as the minorities in Turkey.

Mrs. Salkım's Diamonds is based on a book written by Yılmaz Karakoyunlu, a member of the parliament between 1995 and 2002. After *Mrs. Salkım's Diamonds* in 2009, director Tomris Giritlioğlu collaborated with Karakoyunlu once again, developing his novel *Güz Sancısı/Pains of Autumn* for the cinema. The story this time was about the pogrom of September 6–7, 1955. The film contextualizes the events and provides a brief account of the political climate at the time. The days leading up to the pogrom were dominated by the talks about the status of Cyprus. *Pains of Autumn* chronicles the few months before the September events, as experienced by a Greek–Turkish woman, Elena (Beren Saat), and her lover, Behçet (Murat Yıldırım). While Elena is a prostitute with a high-profile clientele, which includes politicians, Behçet is a research student in law, and comes from a prominent family with ties to the government. He appears to be supporting the nationalists, taking part in their meetings and attending their demonstrations. However, his romantic interest in Elena (as he secretly watches her from his window) forces him to comprehend the possible consequences of their liaison.

"A film like this might be just a film in another country," comments Etyen Mahçupyan, an Armenian columnist who also wrote the screenplay for the film. According to Mahçupyan, because there has been such a long silence and lack of discussion about the pogrom, "the film fulfils an important mission" (*Today's Zaman*, February 21, 2009). *Pains of Autumn* was one of the most watched films in terms of box office success in 2009 in Turkey, and also achieved considerable success in Greece, creating a dialogue about the subject. The director Giritlioğlu said, "The past is the future. Mistakes cannot be faced if we are unable to see the past for what it is. The film also has references to the present day" (*Today's Zaman*, January 22, 2009). Responsible also for a hugely successful television series called *Hatırla Sevgili/Remember My Dear*, which also dealt with the recent past, Giritlioğlu is a director particularly interested in using cinema and television to create public discussion on issues on which a collective silence has previously existed.

Although the interest in facing the past, and talking about the silences, grew in the mid-1990s in Turkey, the trend became distinctly more visible in the early 2000s, as seen in Uğur Yücel's ambitious *Yazı Tura/Toss-Up* (2004), which attempted to combine three traumatic and challenging issues: non-Muslim minorities, the war against the PKK, and the earthquake that killed around

17,000 people seemingly in the blink of an eye in 1999. The film, which is set in that year, is about two young men, Rıdvan (Olgun Şimsek), and Cevher (Kenan Imirzalioğlu), who are doing their compulsory military service in eastern Turkey, where the PKK's armed section is active. Rıdvan, during crossfire with PKK militants, unknowingly kills his high-school sweetheart, who joined the guerrilla force after they parted company. When he discovers what he has done, in shock, he starts to run away, but accidently sets off a mine. In the explosion, he loses his leg and his friend, Cevher, who ran after Rıdvan, is left with his hearing damaged. The film follows these two characters as they return to their hometowns at the end of their military service. The accident not only destroys Rıdvan's aspirations to become a footballer, and causes his fiancé to leave him, but also makes it difficult for him to integrate back into his community.

Cevher, on the other hand, goes back to Istanbul, and uses his combat skills to intimidate others by getting involved with a mafia-like organization, while becoming increasingly more nationalist in his views. When the earthquake hits, killing his uncle and injuring his father, Cevher is reunited with his half-brother, Teoman (Teoman Kumbaracıbaşı), whom he hasn't seen for twenty years. Teoman and his mother Tasula (Eli Mango), a Greek Istanbullite, left their home in Istanbul for Greece because of the rising hostility against Greeks as a result of the conflict in Cyprus at the time. The earthquake brings them back to Istanbul for the first time since they left. *Toss-Up* is undoubtedly influenced by the contemporary political climate as the capture of Öcalan in 1999 allowed the Kurdish issue to be seen in a new light. The earthquake also resulted in improved relations between the Turkish and Greek governments, since Greece was one of the first countries to respond and send humanitarian aid.

With Tasula's return to Istanbul the film highlights the prevailing silence in the lives of individuals, exposing how general consensus on silence works in the society. The audience discovers that Istanbul is where Tasula actually grew up and that the house that Cevher and his father are staying in belonged to her family. The film reminds its audience of the sheer scale of the events of 1999, and we also realize that Tasula's original departure from Istanbul cannot have been voluntary and is part of a larger narrative in which many people fled their homes in fear of their lives. Yet the fact that there is almost no mention of this, neither among the family nor in Turkish society in general, almost makes their story a ghost story. Silence, it is hoped, will keep these specters at bay.

Another film, *Dar Alanda Kısa Paslaşmalar/Offside*, also reflects on society's silence, which functions to maintain "harmony", although it does not explicitly deal with non-Muslim minorities. Instead, it is predominantly concerned with the impact of neo-liberal economic policies on small communities in post-1980 Turkey. In *Offside*, a rich businessman arrives in town to buy the local football team, bringing capitalism to a small and otherwise peaceful town. It is a nostalgic film as it imagines a past in this small town in which the people have lived in harmony and peace. The disruptive force of capitalism arrives in the shape of a businessman to disrupt this. Such nostalgic reflection on the past, according to Suner, often assigns a "collective childhood" to the community, which can only be maintained by "denial, forgetting, and suppression" (Suner 2010: 44). Such denial and suppression is briefly revealed at the end of the film in the character of the football team's coach, Hacı (Savaş Dincel).

A very popular man, Hacı is loved by everyone, but his death toward the end introduces a small twist to the story that makes the film interestingly self-reflexive. When he dies, the townsfolk realize that they, in fact, know nothing about him. Because he has been living alone and has no known relatives, they decide to bury him themselves, which they do according to Muslim custom. However, when his brother arrives to collect Hacı's body, the town discovers that Hacı was in fact Armenian and, therefore, Christian. Although this does not have overt significance for the rest of the story, it does introduce the question of his hidden identity: why did Hacı stay silent about who he really was? It is this question that haunts the narrative and yet it is left unanswered.

While *Offside* adopts a nostalgic look at the past and at small community living, Ümit Ünal's *9* adopts an entirely different approach to the supposedly harmonious life of a small community, turning a story of murder into an allegorical representation of the country, where home is seen as the least safe of all places. The story takes place in a small Istanbul neighborhood, following the brutal murder of a homeless woman, Kirpi (Esin Pervane), who was known to the local residents. The police investigation focuses on six people, and the film takes place in the interrogation room, for the most part. In a Kafkaesque setting, we watch the police interviews with the six different people as secrets are forced to surface, and the corrupt nature of supposedly harmonious relations are unveiled.

Kirpi, who wears the Star of David, is a homeless orphan of whom almost everyone takes advantage. In contrast to *Offside*, and also to the general perception of a close-knit community living in harmony, the people in Ünal's film are exceptionally cruel to each other. While the small town in *Offside* seemingly consists of people living peacefully until the businessman arrives,

Ünal's neighborhood is presented as dangerous, corrupt, and hostile from the start. What is more, whereas *Offside* is about Hacı's—assumed to be voluntarily—hidden identity, *9* comments on how the society itself that cannot allow any deviation from the supposed norm. According to the director, each character represents a segment of Turkish society, and he felt a local neighborhood was the only place that he could bring them together (*Radikal*, November 11, 2002).

The central character, albeit in her absence, is Kirpi, an apparition who appears out of nowhere, walks around singing in an "unknown language," and then disappears again into nowhere. In fact, Kirpi is portrayed as a silent character, who does not utter a single word except when she sings in an unknown language. In an interview that I conducted with the director, Ünal told me that she sings an old Yiddish song, although that fact is never revealed in the film. He added that the choice of the song, and her ambiguous identity, were intentional because his primary aim when making this film was to examine the latent racism in society. While the characters are not sure who Kirpi really is, there is a suspicion that she might be Jewish and this is enough to evoke the existing xenophobia, which then turns into violence against the "other." It is for this reason that Kirpi's status in the narrative is never completely revealed to the audience. She resembles a ghost about whom people know nothing, a figure on which they can project all their irrationality and fear of the other. In fact, her ambiguous status, and the judgment people pass freely on her, with little or no information as the interviews at the police station repeatedly demonstrate, is reminiscent of the status that minorities, whether ethnic, religious, or otherwise, occupy in Turkish society. During the interrogations secrets are revealed, and the audience discovers that each character has his/her own corrupt and selfish perception of the others, while hiding the truth about themselves. For instance, we find out that Firuz is a closeted gay man posing as a conventional "family" man; Saliha, although passing harsh moral judgments on other people, has conceived her only son outside of marriage, and Tunç, self-proclaimed protector of the neighborhood, is, in fact, repeatedly abusing Kirpi.

The film opens with a quote from Kafka's short story *In the Penal Colony*: "[…] but everything was quiet, not the least hum was audible. By operating so silently, the machine seemed to make itself unnoticeable." *In the Penal Colony* is a story about the idea and the mechanisms of justice and the law: the machine that punishes slowly. The story takes place in an unnamed location, and the indifferent character recounts horrific events with detachment. In this sense the director not only alludes to Kafka's short story with a quote from which he opens the film, but also aims to expose the engine of the machine—that is the structural denial. Kafka's machine is not invisible, but because it works silently its existence is deniable. Ünal seems to depart from this idea: the denial of self and others in order to function in a society.

However, toward the end of the film a subtle but shocking image appears on the screen that forces the audience to reconsider what they saw and heard prior to that moment. Kirpi herself appears for a few seconds on the screen, in the interrogation room, which should be impossible since the interrogations are taking place following her murder. Her image remains on screen for no more than a few seconds, and yet it not only further establishes Kirpi as haunting the narrative space, but also introduces another possibility—that perhaps it was the police who killed Kirpi, and that this is all a cover up. The director refrains from providing a clear answer as to what really happened, however, thus maintaining in death the same level of ambiguity assigned to Kirpi by the society in which she lived. A murder story without a narrative closure, *9* does not allow Kirpi's ghost to disappear. In this regard, Ünal's film is not about a murder but rather, to borrow from Derrida, is about how an absent being is brought into the narrative "in the name of justice" (Derrida 1994: xviii); Kirpi's absence haunts the narrative. It is not her murder but her unjust treatment while she was alive that becomes visible in the interrogations, exposing a society that both accepted, and expected, her murder to be insignificant.

The film's release coincided with interest in the "old way of life" in which small communities bond together. There have been countless television dramas produced in small neighborhoods within the last decade,[5] mostly in Istanbul, where the old way of life is imagined as amicable, and, hence, a sense of nostalgia is produced and sold. Ünal's *9* is also disturbing in the sense that it goes against the general assumption that the alienation and violence in society comes from "outside". The film recalls a community that is different than the one generally imagined and accepted, portraying a place in which dark secrets are buried deep.

Another film which maintains the ambiguous status of its main character is Yeşim Ustaoğlu's *Pandora's Box* (2008). The film, which is similar to Ustaoğlu's previous films, asks more questions than it actually answers. The story is centered around an old woman, Nusret (Tsilla Chelton), who is suffering from Alzheimer's. After they receive a phone call, telling them that their mother has disappeared, Nusret's three children, who all live in Istanbul, set out to the village where she lives alone. When Nusret is finally found, they decide to bring her back to Istanbul, as she now needs constant care. However, not only is Nusret's presence in her children's already alienated city lives difficult to maintain, but Nusret herself is also not happy in the claustrophobic setting she is placed in, between the concrete walls of her daughter's flat. She wants go back to her village, back to "her mountain," and it is Murat (Onur Ünsal), her grandson, who finally agrees to take her back home.

Pandora's Box, as the title suggests, is about what happens when the content of the box is released. In this case, it is the event that forces the siblings to spend time together without an escape route, since they now have to collaborate to look after their mother. In the process, we discover that there are many things in their pasts about which they have never spoken. As they are forced to acknowledge the silence that has existed between them, they also face up to the dysfunctional lives that they are leading. However, beyond the film's obvious comment on modern city life and alienated relations, there is an additional element to the film, one that is very subtle, but there, none the less.

The film opens with an idyllic image of Nusret's village, with scenery particular to the Black Sea region. As she goes about her daily chores, she gazes out from the balcony of her house toward the forest and suddenly drops the bag that she is holding: her eyes fixed on something and her expression changes to one of alarm and stress. The director then cuts to her daughter in Istanbul receiving a phone call about her mother's disappearance. What Nusret saw in that moment is never revealed and yet Ustaoğlu hints at this scene at the end of the film.

In Istanbul, Nusret repeatedly attempts to escape the high-rise block that her daughter lives in, and she constantly asks to be taken back to "her mountain." Once back in her village with her grandson, she tries to escape to the mountain again. Murat brings her back, but a confused Nusret says "he is telling me to walk" (*"yürü diyo"*). Although there is no mention of it anywhere else in the film, the earlier scene, when coupled with Nusret's accent—she is played by the French actress Tsilla Chelton and speaks Turkish with an accent reminiscent of non-Muslim minorities—this opens up an alternative reading of Nusret's character.

Chelton reportedly learned Turkish specifically for this role and inevitably her character also speaks with an accent. In a number of interviews director Ustaoğlu mentions her careful search for someone who looked like she was from the region. She failed to find the right actor in Turkey, yet thought Tsilla Chelton had the exact look she was looking for. However, it is almost inconceivable to think that while paying so much attention to the look of the character, she could overlook Chelton's accent. Given the ending of the story, where Nusret does succeed in walking into her mountain, thus answering the mysterious voice she has been hearing, it is almost impossible not to argue that Ustaoğlu cast Chelton on purpose, in order to remind the audience of the history of the region. Nusret's final comments about walking toward the mountain might allude to the forced migrations of Greeks and Armenians.

Although *Pandora's Box* is very subtle in its comment on the forced migration, Ustaoğlu's previous film *Bulutları Beklerken/Waiting for the Clouds* deals with the issue openly and directly. As one of the first films to remind audiences of the problem of those women and children who converted to Islam in order to survive, *Waiting for the Clouds* made an important contribution to the process of rethinking identity through film in Turkey. In what follows, I will provide a detailed analysis of two films, both dealing with the Greek minorities of Turkey, namely Tassos Boulmetis' *Politiki Kouzina/A Touch of Spice* and Ustaoğlu's *Waiting for the Clouds*. Both these films are stories of individuals whose lives are altered by historical violence and although the two films are very different in the ways they deal with their stories they nevertheless share many sensibilities that are outlined in the previous chapter.

Politiki Kouzina/Touch of Spice

A Touch of Spice (2003) was made by an Istanbullite Greek director, Tassos Boulmetis, who was born in Istanbul but was forced to leave the city with his family when he was seven years old. This was the result of the 1964 İnönü enactment, which, in effect, was a "punishment" for the Greeks residing in Turkey, and was triggered by the tension over Cyprus. The enactment cancelled the rights of those Greeks holding resident permits but not Turkish passports, thereby making their status illegal almost overnight. Boulmetis tells the story of a family who left Istanbul for Greece as a result of this enactment. The film, a Greek–Turkish collaboration, was screened and became an immediate success in both countries.

The original Greek title of the film *Politiki Kouzina* conceals a double and untranslatable meaning: it makes reference to the cuisine of the city, as Istanbul/Konstantinopolis is *the* city/polis, but also, depending on how it is pronounced, refers to "the politics of the cuisine". This play on words is lost in both its Turkish and English translations: neither the English *A Touch of Spice* nor the

Turkish *Bir Tutam Baharat* (which literally means "a touch of spice") is able to convey the intended double entendre of the original title. The story does not just recount the impact of exile, but also recalls the director's own memories of *the* city: Istanbul.

A Touch of Spice puts the theme of displacement at its core. The first half of the film takes place in Istanbul, focusing on young Fannis who spends most of his time in the dream world inspired by his grandfather's spice shop. A culinary philosopher, his grandfather shapes Fannis' world and his relationship to food. When the police come to the house one evening to deport his father, following the 1964 enactment, the family decides to leave together, and yet his grandfather, who holds a Turkish passport, chooses to stay behind in Istanbul. Although he makes a few attempts to visit the family, now relocated to Athens, over the subsequent years, the visit never materializes as it transpires that his attachment to Istanbul is thicker than blood. This is illustrated by the recurring pain in his neck, whenever any departure from Istanbul is mentioned. Similarly, when old Fannis describes his grandfather's friends who did leave Istanbul for Athens he refers to them as being diffent then the rest. "They are magnetized," he says, "like a compass, every geographical question reorients their identity, who they are, what their origins are and where they are going." Their magnet is imagined to be Istanbul, the city from which they are.

Fannis and his family are portrayed as misfits, first in Turkey, then, again, in Greece, albeit for different reasons. Although they fit perfectly into their own community (that of Greeks from Turkey), they have difficulty being accepted either as Greeks in Greece or as Turkish in Turkey. In both places the constructed national identity does not include their identity: while in Turkey, they are too Greek to be trusted, in Greece they are too Turkish to be included. In Turkey, Fannis' grandfather is subtly accused of not being "grateful" enough, as he is a guest in the country and not considered part of the nation's make up. In Greece, the family experiences similar exclusion. Fannis' teacher, for instance, complains to his father about his "Turkish" accent, a problem that needs to be addressed. As the director has one of the characters deliver in the film, "they were sent away from Turkey like Greeks and received by Greece as Turks."

What anchors Fannis, and gives him a sense of identity, is food: the sensory experience of cooking and eating, an experience that he and his family are able to bring with them. This is a particular sense of the world that is not ruptured through the experience of displacement. When in Greece, young Fannis tries to maintain the sensory experience that his grandfather's spice shop provided, and one day is found cooking in a brothel—because he is banned from the kitchen at home for fear that he might become homosexual. A police officer writes a "prescription" for the boy, a list of places to visit to make him more patriotic, as he is diagnosed as lacking national pride. Fannis' own answer to the question of belonging does not change, however, since he remains sure that he and his family are neither Greeks nor Turks: they are Greek-speaking Istanbullites. Boulmetis' portrayal of Istanbul is as a world in which the family fits in perfectly until the enactment. The director plays on his characters', as well as his audience's, sensory perceptions: both audio and gustatory knowledge are played upon in order to evoke memories of the place. Since "some of the most poignant reminders of exile are non-visual and deeply rooted in everyday experiences" (Naficy 2001: 28), Fannis' memories of what Istanbul was, and therefore who he is, directly relate to his senses.

The film creates a culinary map of Istanbul, and within that map, a city that belongs to people rather than to specific countries. As Marks writes, "given the cultural differences in the organization of the sensorium, the sensuous geography characteristic of one culture will not be transparent to a viewer from another culture" (Marks 2000: 230). Boulmetis uses a knowledge that is only available to people who are familiar with the gustatory and sonic landscape of Istanbul, hence creating a film that remains largely "shielded from the desire of outsiders to comprehend the culture visually" (Marks 2000: 230), while evoking memories of a place through senses. Similarly when Fannis and his family leave Istanbul behind, they continue to orient themselves, based on the knowledge that they are from Istanbul, which forms the kernel of their imaginary map, their cartography of memory. What they take with them, when they depart, is the memory hidden in the taste and in the smell of food. Food directs the people in the film, telling them who they are, where they are from: when an old woman finds out Fannis puts sugar in stuffed vine leaves, she immediately knows that he is from Istanbul: it is the culinary practice that locates him. Moreover, it is these moments that the older Fannis recalls: the taste, and the bond that is created through taste, forms his memory of his childhood in Istanbul.

Food, in this sense, is the main source of knowledge in the film: through different recipes and ingredients, different memories come to life. Intercultural movies about food, writes Marks, "use food as an entry to memory, troubling any easy access to the memories food represents." Intercultural "food films," he asserts highlight that the "seemingly ahistorical rhythm of cooking and eating food provides an alternative framework for the exploration of cultural memory" (Marks 2000: 234). This sensory aesthetic not only evokes the cultural memory of a city, but also pushes the story beyond historical narrative. It brings to mind a sense of the city as experienced by its inhabitants, which goes beyond their ethnic origins. Using objects, sounds, but most of all tastes, the film creates a sensory memory of the city.

Accordingly, Istanbul's physical beauty is not showcased in the first part of the film in which Fannis' memories of the city are being portrayed. The audience, during these sequences, is not shown anything particularly specific to the visual realm of Istanbul. Instead, a strong sense of Istanbul is created through sound: language and, also, the particular background sound. Although food is the dominant motif in Boulmetis' exploration of cultural memory, sound also functions as a mnemonic device. Yet, unlike the cooking and eating practices that can travel with the displaced, the distinct acoustic environment belongs to the physical environment.

A vital component of the acoustic environment is the language spoken in the film. In Fannis' household, they don't simply speak Greek and Turkish. They speak Greek with many Turkish words and Turkish with a Greek accent. To a certain extent they are able to maintain this part of their sonic experience when they leave, continuing to talk in a similar manner among the family. However, Boulmetis uses another aspect of the sonic environment, which locates his memories as a child growing up in Istanbul. Many of the scenes taking place indoors include a continuous background sound—that of the streets, although the streets themselves are not seen. Children playing, street vendors announcing their goods—these are the sounds of Istanbul, available only to people who "know" the city. These sounds are intentionally part of the film and are not due to filming conditions, i.e. on-location filming. Such quotidian sounds would go mostly unnoticed by the locals, but act as mnemonic triggers for the displaced. Like the original film title, these sounds are untranslatable and are only accessible to Turkish speakers: the sounds *hurdacı*, *zerzevatçı*, and *simitçi*[6] have no equivalent in English, and, even if they did, their function is beyond the simple translation of words. It is the music in which they are sung that sets them apart and makes them of "the city." These sounds, like the culinary knowledge of the city, work as reminders of the daily life of Istanbul for the exile, create a "sensuous geography." Gustatory and sonic knowledge both trigger a collective memory of a place, locating us not just in a particular place, but also in a particular experience of that place. Boulmetis uses both sonic and gustatory knowledge to trigger a memory of the city and also, it seems, to access his own memories of the city through such exploration.

Hence, in his quest to tell a semi-autobiographical story, the director also creates a heavy sense of nostalgia and, at times, uses stereotypical representations of both the city and the people. In other words, the film's—and therefore the director's—relationship to the past is characterized by a restorative nostalgia. As Boym writes, "nostalgia is an ache of temporal distance and displacement", and "restorative nostalgia takes care of both of these symptoms. Distance is compensated by intimate experience and the availability of a desired object. Displacement is cured by a 'return home'" (Boym 2001: 44). Such a return need not necessarily be limited to a literal journey back, as to come up with a narrative of what home means is also part of that return. Fannis makes the journey back to Istanbul in his forties to see his grandfather, who was never able to leave the city, even to visit his children and grandchildren. He dies shortly after Fannis arrives. What is interesting in this segment of the film is that, unlike in the earlier representation of Istanbul, depicting Fannis' childhood memories, the return journey is supported by many landmark images of Istanbul, reproducing a sense of the city as available in travel guides and experienced by tourists. He walks by the Bosporus and meets his childhood sweetheart in Sultanahment Square, also known as the historic peninsula where Topkapi Palace, the Blue Mosque, and Hagia Sophia are located. Boulemetis also includes a taxi scene in which Fannis travels in an old make of car. Considering his visit takes place in the 1990s, it would, in reality, be almost impossible to find a taxi driver still driving that particular car. The image of Istanbul in this second part of the film, imagined through nostalgia, proves more believable than the reality itself, supported by the director's decision to continue Fannis' romantic imagination of the city by including a nostalgic car scene.

In *A Touch of Spice*, director Tassos Boulmetis looks for and restores the Istanbul he remembers from his childhood, before his relationship to the city was disrupted. Because nostalgia is not longing for a place, but rather for a specific time, Boulmetis recreates his Istanbul of the 1960s in the 1990s. Dominated by a heavy sense of nostalgia, the film tells a story of the city, and the experiences of the displaced, through senses and sound. But in its effort to reenact memories of the place, the critical distance is replaced by nostalgic engagement with the city.

Bulutları Beklerken/Waiting for the Clouds

Yeşim Ustaoğlu's *Waiting for the Clouds* takes place in a small village called Tirebolu, in the Black Sea region of Turkey. Set in the 1970s, the film tells the story of a woman, Ayşe/Eleni (Rüçhan Calışkur) in her sixties, who lost her family during the so called "long march," when the Pontus Greeks, living in the Black Sea region, were forced to leave their homes between 1916 and 1923, as part of the population exchange between Greece and Turkey. During these long marches, she loses her parents and she is separated from her brother, Niko. Ayşe, originally called "Eleni," is rescued and adopted by a Turkish family and, in order to hide her identity and avoid further problems, her name is changed to a Turkish one, "Ayşe." When her adopted sister's husband dies, the two elderly women move back to Tirebolu, where Ayşe was born. But her adopted sister also dies, leaving Ayşe/Eleni with no family, and no one to witness to her past. This results in her voluntary isolation from the rest of the village during a seasonal trip to the highlands.[7] She only maintains her connection with a little village boy, whom she loves like a son. However, with the arrival of a stranger, Tanasis, her life changes again. Not only does she speak Greek for the first time in decades, but also through Tanasis finds the address of her lost brother. She embarks on a journey to Greece to find the brother, whose departure has haunted her all her life.

Waiting for the Clouds is a film dominated by a strong sense of loss. The protagonist not only loses her family as a result of the forced migrations, but also loses her home, her name, and her language. The story is about her suffering, her longing for her lost identity, as told through the intense bond between her and the little village boy, Mehmet (Rıdvan Yağcı), who she has to leave behind when she sets out on a journey to Greece to find her lost brother.

The film relies predominantly on the audience's active engagement with the image, asking more than it answers. The opening sequence is of particular importance with regard to how the film positions its audience. The very first image of the film (also the very last) is black-and-white footage showing a large group of people walking, and boarding boats and trains. There are a number of close ups on random individuals among the crowd. Before fading into the narrative's present time, an image of a young girl holding a little boy appears on screen. This is also the image that concludes the film (see Figures 3.1 and 3.2). However, this time the image says more, testifying to Ayşe's/Eleni's ordeal as the audience now knows that she was separated from her brother as a result of the long marches. This is the director's approach to the story throughout: important details become comprehensible only later on—not when they are first presented.

The director, by demanding that the audience must "remember" the beginning of the film in order to make complete sense of it, forces her audience to go "back to the beginning." to engage with their memory. This approach has wider implications since the film is about the present as much as it is about the past, like memory itself. Moreover, it is not simply a story of a personal ordeal, but is about an event that affected thousands that has not been properly recognized. The film, in other words, attempts to recognize the suffering and to bring it into the realm of the visible.

A striking example of this occurs when the census takes place, which allows the audience to find out about Ayşe's/Eleni's identity very early on in the film. In this early sequence, the television news (which plays an important role throughout the film) informs both the citizens of Turkey at the time, and the audience of the film, about the census that will determine statistics on language and religion (it also happens to be the first census that includes questions on these issues). When the census officials arrive, they ask questions about Ayşe's/Eleni's "identity," such as her family name, and so on. These questions, seemingly insignificant, cause a momentary silence to fall between her and her sister. Ayşe's/Eleni's answers to these questions are based on what is written on her official identity card, rather than what is reality. Although this sequence supplies

Figure 3.1 *Waiting for the Clouds* (dir. Yeşim Ustaoğlu, from Silkroad Productions, 2003). The opening image.

Figure 3.2 *Waiting for the Clouds* (dir. Yeşim Ustaoğlu, from Silkroad Productions, 2003). The closing image.

the first pieces of information about her, the information given will ultimately prove to be "fake," as the audience gradually discovers. Similarly, the scene in the mountains (which is examined in detail below) becomes momentous for the audience, when she reveals her "true identity," not the one she has been forced to assume in order to escape exile. The way the director forces her audience to process this information requires active viewing: rather than providing answers, the information poses a challenge to the legitimacy of those answers concerning her identity, and also that of the Turkish identity.[8]

Ustaoğlu, by contrasting certain elements, positions her audience as active viewers, rather than passive. The film puts an emphasis on the oral, as opposed to written history, and gives a subjective account of a certain part of recent Turkish history. In doing so, Ustaoğlu also creates a contrast to her imagery. While the story is a painful one, the imagery is poetic: the director repeatedly uses beautifully captured shots of the mountains and the sea. This contrast seems also to mirror Turkey's attitude toward its past. Where the surface, the place called "home," appears poetically beautiful, there is so much pain and suffering if one digs beneath the surface and listens to individual stories. This suffering has never been properly integrated into the official discourse, and in the mainstream representation of that part of the nation's history. However, these shots also provide Ayşe's/Eleni's subjective view of the land, showing the landscape as she sees it. Her relationship to the place is an emotional one: she starts treating it as a canvas on which her past is inscribed.

Ustaoğlu's approach to the story is one that is based on challenging the audience, not only about the past, but also, and perhaps even more so, about the present. In this respect, allegorical representation becomes an important motif in the film, which allows the director to challenge the traditional forms of representation, and creates an opportunity to problematize particular concepts. Allegorical representation, in Walter Benjamin's sense of the term, becomes particularly significant here, as it allows the story, in its representation of the past, to pose questions that are relevant to the present.

Allegory, according to Benjamin, differs from symbol. As opposed to romantic symbol, in which "the beautiful is supposed to merge with the divine in an unbroken whole," allegory "declares itself to be beyond beauty" (Benjamin 1998: 160, 178). According to Benjamin, the basic characteristic of allegory "is ambiguity, multiplicity of meaning," and "ambiguity is always the opposite of clarity and unity of meaning" (Benjamin 1998: 177). In his later essay, "Theses on the Philosophy of History", he makes a similar distinction, this time between historical materialism and historicism.[9] Accordingly, "historicism gives the 'eternal' image of the past," while "historical materialism supplies a unique experience with the past" (Benjamin 2008: 262). Historical materialism forsakes "historicism's homogenous, empty time" in favor of what Benjamin refers to as *Jetztzeit*. "History is the subject of a structure whose site is not homogenous, empty time, but time filled by the presence of the now (*Jetztzeit*)" (Benjamin 2008: 261). And, according to Adam Lowenstein, the moment of *Jetztzeit* "is an allegorical moment, an instant in which an image of the past sparks a flash of recognition in the present" (Lowenstein 2004: 149).

Following this distinction between allegory and symbol, as well as historical materialism and historicism, certain moments in *Waiting for the Clouds* can be argued to create allegorical moments: through a specific use of language and imagery, the past becomes recognizable in the present, as well as the present being recognized in representations of the past. These allegorical moments not only tell us what happened in 1916, and the following few years (the beginning of the forced migrations in the region), or what was happening in the 1970s (the time in which the story is set), but they also echo present-time politics about ethnic minorities and national identities in Turkey. Therefore, the story is never about the "then" only, it is simultaneously about both "then" and "now." Moreover, these moments demand contemplation rather than the provision of answers. They open up new representational possibilities. It is in these allegorical moments that the film becomes centered in today, about the politics of memory in today's Turkey, rather than about the past. The past and present become interwoven, informing each other, a striking example of which occurs during an exchange between the little boy, Mehmet, and Ayşe/Eleni.

At the very beginning of the film, Mehmet comes to Ayşe's/Eleni's house and tells her a story about goblins. These creatures, which he calls "karakoncolos," come and hide under his bed every time he wets his bed. Ayşe/Eleni responds with a story about a little girl whose family died while they were trying to flee from the "goblins," for which she also uses the word "karakoncolos" in Turkish. According to Ayşe's/Eleni's story, there used to be "karakoncoloses" in the village who cursed the place. "Trying to escape, the villagers walked from mountain to mountain. There was a little girl who lost all her family in a snowstorm because of the karakoncoloses, but was saved by a little angel."

Although the full extent of her story is not yet revealed to the audience, the director plants the seed of doubt with the use of an unexplained silence accompanied by a caring and sorrowful look exchanged between Ayşe/Eleni and her sister, who knows this is in fact her story. This silence, as well as the meaning of the story (in effect, an allegory for the forced marches), is revealed later on in the film, when Ayşe/Eleni decides to lift the veil that has been hiding her identity. The story about the past sparks a flash of recognition in the present.

It should also be noted that the word "karakoncolos" is an unfamiliar word to the average Turkish speaker and is specific to that region: an area that was once inhabited by large numbers of Pontus Greeks. The origin of the word is the Greek Kallikantzaros (Καλλικάντζαρος), which is used to describe a goblin-like creature that would live underground and come to the surface of the earth in winter. The director is clearly creating the link here between the past and the present, as well as between myth and reality. However, this is only a spark rather than a clear statement. The use of the word by both Ayşe/Eleni and the little boy, who not only have different ethnic origins, but also belong to different generations, creates an allegorical moment—a moment of *Jetztzeit*. The existence of this word in both languages shows the presence of the absence: the dialogic relation between the two languages that has left its mark in the type of Turkish spoken in the region. However, those people who spoke one of those languages, i.e. Greek, are no longer present.

The little boy Mehmet, in addition to his position in Ayşe's/Eleni's life as a substitute for her lost brother, also serves an important function in the film: to provide an account of the world as seen though a child's eyes. The director states that she based the experiences of the little boy on her own as a little girl in the 1970s. She adds, "I learned the same nationalistic chants as shown in the school scenes. I remember Turkey was going through a tumultuous period politically" (Ustaoğlu, Press Kit). Contrary to the typical use of children in films as the bearer of innocence, Mehmet's journey is that of a discovery of atrocities, unfair treatment, and confusion. He witnesses Ayşe's pain, survives an attack by nationalists, and helps his friend to escape the detention center in which he was put for stabbing the men who molested him and Mehmet. In this respect, the director does not allow a nostalgic look back to the past, to childhood; she forces the childhood memories to come back to the audience, whatever they may be. In other words, the story becomes a story of the dark places of childhood, both Mehmet's and Ayşe/Eleni's.

In investigating Ayşe's/Eleni's identity, and her sense of "home," the film also questions Turkish identity. The scenes at the school where Mehmet goes through little daily ordeals are used as opportunities to communicate deeper social commentary on the education system. Although not given special

significance and taking place in the background, these instances subtly mark
the nationalistic tone of the education system that is familiar to many of those
educated in Turkey. Because they are part of a "normal" school day, they are
also likely to go unnoticed, but become alienating forces within the context
of the film. It is not a coincidence, for example, that the director cuts to Ayşe/
Eleni looking out from the window aimlessly, while the children are heard in
the background making their routine daily oath, a requirement in schools in
Turkey. The oath translates as follows:

> *I am a Turk/ I am honest/ I am diligent/ My law is to protect the younger/ Respect
> the elders/ To love my country/ and my nation more than I love my self/ I dedicate
> my existence to the existence of Turkish nation/ What an honor to say I am a Turk.*

Although it is part of the daily routine for primary school children in Turkey,
it gains a new meaning with Ayşe's/Eleni's story. Similarly, when the children
are singing a song that most Turks would also remember from childhood, the
sensation is not a simple memory of the old days: it becomes an almost violent
reality. The song goes:

> *If surrounded by enemy / If abandoned on their own / Do the Turks give up? /
> Turks never give up. / Until the end of time / Turks never give up.*

These moments become allegorical instances that at the same time estrange
the audience from these otherwise daily and "normal" occurrences. They come
to represent the politics of the education system and how the past is shaped
through such repeated daily activities in the mind of these school children.

The notion of home is also continuously questioned in the film and haunts
the filmic space. When Ayşe/Eleni's sister falls ill, the doctor reveals that there is
nothing he can do to save her and she should be taken "home." The idea that the
best place to die is "home" arises again later in the film, when, shortly after her
sister dies, Ayse/Eleni retreats to the house in the highlands, waiting to die. This
wish, the desire to die at home, is voiced one more time at the end when Ayşe/
Eleni travels to Greece and meets an old woman who used to live in Turkey
before the population exchange, who wishes to be buried "under the cheery tree
there." Home, no matter how much hostility it involves, is a place that is remembered with a nostalgic feeling. This attachment appears to be enhanced when a
person is forced to leave his/her "home": forced departure creates a rupture.

In a similar vein, Ayşe/Eleni's decision to go back to the village she was
born in can be read as a manifestation of her longing for her "home." This

nostalgic act is an act that will fail to satisfy her longing for her lost memories. As nostalgia is about being cut off not only from a certain place, but also from a certain time, the moment before rupture, before displacement, is equated with the place itself in the mind of the nostalgic. In Ayşe/Eleni's case, reunification with the house in which she was born does not end her suffering. She then attempts to claim her past by suddenly switching to her mother tongue, Greek, which takes place simultaneously with her flashbacks, providing the temporal shifts she needs in order to "go back."

The flashbacks begin when the entire village goes to the highlands to spend the summer. Although seasonal migration to the highlands is common practice in the region, coupled with her sister's death and her past slowly surfacing, this journey triggers Ayşe/Eleni's flashbacks and function as the repetition of the initial moment of forced migration. Once there, Ayşe/Eleni stops talking to people and spends the first day and night outside, her eyes fixed on the mountains/clouds (see Figure 3.3). Worried about her, Mehmet hugs Ayşe/ Eleni to comfort her. However, mistaking the boy for her lost brother, Niko, she responds, in Turkish, saying: "Niko! Don't go." In another scene at the mountain, in a moment of "transition," she opens her arms as if she was going to let herself go from the edge, and the boy arrives and hugs her again (see Figure 3.4). This time she speaks in Greek to him, saying: "God forgive me, please help me." These are moments in which Ayşe/Eleni is temporally displaced, not only remembering, but also being in her past. Her flashbacks are not visually created for the audience, positioning them as *witnesses* to her pain.

The decision not to recreate these moments of flashback is also in accordance with Ustaoğlu's general approach to narrative and how she positions the

Figure 3.3 *Waiting for the Clouds* (dir. Yeşim Ustaoğlu, from Silkroad Productions, 2003). Ayşe/Eleni in the highlands.

Figure 3.4 *Waiting for the Clouds* (dir. Yeşim Ustaoğlu, from Silkroad Productions, 2003). Ayşe/Eleni experiencing a flashback.

audience. Flashbacks in film, according to Maureen Turim, are usually associated with "subjective truths" and an "emotional charge of memory."

> These charged sequences are inserted into the less individuated, more "objective" present unfolding of events, often combating and overturning a certain view of the law. Knowledge of the past is often presented as a privilege afforded by the fiction, access to which is transformative, but temporary and didactic. [...] Made aware of the past, the spectator is freed to forget once again. This symbolic order vacillates between knowing and forgetting, the shifts determined by the positioning of the spectator within the structured operations of narrative temporality (Turim 1989: 12).

By not providing the images of the flashbacks to the audience of the film, Ustaoğlu renounces her all-knowing and all-seeing position as a director and leaves the audience with their own imagining processes. This, in turn, creates a more arresting image of the past: made aware of the *questions* regarding the past, the spectator is arrested and has to *become* aware. Moreover, the lack of images of flashbacks also indicates the absence of these stories in the public sphere. According to Turim, "if flashbacks give us images of memory, the personal archives of the past, they also give us images of history, the shared and recorded past" (Turim 1989: 2). The lack of shared images in the filmic space, when it is clearly indicated that the protagonist is experiencing a moment of flashback, marks, then, the absence of the "shared" and "recorded" past.

Ayşe's/Eleni's flashbacks are the audience's entry into her past, and in that articulation another important occurrence takes place, that is, the language switches. According to Naficy, "one of the greatest deprivations of exile is the gradual deterioration in and potential loss of one's original language, for language serves to shape not only individual identity but also regional and national identities prior to displacement" (Naficy 2001: 24). Ayşe's/Eleni's language switches are also centered around a sense of loss which has shaped her identity. Her switches back and forth between Turkish and Greek signify the cracks in her identity. Her language is broken up simultaneously with her escapes to her past. The rupture created by loss of family, and the loss of language along with them, is relived this time voluntarily: Greek is the language of her past and these switches are also temporal switches. Moreover, her refusal to speak to anyone after her sister's death marks her departure not just from the Turkish language, but also from the present time. It is first complete silence, then the refusal to speak Turkish that becomes her method of rebellion, a method used to reclaim her identity.

Moreover, representation of these switches between Turkish, the language of the perpetrator, and Greek, which is her mother tongue, is only possible in visual media for it allows subtitles to exist together with image and sound. As the nature of the medium allows two languages to exist simultaneously, the director can point to the split identity of the protagonist through the use of both. These moments are the moments in which the audience is given significant information about Ayşe's/Eleni's past, present, and her emotional state. They are also liminal moments for her as she is neither "here," nor "there," neither "Ayşe" nor "Eleni." The mountains and the clouds mark this emotion with their dream-like quality.

Her language switches reach a climax when Tanasis (Dimitros Kanperidis), a stranger, arrives in the village. Tanasis, it turns out, is also from there, but left, in 1916, to go to Russia. Mehmet, recognizing that he speaks the same "strange language" as Ayşe/Eleni, takes him to her. Ayşe/Eleni, who has remained in the highlands, even after everyone else has left, is found staring at the mountains when the two arrive, and suddenly starts speaking in Greek again. Thinking she is talking to her lost brother Niko, the following monolog takes place:

Niko, you came back. See mother in the clouds? She is carrying Sofia on her back. But I can't see Sofia clearly. Her head bounces lifelessly. I can't tell if she is alive. Father isn't there to protect them anymore. He was shot with other rebels, remember? Look! Mother put baby Sofia in the snow. She's leaving her there. Oh little Niko! Remember how we feared for our souls every night? We used all our strength to walk each day, only to watch each other die at night. Why did they do this to us Niko? They told us "only two days". You'll have to walk only two days. But what happened? We walked weeks and weeks to get to Mersin. They watched us bury our dead along the way. Should we tell him who you are? Niko is my brother. I am Eleni Terzidis, the daughter of Prodromos and Marika Terzidis. Before my father died, he made me promise to protect Niko. He trusted me.

The speech is not only in Greek, but also takes place at a time when she is able to speak Greek, suggesting a temporal displacement. These words inform us about everything that Ayşe/Eleni has repressed, and has had to bury inside. The speech brings past into present, and in a way brings the inside to the outside, revealing the identity shift that had to be made in order for her to survive.

The distinction between inside and outside is emphasized in a number of scenes. For instance, when Ayşe/Eleni relives the initial moment of her great trauma, the moment in which she lets go of her brother, as she enacts the scene of him being taken away. She says: "My betrayal of Niko keeps torturing me. Niko [...] looking at me behind the window. This is etched on my mind." Similar recollections are repeated with different characters functioning as triggering forces to her memory flashbacks. In all these instances, the space that confines her, which is supposed to protect her, represents a force that separates her from what she wants to reach out for. As Gaston Bachelard describes beautifully: "The fear does not come from outside. Nor is it composed of old memories. It has no past, no physiology. [...] Fear is being itself. Where can one flee, where find refuge? In what shelter can one take refuge? Space is nothing but a horrible outside-inside" (Bachelard 1994: 218).

Finally, the film puts a great emphasis on photographs, and these photographs become central to the film's final resolution. The relationship between memory and photographs is a peculiar one. *Waiting for the Clouds* plays on this relationship in its final scene as the photographs' status as "evidence of existence" is questioned. For Ayşe/Eleni, a single remaining photograph from her childhood, a picture of herself with her brother and their father, is a proof of her past, and an important part of the puzzle. However, photographs on their own cannot narrate a story, they are used to illustrate stories. In Tom Gunning's words "the apparatus, in itself, can neither lie, nor tell the truth. Bereft of language, a photograph relies on people to say things about it or for it" (Gunning: 42).

At the end of the film, she travels to Thessaloniki hoping to find her brother. She finds Niko and reveals her identity, but he is not convinced that she is his sister. The following day, he shows her old pictures of himself from childhood to the present time, trying to prove that she did not exist in his life, simply because she is in none of these photographs. Niko remarks: "These photographs represent my life. You aren't in any of them. [...] If you were really my sister, you would be in these photos." Ayşe/Eleni, then, shows Niko the picture she has been carrying around all the time, in which they are together as children (see Figure 3.5). As Barthes asserts, photographs say "this has been." It is a proof of what was "then" and "there." In the final scene, the film plays with this aspect of photography from both sides. Niko's attempt to prove she "was not there" is disproved with another photograph that says "this has been."

Writing on life and death in photography, Mulvey says that Barthes "combines the materiality and flexibility of the shifter with tense: 'then' the photograph was 'there' at its moment of registration, 'that' moment is now 'here'. He sums up photography's essence as 'this is now'" (Mulvey 2006: 57). This is somewhat

Figure 3.5 *Waiting for the Clouds* (dir. Yeşim Ustaoğlu, from Silkroad Productions, 2003). Nico and Eleni together as children.

reminiscent of Benjamin's *Jetztzeit*, in which the image of the past creates recognition in the present. What is also remarkable here is how photographs are used to mark the narrative time. While the film itself is perceived as representing the present, photographs come to represent the past. Interestingly enough this tendency can be found in many films dealing with characters who have experienced a personal loss and developed a feeling of nostalgia. As nostalgia is longing for a specific time, the nostalgic usually hangs on to a photograph, which is frequently a picture of a person or a place. What these photographs are representing is, in fact, a time that is captured in the form of a photograph, a slice of the past that the nostalgic is longing for: a picture of how s/he remembers herself/himself. Peter Wollen writes that still photographs "cannot be seen as narratives themselves but as elements of narrative" (Wollen 2007: 110). Niko's remark about how the photographs represent his life, his past, is in fact about how he narrates his life through these photographs. However, from a different perspective and with an additional photograph they narrate a different story, that of Ayşe's/Eleni's.

Ayşe/Eleni and Niko are not only using photographs to establish their pasts in the present, but this moment becomes an allegorical moment of the denial of the human suffering on the part of both states. National history is written with documents, but only with the ones that were supportive of the existing discourse. For this reason it is equally important that the director cuts back to the archival footage at the end of the film. The importance of this scene does not lie in the question of whose story is the "true" version, but in the way the director acknowledges the contestation.

The archival footage and the decision to end the film with this frozen image can also be read as a statement on the constructed nature of memories, and the obsession with documenting them. What said very little at the beginning is now saturated with significance. Similarly, in order to believe her story both Niko and the audience need a "document." There is an affinity between Niko's initial reaction to his sister, and Turkey's reaction (and many other nation-states for that matter) to its own past. "In this light, documentation no longer serves as a useful means for recording actualities in order to enable discourse based empirical authority. Instead, documentation becomes an end in itself, a goal of self fashioning for ongoing retrospection" (Pence 2003: 246). Ayşe/Eleni's obsession with this photograph, how she places this very picture behind the only candle that illuminates the room when she is in the highlands to see the photograph day and night, Niko's carefully and chronologically ordered family album that narrates his life are all precursors of this self-fashioning.

Waiting for the Clouds is a film that deals with a sensitive issue in recent Turkish history, one that had devastating effects on a certain part of the community. Through Ayşe's/Eleni's individual experience, her loss of family, loss of home, and loss of language, we are given a subjective account of a part of history. As she brings back her memories, the audience is also forced to bring back certain memories of their own, or to "learn" about them. The film's comment on identity and memory is, therefore, not limited to that of minorities but is also about the complex and multicultural make up of Turkey. What Ustaoğlu challenges is not the authenticity of Ayşe's/Eleni's memories, nor the memories of anyone who has "experienced" the event, but the politics of memory, then and now; what we remember and how we remember it, how much of those memories are allowed to be remembered. As the director also states, if Ayşe/Eleni were to live in a less hostile environment she would not have had to hide her identity and her memories (Ustaoğlu, Press Kit).

The film questions the existing discourses on the idea of Turkishness, Turkish history and the questions around identity by means of allegorical represen-tation. Its narrative strategy makes use of the filmic space and its possibilities in relation to time and space to comment further on the audience's memory both of the history of Turkey and of the film itself. The film asks important questions about the political and social attitude of Turkey toward its memory of the past, and its representations in the present.

* * *

Since the end of the 1990s, there has been increasing interest in the experiences of minorities in Turkey, and in that an interest in questioning the Turkish identity. These films, on the one hand, openly deal with the past, and on the other reconsider issues related to identity in Turkey, often challenging the understanding of the unified nation under the category of Sunni-Turk. Polyglossia, that is, the use of more than one language, is an important device in this process. More often than not such "pureness" does not exist, which then opens up new ways of understanding the complex forces at work.

One of the most salient aspects of these films is the way they deal with, and understand, the existing silence in Turkey about the past and the different ways of breaking such silence in its representation. This is also tied into the issue of language. In *9*, for instance, the only time we hear Kirpi say anything is when she sings the song in an "unknown" language. Similarly, in *Waiting for the Clouds*, Ayşe's/Eleni's silence is related to her native language surfacing. *Offside*, on the other hand, does not necessarily focus on a silent character but brings the existing silence to the fore regarding minority identities. Journeys are also used often in these films and are taken by characters who are torn between two places: while Ayşe/Eleni embarks on a journey to Greece to find her brother, Fannis in *A Touch of Spice* and Tasula in *Toss-Up* take the journey in the opposite direction and come back to Turkey. These journeys also mirror each other. While Ayşe's/Eleni's is completion of an interrupted journey, one that she could not make when her brother left for Greece, Tasula's and Fannis' journeys are back to a place from which they are separated.

These films, influenced by, as well as influencing, the processes that Turkey is going through, bring particular moments of crisis back into current memory, and in doing so, they open up further discussions. What needs to be remembered is that the experiences these stories represent are not new; however, their visibility in the public sphere is a new phenomenon, which has surfaced at the first available opening. It is perhaps in their willingness to bring the ghosts of forgotten languages that these films are at their most powerful: in a flash, even a single a word can bring to the present the knowledge of absent people.

4

Representing the Armenian Genocide:
Ararat and Beyond[1]

This chapter, as the title indicates, focuses on the representations of the Armenian genocide in film, putting Atom Egoyan's *Ararat*, and its reception in Turkey, at its center. As I have been arguing throughout the book, narratives outside the borders of Turkey are as relevant and influential as the ones coming from within when examining the country's relationship to its past through film. Yet, before going any further, the centrality of the film to the chapter, as well as the reasons for discussing the Armenian genocide in a separate chapter, might benefit from further clarification. Armenians are, after all, members of the non-Muslim minorities, as well. Is the representation of the Armenian genocide different to representations of other such massacres or genocides in film? And, why does *Ararat* form the kernel of this chapter?

Although Armenians made up part of the non-Muslim population living in the Ottoman Empire, the genocide claims and subsequent denial that exists in Turkey regarding genocidal intent is an ongoing issue, with its own separate political and social ramifications. Hence, the weight of the subject in contemporary Turkey requires a separate discussion in order to be able to tackle its own particular context and the various discourses produced on the subject. Unlike other issues related to the minorities in Turkey, or other catastrophic events, in general, outside of Turkey (or modernist events à la Hayden White), the denial on the part of the Turkish government, and the anguish created by the denial of pain and suffering on the part of Armenians, are what distinguish the Armenian genocide from similar traumatic episodes in history. In other words, the context in which the works on the Armenian genocide are produced and dealt with is one in which there is an ongoing denial of the fact itself. The erasure and the denial of history in relation to the Armenians often make the works on the Armenian experience different from similar works, since in this case the already debilitating nature of the event is taken further since the survivor is put in an agonizing position of having to prove his/her suffering in order that he/she can mourn it. This denial, combined with an extremely long struggle to end that denial, shape much of the discussion and the representation of the event. The film *Ararat* not only deals with various representations of the genocide, but also, unlike any other film discussed in this book, lies at the center of intense debates in Turkey.

Discussions about the film started in Turkey months before it premiered at the Cannes Film Festival in 2002, as *Ararat* was already making the news during the production and the post-production phases. When the film was released in 2002, it continued to create heated debate in Turkey and elsewhere in the world. Part of the reason why Egoyan was able to create such turmoil, in addition, or perhaps in relation to Turkey's denial of the genocide claims, is the film's unusual take on the historical epic genre. While questioning the genre and its limits, *Ararat* tries to understand the past through today, interrogating the notions of truth and testimony. It explores the present time and how present conditions influence the memory of a traumatic event that is not only the subject of social and cultural debate, but also that of historical, political, and juridical contestation.

This chapter is divided into five sections. While the first section aims at providing a brief background to the events of 1915, and their aftermath, the second discusses representability—and the representation—of the event in film. The section briefly looks at Fatih Akın's *The Cut* (2014), and the Taviani Brothers' *La Masseria Delle Allodole/The Lark Farm* (2007), with the aim of situating *Ararat* among other films on the subject. The chapter then discusses the themes of absence, denial, and memory in Egoyan's filmography. The final two sections focus specifically on *Ararat*: a close textual analysis of the film is followed by an analysis of its reception in Turkey.

Historical overview: 1915, and its aftermath

The Ottoman Empire was governed by a *millet* system, allowing relative autonomy to religious communities, and the Armenians were one of the non-Muslim communities living under the protection of the Sultan. During the first half of the nineteenth century, many ethnic groups demanded independence, and established their own nation-states. The Armenians, however, remained part of the empire, with no serious claim to a separate state; they were also known as the "loyal nation" (*millet-i sadika*). This changed in the second half of the 19th century, as they, too, started to express similar demands regarding independence, and were backed by several Western countries and Russia.

The growing anxiety and conflict among the Empire's subjects caused continuous bloodshed. While the Balkan Wars (1912–13), and the defeat that followed, were important in relation to the development of Turkish nationalism, both Christians and Muslims were involved in violence, looting and massacring villagers. According to Taner Akçam, the Rumelian Muslim refugees, trying to escape massacres in Christian-dominated areas, started arriving in Anatolia from 1912 onward, and contributed greatly to the already existing desire for revenge in the minds of the Muslims. This, according to Akçam, was crucial in creating the necessary conditions "for the subsequent Armenian genocide, because it was precisely those people who, having only recently been saved from massacre themselves, would now take a central and direct role in cleansing Anatolia of 'non-Turkish elements'" (Akçam 2007: 84).

However, the massacres of 1915 were not the first that the Armenians had suffered under the Ottoman Empire. Historians often cite two distinct events prior to 1915: the Hamidian Massacres, between 1894 and 1896, and the Adana Massacres of 1909. The Hamidian massacres were carried out by Hamidiye regiments, that is irregular Kurdish cavalry forces, backed by Sultan Abdül Hamid II. The regiments were created in order to ensure security near the Russian border, but the real reason for their existence was to keep Armenian revolutionary activity under control (Akçam 2007; Hovanissian 2004). The Adana Massacres, on the other hand, erupted after a counter-coup against the CUP government by Abdül Hamid supporters. Local Muslims in the province of Adana attacked Armenian villages, which, in their eyes, represented the "evil Western values" that were being imposed on the Ottoman Empire. According to Akçam, even though "the CUP had no direct connection to the events in Adana, there are a number of accounts that claim local Unionists leaders [CUP members] were involved" (Akçam 2007: 63).[2]

It was after the Battle of Sarıkamış (1914) and the defeat by Russia that the situation worsened. Enver Pasha, who was one of the leaders of the CUP, and who is often regarded as one of the architects of the massacres, ordered Armenian conscripts to give up their arms, as he blamed the Armenian soldiers for collaborating with the Russian Army. A secret branch within the governing party called *Teşkilat-ı Mahsusa* (Special Organization) planned the deportations of Armenians between 1915 and 1918, according to many scholars, with the intention of clearing Anatolia of Armenians. Many died during these long marches due to starvation and illness, and this later formed part of the accusations made against the authorities as it is claimed that they intentionally did nothing to protect the people. There are also eyewitness accounts claiming to have seen soldiers massacring and torturing Armenians, to which the authorities reportedly turned a blind eye.

The military tribunals of 1919 and 1920 sentenced Talat Pasha, Enver Pasha, Dr. Nazım, and Cemal Pasha, the four main agitators in the massacres, to death in their absence. Talat Pasha and Cemal Pasha were assassinated later by the Armenians. Although the massacres were admitted and the responsible bodies were tried, Turkey later took a step back. The birth of the newly established Turkish Republic as a nation-state, and its desire to narrate a heroic past, resulted in the erasing of certain events from the public discourse.

The historiography on Armenians and the silence that exists in Turkey go through different stages. According to Fatma Müge Göçek, the historiography of the Armenians in Turkey can be viewed in three historical periods: the Ottoman investigative narrative; the republican defensive narrative; and the post-nationalist critical narrative. Each of these periods produces a distinct historiography, shaped by the political climate in which it emerges. The first period, the Ottoman investigative narrative, covers the period of the genocide and its immediate aftermath. The most salient aspect of these works (memoirs, reports, and so on) is that they do not question the occurrence of the massacres (Göçek 2003: 211). This was followed by a period of silence until 1953, which was broken briefly by the publication of a few works on the subject, which formed the defensive narrative. There is then another twenty years of silence, until 1973, after which the majority of the works disseminating the republican defensive narrative were produced. The works that are written in defense of the republican narrative are dominated, in tone, by Turkish nationalism. These works blame Western forces and Armenian revolutionaries for the loss of Armenian lives, thus disowning all responsibility on the part of the Ottoman–Turkish authorities. Göçek connects the emergence and popularity of these works to the political climate in Turkey: the nationalist narratives concerning the events of 1915 were written predominantly during the 1970s, the period in which ASALA emerged, and carried out a number of attacks on

Turkish embassies abroad. The organization also attacked an airport in Turkey killing and wounding many civilians. Its aim was to create awareness of and recognition for the Armenian genocide, but in Turkey it created a counter-response, and a nationalist discourse was reenacted. In other words, although the need to form a discourse countering genocide claims was already felt by the Turkish authorities, it was the formation of ASALA that made it impossible to maintain the silence on the subject. Hence, after the period of silence on the matter, Turkish state policy has been revisionist. Within its official discourse, Turkey denies the accusations of genocide, and maintains the position that the events of 1915 took place during World War I and should be examined and treated accordingly. A number of international scholars also support this position, most notably Bernard Lewis and Stanford Shaw. In short, the counter-arguments usually state that genocide requires intention and, in this case, that the Ottoman Empire intended to wipe out its Armenian population cannot be proved. Another line of argument rejects the accusations of genocide altogether, maintaining that the loss of lives was due to intercommunal clashes, combined with bad weather conditions during the deportations.

Until very recently, it was almost impossible to argue against the official discourse in Turkey without facing serious problems. This is also what Göçek refers to as the third period, when she describes the post-nationalist critical narrative that emerged in the early 1990s, with a lessening military influence over politics and accession talks to the EU intensifying. According to Göçek, "the most significant factor that unites the works in this category is that none is written to defend a particular thesis or is supported for publication, in one capacity or another, by the Turkish State"; they are all "products of emerging civil society in contemporary Turkey" (Göçek 2003: 225). The author's argument is applicable to a wide range of cultural production in Turkey, and *Ararat*'s release coincides with this third period. However, as Göçek also reminds us, the discursive space that allowed post-nationalist critical narrative to emerge does not necessarily make the republican narrative disappear. Rather, these two discourses continue to coexist and works falling in line with both narratives continue to be published.

Representing genocide, situating *Ararat*

The representation of events that are considered to be historically tragic and socially traumatic, such as massacres and genocides, is a much discussed issue.

It is often suggested such traumatic experiences escape our capacity to attach meaning to them, and, therefore, are not representable as they escape language and reason.[3] Another line of argument suggests that such events escape representation because they are a different type of experience and ask for their own mode of representation. Writing on the representability of the Holocaust, Hayden White argues that genocide is not "any more unrepresentable than any other event in human history. It is only that its representation, whether history or in fiction, requires the kind of style, the modernist style, that was developed in order to represent the kind of experience which social modernism made possible" (White 1992: 52).

When we look at the actual representations of traumatic episodes in history it is possible to examine them under two, albeit large, categories: the "historical realist narratives," as Joshua Hirsch calls them, and the narratives that employ the modernist style, as defined by White. The historical realist narratives assume a certain authority over truth, representing "the past unselfconsciously, drawing attention to the events represented, and away from the [text's] own act of presentation" (Hirsch 2004: 21). Narratives employing the modernist style, on the other hand, question the notions of truth produced by historical knowledge, and are aware of their own participation in the process of representation.

White argues that telling a story about such events may provide "a kind of 'intellectual mastery' of the anxiety which memory of their occurrence may incite in an individual or a community. But precisely insofar as the story is identifiable *as a story*, it can provide no lasting 'psychic mastery' of such events" (White 1996: 32). What White refers as "intellectual mastery" is in fact failure to grasp the truth about the event as a result of its narration. It is the kind of mastery that the representation of the event provides for the audience without the audience going through the trouble of engaging with the event represented. According to White, it is through the "antinarrative nonstories produced by literary modernism" that adequate representation of such "unnatural" events might be achieved (White 1996: 32).

Such style is observable in Egoyan's approach to the subject in *Ararat*, as he creates a complicated and fragmented narrative structure, as well as questioning the process of representation through the inclusion of various representations of the event, from the "film-within-the-film" to Arshile Gorky's landmark painting. The film requires the audience to be pensive, to engage with absences, with the ghosts of history, and asks them to question the disabling nature of denial. Such narration is specific to neither *Ararat*, nor to works attempting to deal with the

Armenian genocide. On the contrary, most works dealing with displacement and historical traumas resort to absences and specters. Nevertheless, dealing with a denied trauma might be said to introduce additional challenge to the text. Thus, introducing absences to the texts, that also aim to expose the existing denial, forms the most enabling narrative element when dealing with the debilitating nature of the event.

From Hrair Sarkissian's photographs to Egoyan's video installation *Auroras* (2007), works on the Armenian genocide repeatedly visit the notion of absence. Sarkissian, for instance, in a series called *Unexposed* (2012), photographed Armenians living in Turkey who converted to Islam in order to escape genocide in 1915. Although the later generation reconverted back to Christianity, they had to conceal their identity. The series consists of underexposed "portraits" in which the subjects' faces are not revealed and only parts of their bodies are seen due to the underexposure. What would ordinarily be considered an error in a portrait becomes the most important feature in these photographs. It is in their absent identity that the truth, only as a possibility, is exposed.

Similarly, *Ararat* is not only part of a body of work by Egoyan that deals with the history of Armenians, but also a product of an ongoing exploration into the notion of truth, i.e. who tells the truth and the ways in which it is performed, particularly in relation to the historical and unrecognized pain that continuously ruptures the later generations. In addition to his feature length films, Egoyan also created a number of installations and short films dealing with the issue. In *Auroras*, a video installation about a survivor of the genocide, young Aurora Mardiganian, Egoyan casts seven different women of various ethnic origins, speaking English in different accents, to read an extract based on Mardiganian's memories. Escaping Turkey for the Unites States, Aurora Mardiganian was encouraged to write her story. The book was then turned into a film, *Ravished Armenia* (Oscar Apfel, 1919; also known as *Auction of Souls*), in which Aurora was cast as herself.[4] She was asked to travel with the film to promote it, but had an emotional breakdown and had to withdraw. As a result, the production company hired seven different Aurora lookalikes to replace her.

Ravished Armenia, the first film on the Armenian genocide, asks the victim to act as herself, to perform, to prove, and to legitimize her pain, and when she collapses, she is replaced by actresses who play out her pain in her absence. Egoyan's installation, in return, comments on the forced performance of pain for audiences. Using seven different women to act as Aurora, Egoyan asks some of them to be overtly emotional in their recitals, while others appear indifferent to what they are reading. Together, they expose an aspect of such representation: history is an unstable notion and our experience of it depends heavily on how it is narrated and represented. Yet, as discussed, the approach that questions its own act of representation is neither the only approach to representation of genocide, nor is it the most common. Below, I discuss briefly two films dealing with the Armenian genocide that differ, in their approach, from the aforementioned examples, as well as from *Ararat*: the Taviani Brothers' 2007 film *La Masseria Delle Allodole/The Lark Farm* and Fatih Akın's 2014 *The Cut*.

The Lark Farm is based on a book by an Italian–Armenian writer Antonio Arslan, whose family migrated to Italy after they fled from Van, Turkey. Featuring an international cast, and both Armenians and Turks speaking in Italian, the film is set in a small town during the months leading up to the massacres. It tells the story of the Avakians, a wealthy Armenian family, who fail to read the signs of what is to come. Betrayed by their Turkish friends in powerful positions, the Armenian men in the family, and in the town, are killed, while the women are sent to the Syrian desert, Der Zor, on foot. The plot features a love story between Nunik (Paz Vega), the daughter of the Avakian family, and a Turkish soldier, Egon (Alessandro Preziosi). Knowing what is to come, Egon tries to save Nunik, but after his plans are discovered by his superiors, he abandons her. The film ends with the children of the family arriving in Italy after much effort by their uncle in Venice to save his family from the camp. No other family member manages to survive. With a sense of mastery over historical truth, and an omniscient narrative, which does not allow any critical distance, *The Lark Farm* relies heavily on emotion and does not fall short of gory depictions of the events. The film, like many other conventional historical films, attempts to turn the incomprehensible into a comprehensible story.

One of the main problems of the film in its representation of the event is the lack of responsibility that it imagines on the part of the perpetrators. It produces one of many examples of a type of narrative that I call "reconciliation-gone-wrong." The film depicts those who actively participated in the massacres, as well as those who facilitated it, as individuals with no apparent agency. This becomes most salient when another Turkish soldier (Moritz Bleibtreu) develops feelings for Nunik at the camp. He not only refuses to have intercourse with her in exchange for food, but also wants to save her, and expresses his disappointment and upset for what is happening at the camp, i.e. abuse, rape, and murder, thus giving a portrayal of a compassionate soldier. He has joined the army to fight the enemy and "not for this." Although he disagrees with the treatment of the Armenians, he also appears to be helpless in his participation in the events that follow. Hence, the film ends up, in its efforts to understand what might have happened to turn people against their neighbors, producing a narrative in which nobody is really held accountable for the massacres. The official rhetoric that the "Armenians were assisting Russians against the Turks" seems to be the reason why hostilities started and, according to the film, ordinary Turks were caught up in this narrative. And, although many Armenians were peaceful, the Ottoman Army still carried out their plans of clearing the land of Armenians. To end the film with a Turkish soldier's confession in the court martial, blaming both himself for taking part in the massacres, and also his superiors for giving the orders, produces an uncritical narrative that fails to understand the rupture caused by the denial of the event in contemporary Turkey.

In comparison to the Taviani Brothers' film, Fatih Akın's 2014 *The Cut* deals with the question of representation in a less assuming manner. Yet it refrains from scrutinizing and questioning its own participation in producing a comprehensible representation of the event, as well as dealing with the event's ramifications in contemporary Turkey. The film is the third in Akın's love (*Gegen Die Wand*, 2004), death (*The Edge of Heaven*, 2007), and evil trilogy. It is also the first film made by a Turk (albeit a German–Turk) on the subject that does not reproduce the official Turkish discourse.

The Cut focuses on one man's journey, that of Nazaret (Tahar Rahim), an Ottoman–Armenian blacksmith from the city of Mardin. After Nazareth and his brother are forcefully taken from their home by Turkish soldiers, they are brought to a construction site to work with other Armenian men. During their time in the labor camp, they see Armenians from surrounding villages on forced marches and witness crimes committed by thugs, and soldiers accommodating the criminals. When finished with the construction work, the soldiers leave them to the criminals to be slaughtered, but Nazaret lives because Mehmet, the man who was meant to kill him, is unable do so. However, he does receive a deep cut to his throat and, as a result, loses his ability to speak. With Mehmet's help, he survives, and starts searching for his family on foot. When he finds out that his daughters are still alive, he once again has a mission in life, and from then on the film follows his dedicated journey to find them. The second half of the film chronicles his epic journey from Aleppo to Lebanon, then on to Cuba and finally to America, in search of his daughters.

Akın's decision to have Nazaret as a silent character is an important one. As discussed in Chapter 2, silent characters are used for various reasons in film, often as bearers of unspoken knowledge, and here Nazaret is the ultimate witness to a massacre. Their silence is unstable and has the power to destabilize the text. In narratives on displacement, silence often denotes what cannot be said, that which cannot make itself known within the structure of language. *The Cut*, in this sense, is a film aware of the perils of witnessing such an event on the human psyche; here it is translated into a physical wound, which is the embodiment of what cannot be described. Nazaret is not refusing to talk; he is simply unable to. He is a silent character, who cannot voice his loss in words. Although this inability appears directly related to the physical wound that he receives to his neck, it is, in fact, the result of surviving, and having to testify to, the event. Thus, despite the various conventional decisions he makes, the director, Akın, does not have Nazaret recite his story. Yet, while Nazaret cannot turn his experience into a story, this, on its own, does not necessarily translate into admitting that *it* cannot be turned into a story. Although Nazaret is no longer able to function within language as a witness, it is assumed that the film can and should do so.

Hence, Akın focuses on what the massacres did to the survivors, to Nazaret, rather than trying to explain the events that happened. In this sense, *The Cut* is different from *The Lark Farm*, since, unlike the Taviani Brothers, Akın knows the limits of representation. He has stated in a number of interviews that *The Cut* is not a "genocide film," but rather his take on the Western genre. During a Q&A session at the London Film Festival (2014), he repeated this position, adding, "if I wanted to tell a story of the genocide I'd probably make a documentary for at least twelve hours long and tell the story of not only 1915, but the last few hundred years."[5] We do not know what that documentary would look like, but *The Cut* limits its representation to actions, not establishing a cause-and-effect relationship between those actions as to why they happened. In a similar vein, Nazaret does not have to prove his pain to others nor explain what he has gone through. What is more, contrary to the claims that Akın's film does not show an act of genocide, a centrally organized crime, the film repeatedly makes it clear that the authorities were aware of what was going on, but that they either facilitated, or turned a blind eye to, the massacres of the Armenians.[6] The film also hints at German complicity in the events.

In addition to reactions that are heavily shaped by the politics of the subject in Turkey (reminiscent of the response to *Ararat*, which is discussed in the following sections),[7] Akın has been criticized for making a number of aesthetic and narrative decisions. Among them is the decision to make the film in English and have his Armenian characters, who would, in fact, speak Armenian to each other, speak English with an accent. While using English-speaking characters may increase the size of the potential audience, it also becomes a source of unintended alienation in the film, particularly when Nazaret arrives in the United States and is unable to understand the language. Alas, this is also the only connection made to the "now" of the film: that the film aims to address a large market. Unlike *Ararat*, or some of the other films dealt with in this book, *The Cut* does not make connections to contemporary political and social contexts, which is a glaring absence given that the issue is very much an ongoing one for both Armenians and Turks.

Yet, Akın's decision to have his Armenian characters speak in English is not the only cliché to be found in the film. Nazaret's representation as a hard-working man, devout father, a loving husband, an almost perfect human being who is dedicated and committed, is equally, if not more, problematic. Nazaret's portrayal not only employs a tiresome cliché, but it is an ethically problematic approach as well: a historical wrongdoing is not less of a crime when it is suffered by a less likeable character. The decision to deal with such a complex and contested chapter of history in film results, in Akın's case, in disregarding those very complexities. In this sense, *Ararat* can be read as a film with an opposing attitude to the subject matter, as it explores the nature of the event, while questioning the representation of the historical truth. Creating not only complex charaters, but also a very complex narrative structure, *Ararat* insists on the "now" in order to understand the meaning of the past, and employs a number of narrative decisions that tackle the question of absence and denial.

Egoyan: Absence, denial, and memory

Ararat, in many ways, is part of an ongoing "discussion" in Egoyan's films: that of being displaced, its ramifications on the subject, and how memory is stored and reshaped in this process, which resonates with Egoyan's own identity as it was also shaped by displacement. His grandparents were both survivors of the massacres, and fled to Egypt from Turkey. Later, his parents migrated from Egypt to Canada. However, like many migrant parents, they wanted him to integrate, raising him as a Canadian, so much so that he didn't learn Armenian until he was studying at the University of Toronto. It was during this time that he also became interested in the history of the Ottoman Armenians. Whether as a result of the rupture that forms the kernel of his Armenian identity or for other reasons, Egoyan's work often deals with how memories are stored and how identity is constructed in his films. *Next of Kin* (1984), *Family Viewing* (1987), *The Adjuster* (1991), *Calendar* (1993), *Exotica* (1994), and *Adoration* (2008) all deal with memory, loss, and the idea of the substitute, as well as various forms of absences.

In *Next of Kin*, an Armenian family finds a substitute for their son, who was given away for adoption, while the new son invents a new identity and takes on the memory of the others. In *Family Viewing*, Van, a young man, tries to look after his grandmother who has been put into a nursing home by his father. The grandmother is Van's only connection to his own past and to his dead mother. His father, in an attempt to divest himself of the memory of both women, refuses to visit the grandmother and also tapes his intimate life with his new wife over the old family videos, which are the only testimonies to Van's happy childhood with his mother and grandmother. In *Calendar*, Egoyan puts himself and his wife in front of the camera as a couple going through a breakup. His first film that is explicitly about Armenia—the absent, imagined homeland—and his relation to it, *Calendar* questions the idea of home(land) through epistolary narrative, as the film largely consists of telephone conversations and letters. Running through most of Egoyan's films as a central concept, the themes of loss and memory features as the loss of home or a loved one. Displacement and its two siblings, grief and nostalgia, are strong and recurring motifs in Egoyan's films.

Films such as *Family Viewing*, *Calendar*, and *Adoration* are films explicitly about how the past is stored, as photographs and video cameras are very central to the narrative. In *Family Viewing*, Egoyan plays with the idea of family videos, as the protagonist cold-bloodedly erases his own and his family's past, recording his intimate "present"—his sexual encounters—over his past. *Adoration*, on the other hand, explores the idea of the "prosthetic memory,"[8] as an adolescent boy in the film invents a past that never existed, using gadgets that are available to almost everyone, and the social media. In most of his films, Egoyan investigates the technologies of memory as extensions of the body. From this perspective, his films provide an interesting journey when watched chronologically. As the technologies develop, they become smaller in size and much less tactile. For instance, at the end of *Adoration*, the boy decides to burn the cellular phone on which he has been recording his grandfather's memories as a way of disposing of the recordings. In contrast, in the earlier *The Adjuster* it is the family photographs that are burned. Thus, in *Adoration*, it is the apparatus that is destroyed, not the product; hence, the distinction between the two is blurred. Moreover, unlike the scene in which Seta burns the photographs in *The Adjuster*, the scene in *Adoration* is charged with far less pain and yet with more ambiguity. What was once a tactile object, a videotape or a filmstrip, and subject to deterioration, is now stored in the digital apparatus itself.[9] All of these characters are mourning a loss, longing for a specific time in a specific place. Moreover, their nostalgic longing is translated into image as destruction: erasing and burning. In Boym's words, "a cinematic image of nostalgia is a double exposure, or a superimposition of two images—home and abroad, past and present, dream and everyday life. The moment we try to force it into a single image, it breaks the frame or burns the surface" (Boym: xiv).

Mourning a loss is perhaps most visibly haunting when a migrant idealizes the homeland he/she has never been to, which is what Egoyan deals with in *Calendar*. The film explores how the memory of a place is constructed and maintained as the characters try to come to terms with the memory of the idealized land of Armenia, while producing photographic images of the churches in Armenia for a calendar. The photographer (played by Egoyan himself) and his wife (played by his real-life wife, Arsine Kanjian) are both Canadian citizens of Armenian decent, visiting Armenia for the first time. The wife, who can speak Armenian, acts as a translator between her husband/the photographer and their driver/guide. During their trip, she develops a romantic interest in their local Armenian guide, which eventually leads to the couple's separation. While she stays in Armenia, the photographer goes back to Canada. It is through their interaction with this foreign and yet familiar land that the film explores the idea of homeland, as well as the memory of it.

In *Calendar* Egoyan frequently rewinds, fast forwards, and freezes frame, while switching back and forth between the video screen and the cinematic screen, leaving the audience baffled about the temporality, as well as the spatiality of the narrative. Significantly, his playful attitude toward time works extremely well against the timeless monumental structures that his character seeks to photograph. In an interview, Egoyan admits that he finds the "whole notion of time being fluid as opposed to the timelessness of these monuments" very appealing (Egoyan 2004b: 221). Moreover, there is an undeniable sense of loss brought with these centuries-old churches, now largely in ruins.

Egoyan, in *Calendar*, not only plays with the concept of the calendar, which is essentially a timetable designed to structure our entire year, but also with the notion of subjective time: as each monument also marks a significant moment in the characters' lives as a couple, the photographer recreates these moments in order to "remember." *Calendar* is not only Egoyan's first attempt to represent Armenia on screen, but also the precursor of *Ararat*: both films are explicitly about Armenia (historical and contemporary) and Armenian identity. Moreover, there are significant similarities between the two films in terms of plot structure and the representation of time. Both *Calendar* and *Ararat* rely heavily on flashbacks in order to structure time. However, Egoyan does not use flashbacks in a conventional sense when the shifts between temporal zones are clearly marked. Although flashbacks in film have immense potential to expand the temporal dimensions of a narrative, they are usually used "in order to naturalize them as personal memories," rather than exploring their potential "for disturbing a participatory viewing" and "encouraging a greater distance" (Turim 1989: 17). In this sense Egoyan uses flashbacks to raise questions and to encourage intellectual distance. In both *Calendar* and *Ararat*, he turns the technologies of memories into devices that introduce flashbacks rather than the conventional methods of wipe or fade. The recording devices become sources of flashbacks, as recorded events are watched and remembered. This, in turn, makes it more difficult for the audience to figure out the temporal location of the events as well as the chronological order. The technological possibilities available for re-storing and re-presenting memories inevitably have political meanings, and Egoyan's films do not fall short of them. This gains a new significance in *Ararat* when he introduces painting, photography, video recording, and film-within-the-film all at once as different ways of technological reproduction and representation of the past in film.

Ararat: Close-up

Ararat deals with the events of 1915 from an unusual perspective: rather than producing a representation of the event, the film focuses on the representation(s) of it, questioning the ways in which knowledge, memory, and identity are produced and represented. It is a film that is particularly difficult to provide a plot summary for, predominantly due to its complicated narrative structure. The film switches back and forth between different temporalities without clearly marking them, leaving it to the audience to fathom. In an effort to explain the complicated narrative of the film, for which he was often criticized, Egoyan said that the grammar of *Ararat* "uses every possible tense and mood available to tell its story, from the basic pillars of the past, present, and the future, to the subjective, the past-perfect, and past not-so-perfect, and the past-would-be-perfect-if-it-weren't-so-conditional" (Egoyan 2004a: 901–2). He explains that his decision to create such a complicated grammar was due to the nature of the issues he dealt with in *Ararat*, asserting that "this was the only way the story could be told. It is dense and complex because the issues are so dense and complex" (Egoyan 2004a: 902).

The film consists of three parts: Edward Saroyan's (Charles Aznavour) historic epic film, which is made during the film; the events that take place during the filming of Saroyan's film; and the more ambiguous sequences that take place in Arshile Gorky's studio as he is creating his most famous painting, *Artist and His Mother*. While the film-within-the-film structure allows the director to create a space for comparison between different representations of the past and enables the audience to challenge different viewpoints, the self-reflexive qualities and the complicated plot structure allow the film to stay at a critical distance from its subject.

Ararat attempts to tell this complex history in a narrative set in contemporary Canada, creating a complicated network of relations between various characters. The director of the film-within-the-film, Saroyan, is a filmmaker of Armenian descent, whose most successful days are now behind him. His film is about the Armenian uprising against the Ottoman army in the city of Van in 1915, and is based on his mother's memories, as well as on a book written by Clarence Ussher,[10] who was a physician in Turkey at the time (played by Bruce Greenwood). The making of Saroyan's film brings a number of characters together, as they are directly or indirectly related to the process. While the-film-within-the-film attempts to represent the event itself, the rest of the film tackles the daily encounters of the characters, questioning the problem and/or possibility of the representation of the event. Thus, *Ararat* not only explores the legacy of the genocide through a number of people who are in one way or another connected to each other, but also through various representations of the genocide—Saroyan's film and Gorky's painting are just two of the representations dealt with.

One of the central characters in the film is Raffi (David Alpay), whose mother, Ani (Arshine Kanjian), has written a book on the Armenian painter, Arshile Gorky. Having heard Ani's lecture on Gorky and that he was a little boy in Van at the time of the uprising, Saroyan decides to include the young Gorky as a character in his film. Through his mother, who is now involved with the film as an advisor, Raffi also becomes part of the film crew and starts working on the set. Yet Ani's relation to the history of the genocide is not limited to her book on Gorky. In addition to being an Armenian herself, her first husband, Raffi's father, was killed while he was trying to assassinate a Turkish diplomat in an attempt to raise awareness about the Armenian genocide. While Ani considers her ex-husband a hero, who "died for what he believed in," rather than an assassin, Raffi struggles to accept either of these definitions fully. The figure of the absent father is also related to Celia (Marie-Josée Croze), Raffi's girlfriend and the daughter of Ani's second husband. Celia's father also died in an "alleged" accident. Although she believes he killed himself because of Ani, her stepmother maintains that it was an accident.

The official Turkish discourse enters into the story through the half-Turkish actor Ali (Elias Koteas), who plays Cevdet Bey in Saroyan's film and lives with his boyfriend, Phillip (Brent Carver). Through Ali's conversations with Saroyan and Raffi, the audience is exposed to the defensive Turkish narrative. Finally, Phillip's father, David (Christopher Plummer), is a customs officer at the airport and becomes central to the story when he questions Raffi about his possessions at the airport, suspecting that he has brought illegal substances into the country from Turkey.

As much as being a film about the legacy of the genocide, *Ararat* is also a film about the consequences of the past being buried under a carpet, and how simple personal encounters can shape and change perceptions and reactions. Hence, there is particular attention paid to "now": the encounters and denials of the present day. Egoyan explains his decision to focus on "now" as his desire to show that "the truth is not to be found in the epic scenes of deportation and massacres, but in the intimate moments shared by individuals" (Egoyan 2004a: 903). Yet, his insistence on "now" is not merely a narrative device; it has an immediate connection to the "now" of the film. Turkish authorities have been denying much of the claims about the "genocide"—or the "alleged Armenian genocide", as it is called within the official discourse in Turkey. This, according to Marc Nichanian, is precisely the "fact" at the heart of the issue. The fact is not the "extermination" of Armenians, he writes, but rather it is "the erasure [of memory]. And this is exactly why the result of genocidal will is catastrophe for the victim" (Nichanian 2004: 155).

The title of the film, as well as the title of the film-within-the-film, comes from the name of a mountain, Mount Ararat: an important symbol in Armenian culture, which lies within the borders of Turkey today. The importance of Mount Ararat for Armenians manifests itself throughout the film as Egoyan not only names his film after the mountain, but also opens the film with an image of Ararat, almost using the image of the mountain as a reference point, which both locates and dislocates the anxieties created around Armenian identity. Similarly, in the film-within-the-film, Saroyan decides to have the image of the mountain visible from Van, which it is not in reality. When challenged by Ani, Saroyan cites "poetic license" and that it is true "in spirit." The scene locates Saroyan's own anxiety around the image of Ararat as he relocates the mountain: the issue here is not geographical, but rather temporal—it is about what is needed today, rather than what really happened in the past. This, namely the need to locate one's identity in relation to the past and the present, also determines how Egoyan deals with the issue of time in the film as it moves freely between different temporalities.

When dealing with the latter in the way that Egoyan does, the film-within-the-film becomes a useful device. A film within a film, as Deleuze writes in *Cinema II*, is an example of what he calls a "crystal-image," that is, an image with two sides, actual and virtual, but no longer indiscernible, "each side taking the other's role" (Deleuze 2000: 69), giving the image its crystallized state. What becomes visible in the crystal-image is something that is otherwise not visible which, according to Deleuze, is time. In a lengthy but explanatory paragraph, Deleuze writes:

> What constitutes the crystal-image is the most fundamental operation of time: since the past is constituted not after the present that it was but at the same time, time has to split itself in two at each moment as present and past, which differ from each other in nature, or, what amounts to the same thing, it has to split the present in two heterogeneous directions, one of which is launched towards the future while the other falls into the past. Time has to split at the same time as it sets itself out or unrolls itself: it splits in two dissymmetrical jets, one of which makes all the present pass on, while the other preserves all the past. Time consists of this split, and it is time that we *see in the crystal*. The crystal-image was not time, but we see time in the crystal (Deleuze 2000: 81).

Ararat, and, in fact, most of Egoyan's films, are filled with crystal images with two distinct but indiscernible sides, "each simultaneously capturing and liberating the other" (Deleuze 2000: 68). Without Saroyan's film, the rest of *Ararat* would become disabled in the way it deals with time and its representation: it is in their relational perception that time becomes visible. Cinema's ability to make time visible, to show the existence of present and past together, is especially important in a film such as *Ararat* for its subject matter does not have a settled and accepted history; its perception and narration vary and change rapidly according to changes in the present time.

While in *Ararat* the film-within-the-film constantly marks the difference between two temporal zones; they are not the only moments at which time becomes visible. Most of the scenes with Gorky also function as crystal moments. Gorky, a ghostly character played by Simon Akbarian, acts almost like a bridge (or corridor) between the two different time zones: the time in the film being made, 1915, and the time of the making, 2001. Although Gorky exists in Saroyan's film as the little boy in Van and in the rest of the film as an influential figure through his painting, it is not clear to which of the two sections these sequences, which take place in his studio in the 1920s, belong. This not only gives Gorky a "liminal" existence in relation to the two films, but also allows the character to both locate and dislocate the two temporalities. In addition to occupying his own space within the narrative of the film, Gorky's character also functions almost like a mirror (as well as a screen) for both narratives.

Gorky, who today is considered one of the most influential figures in Abstract Expressionism, was originally from a village near Van, which is part of modern-day Turkey. In 1915, he escaped to Russia with his family. His mother later died of starvation, and at the age of 16 Gorky was reunited with his father in the United States, where he lived for the rest of his life. The film focuses on the part of his life when he took on the project of painting his mother, based on a photograph that was taken in Van when he was a young boy, and sent to his father. Gorky later took repossession of the photograph when he was reunited with his father in America. However, it took him more than a decade to take up the painful task of trying to remember and represent his and his mother's experiences in a painting. Losing his homeland, where the memories of his childhood and his mother are inscribed, Gorky is portrayed in the film as a man in agony, attempting to translate his memories into images.

In the film, Ani reads from her book on Gorky: "With this painting Gorky saved his mother from oblivion, snatching her out of a pile of corpses to place her on a pedestal of life."[11] The painting slows down the decaying process and gives the dead a place in history. Gorky's attempt, as well as Egoyan's attempt at representing it, is not merely to create an art object. It is an attempt to give the image of the mother back her auratic existence. However, it can also be read as an attempt to "turn the incident into a moment that has been lived," by actively and intellectually being involved in the recreation of it, by creating a painting of a photograph and, therefore, highlighting the inconsumable nature of the experience which the photograph fails to achieve. This evokes Benjamin's distinction between photography and painting: once the hunger is fed and the thirst is satisfied the object will be forgotten, disposed of. "What prevents our delight in the beautiful from ever being satisfied," writes Benjamin, "is the image of the past. [...] Insofar as art aims at the beautiful and, on however modest scale, 'reproduces' it, it conjures it up (as Faust does Helen) out of the womb of time. This no longer happens in the case of technical production" (Benjamin 2007: 187). Gorky, with this painting, "conjures up the beauty from the womb of time," and snatches it out of a pile of corpses to give it life.

Benjamin suggests that photography destroys the aura of the artwork in the process of mechanical reproduction. What it creates is, however, an urge to search "for the tiny spark of contingency. [...] It is through photography that we first discover the existence of this optical unconscious, just as we discover the instinctual unconscious through psychoanalysis" (Benjamin 1999: 511). It would not be wrong to assume, then, that when a reverse takes place, when a painter reproduces a photograph, the subject gains its aura. Yet, what is lost in translation is that the unique ability of photography, the ability to allow space for the contingent to be registered, is destroyed in the process of painting; it is taken under control. When a photograph is reproduced in painting, although it makes its subject eternal, it also destroys what photographs bring to life: the desire of the artist to master the situation rids the contingent from the photograph. This dialectical relation will become visible in Egoyan's *Ararat* when Arshile Gorky is depicted in the process of painting. Egoyan scrutinizes each step toward the final painting, from the moment of the photograph being taken to the process of painting it.

The photograph of Gorky and his mother is also one of the first images of *Ararat*. The film opens with the camera gazing across the artefacts and other materials in Gorky's studio, including the sketch, and the finished version of the painting. The camera moves across the room to stop, momentarily, on the painter himself looking outside the window, before dissolving into another image, into a different temporality: first to appear are silhouettes of people at the airport, a pensive Saroyan among them. According to Sylvie Rollet, with this scene the ghosts of history that connect/haunt these two men also haunt the filmic space: "Although these fugitive silhouettes assume, after several long seconds, the form of harmless travellers, they nevertheless inscribe the phantoms of Saroyan's and Gorky's shared history on the surface of the filmic signifier" (Rollet 2004: 68). However, although she limits her analysis to the image, the ghosts of history also haunt the soundtrack in this sequence, albeit very discreetly: while the image slowly dissolves into people walking at the airport, the sound also dissolves. What seems, at first, to be the sound of people walking at the airport reveals itself to be two superimposed sounds, the sound of people walking accompanied by horses, which dissolves into the noises of the airport: the displacement connecting the two men is given away subtly with the sound bridge that also connects the two images. While the forced marches of Armenians accompanied by soldiers on horses mark Gorky's past, a ruptured sense of space and time marks Saroyan's.

Egoyan returns to Gorky's studio a few more times as the story develops, and the audience begins to understand the centrality of the painter, and his most famous painting *Artist and His Mother*, to the narrative. Throughout the film, Gorky paints the picture of his mother, Shushan, and himself from the photograph, erasing, adding, and finally leaving it "unfinished." According to art critic Jonathan Jones:

> This painting is testimony to how much it anguished him. The transfiguration of the image into cubistic planes of color emphasizes Gorky's complex reaction to the photograph, as he remade it in his mind. He gives it color, animation, but cannot bring his mother back. While the boy moves in three dimensions, she remains fixed, a flat ghost. Armenia itself is a no-place. Gorky paints a brown square behind his mother's head resembling a window. But it is opaque, no view. Her landscape is gone (*Guardian*, March 30, 2002).

The absence that marks the painting, the absence of the mother, the absence of the land, is not mastered by the painter, but lived. A similar absence marks the lives of the characters in the film as the ghosts of dead fathers, and a ghost of long gone history, haunts each character in different ways.

Gorky, in *Ararat*, is portrayed as a silent character, embodying displacement and loss: a man who is "mute," who cannot find a way to mourn the loss of his homeland, his mother's death, or the past. His "worldlessness" becomes his "wordlessness."[12] Yet, the puncture the photograph creates says more than Gorky can with words. His attempt to paint it, and the film's ability to show both the photograph and the painting at the same time, make those gaps visible between the images. Gorky's spectacular failure to represent his pain is precisely the moment he is able to convey his agony. This, in return, allows Egoyan to reflect on his own inability to represent the event. In *Ararat*, Egoyan imagines that Gorky erases the hands of his mother, which he had already painted. This is an act that allows Gorky also to "touch" his mother at the very moment of destroying her painted hands. Egoyan moves his camera behind the canvas, capturing the momentary trace Gorky leaves on the painting; a sense of touch develops in relation to the painting.

Laura Marks, when discussing the ways in which intercultural cinema communicates embodied knowledge, asserts that "cinema itself appeals to contact—to embodied knowledge, and to sense of touch in particular—in order to recreate memories" (Marks 2000: 129). She calls these images "haptic images," images that create a visual experience that asks the eyes to temporarily function as organs of touch.[13] These images suspend an unproblematic engagement with the narrative, and asking for an engagement which forces the spectator to relate to his/her own knowledge and memory in addition to the knowledge (re)presented on the screen. Moreover, "haptic visuality, in its efforts to touch the image, may represent the difficulty of remembering the loved one, be it a person or a homeland" (Marks 2000: 193), and it is precisely this difficulty, the difficulty of remembering a loved one, no matter how many photographs and

Figure 4.1 A photograph of the painter, Arshile Gorky, and his mother, in Van, 1912. Uncredited. The painting based on this photograph can be viewed at the Whitney Museum website: http://collection.whitney.org/object/2171.

paintings are reproduced, Egoyan imagines Gorky to be experiencing. After finishing the painting, Gorky looks at it with a degree of dissatisfaction and frustration. Appearing almost at the edge of a nervous breakdown, he puts paint on his hands and touches his mother's hands tenderly, as if he is holding them at first, and then with more rage, as if he is trying to erase them. This moment, although it is the moment of a partial destruction of the painting, is also the moment Gorky touches his memories of his mother and, inevitably, also the pain surrounding her death, a gesture that enacts both tenderness and violence at the same time. When asked about this scene Egoyan stated that to find a way "to deal with images of physical violence" and to show "the after effect of the brutality of the Armenian genocide" was a huge challenge.

> [W]hat Gorky is doing by erasing the hands is by its nature a very violent gesture, but it is done with great tenderness, with almost a sense of communion and transference. [...] There is a sense of something pressing against something else; there is obliteration at that point of contact. I think the film charts a number of obliterations, a number of places where the mere act of touching cancels out the latent physical properties of the materials that are being studied (Egoyan 2008: 252).

Similarly, in the film, when the original moment of the photograph being taken is reenacted, the photographer, unhappy with the image, rearranges the mother's hands, resting them on her lap. This moment, the moment of touch, right before the production of this photographic document (a document that will outlive his mother) is reproduced from the young Gorky's point of view with a close-up shot (see Figure 4.2). Later in the film, when Gorky touches the painting, this touch is repeated, this time by the "looker," Gorky himself. It is not an image that comes directly after the sequence with the photographer. It is a haptic image, which the spectators have to remember with the earlier moment of touch (see Figure 4.3). The film, in Marks' words, demands a "Bergsonian form of film spectatorship," which demands a "viewer's 'attentive recognition' of the images on screen. Perception takes place not simply in a phenomenological present but in an engagement with individual and cultural memory" (Marks 2000: 147).

Gorky's portrayal in the film is dominated by a heavy sense of grief caused by his mother's absence. Her absence, along with others (absent fathers and absent land, for example), haunts the text. An image that is marked by "silence, absence and hesitation" (Marks 2000: 21) is always already a ghost story, and ghosts serve as metaphors for unresolved past events and unjust treatments. They push boundaries that are not meant to be pushed. Ghosts destabilize the narrative, defy definitions and mark the present by their uninvited presence that is simultaneously a "significant absence." Yet, Gorky is not the only character dealing with the ghosts of the past. Raffi and his girlfriend Celia, with their rejection of the narratives offered to them, challenge the burden the past brings with itself.

Most of the film is based on Raffi's flashbacks and his search for "some kind of explanation," while Celia is on a mission to have Ani accept the "truth." Celia's way of dealing with her father and his death is also very much like carrying his ghost around. She refuses to let him go unless she receives a closure to her "story": the truth behind his death. She believes that Ani's unjust treatment of her father during their relationship is the reason why he committed suicide. However, Celia's story also hits the wall of denial head-on, as Ani categorically denies her accusations. During one of their arguments, Celia asks Ani to admit that, on the day her father died, she had told him that she was having an affair with another man and that she was going to leave him. According to Celia, her father would have wanted to kill himself if Ani was having an affair. Ani's answer transcends the specific conversation they are having. In response to Celia's question of whether he jumped of the cliff, Ani says: "I can't remember what you want me to remember. Even if I could, I wouldn't. I don't need to." During this conversation, Celia is standing in front of a mirror and within the frame we see Ani and Celia's reflection in the mirror (see Figure 4.4). Although Ani also suffers from the pain caused by denial, she fails to recognize the reflection of this very same pain in the mirror. Celia appears like a spirit trapped in the mirror. Ani, by refusing Celia's request categorically ("even if I could, I wouldn't") also

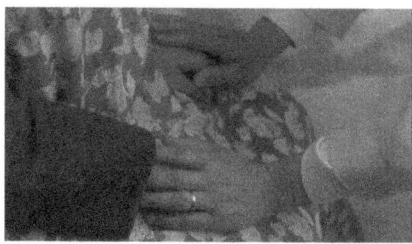 

Figure 4.2 The photographer touching Gorky's mother's hands in *Ararat* (dir. Atom Egoyan; from Miramax, 2002).

Figure 4.3 Gorky touching his mother's painted hands in *Ararat* (dir. Atom Egoyan; from Miramax, 2002).

refuses to hear her, to help her move on, and fails to provide an explanation to Celia about her father's death. Ani, rather than trying to understand Celia, is interested in defending herself, which makes their encounters about shifting the blame, not about a humane response to a personal tragedy. Not being able to discover the truth about her father's death and being refused an answer by the only person who can provide an answer, Celia has no choice but to continue carrying the ghost of her father with her. Enraged by Ani's answer, she storms into the exhibition room and attacks Gorky's painting with a pocket knife, attempting to cut through the canvas, stabbing the painting. This is the painting that, in Ani's words, framed Armenian identity and suffering for many Armenians, and that explains who they are and how they got there. However, whether Celia is able to "tear" the image remains unclear. While Egoyan does not show the actual rip (the camera moves toward the paintingm but cuts away just before it gets close enough to reveal the information), he does provide the sound of the canvas being torn. According to Nichanian, this is how Egoyan avoids the slash: through imagination. "The real laceration could not be brought into representation. It persists and insists, however, in its very erasure. It is a glaring absence" (Nichanian 2004: 6).

Raffi's father, on the other hand, has a different story, as there is no question about how he died. What haunts Raffi is the reason why his father followed the path he did, which caused him to die the way he did. Raffi constantly moves back and forth between his father being a "freedom fighter" and a "terrorist." Taking Celia's advice ("You look after your ghost, I look after mine"), he decides to go to Turkey, to the city of Van, the land of his ancestors and the city where the siege in the film-within-the-film takes place. This is the journey that will also lead to his troubles at the customs on his way back to Canada, as he is stopped by the customs officer, David, on the suspicion of drug smuggling. During a very long and tiresome interrogation about what Raffi has brought from Turkey in the cans that "look like" film cans, Raffi maintains his innocence and insists that the cans contain unexposed film, which would be ruined if exposed to daylight. He tells David that he is working for Saroyan's film and had gone to Turkey "to film the original locations so the people could be added later digitally". In reality, the film is already finished and premiering on the very same day that Raffi is at the Toronto airport, being interrogated. It is revealed during the interrogation that he recorded his entire trip with his digital camera as a visual diary and plays this footage to David at his request, while he tells his story. Shot in Van, and mostly in the historic Akhtamar Island where a tenth-century Armenian church is

Figure 4.4 *Ararat* (dir. Atom Egoyan; from Miramax, 2002). Ani is challenged by Celia, about her father's death.

located, the images visible to the spectator as well as to David serve neither to prove nor to disprove his story.

The scene, according to Nichanian, represents a symbolic encounter between the law and belief, as well as Armenian history forcing its entry to the civilized world.[14] This long conversation, during which David listens to Raffi's reasons for going to Turkey, is practically unnecessary in order to expose the "truth." In an effort to explain himself Raffi starts talking about his ancestors, the denial of the suffering they were subjected to, as well as his father, "illustrating" his points with the video recordings in which "there is nothing but ruins." Combined with Raffi's desperate attempt to tell the story of his ancestors, these images of the ruins haunt the narrative. Nevertheless, the question for David is simple: has Raffi brought cocaine to Canada? As David also states, he could bring the dogs in and they would tell him immediately, but he prefers to hear what Raffi has to say. Having listened to Raffi's inconsistent story, David decides to open the cans. Raffi asks him to do it "at least in dark so they won't be ruined". The officer agrees and "interrogates" them with his touch in the dark room. Egoyan does not disclose the contents of the cans, but does show Raffi set free.

It is revealed to the audience later that the first can contained unexposed film, but the rest contained cocaine. David's decision to free Raffi is based solely on his perception of the events as told by Raffi, since the story reaches the point at which it is simply impossible to determine the truth, whether Raffi knew what was inside the cans. When asked why he let Raffi go, when he was clearly trying to smuggle drugs into the country, David says: "I trusted him; he didn't believe he would do such a thing."

Egoyan, in an article, maintains that trust is what his film is about.

> Raffi appeals to David, the customs officer, to accept his testimony in an act of faith beyond any proof. After the collapse of his story, he is left only with his words. This moment that is shared between the customs officer and the young man he has been interrogating has come from a deep sense of compassion, and I firmly believe that it is only from this capacity—the ability to feel someone else's experience of the world—that we can draw any hope for reconciliation (Egoyan 2004: 903).

Trust was not only missing throughout the film in the relations between the characters, but also is lacking in reality between the two sides of the political argument. Yet, according to Paul Ricoeur, most of our institutions rely on trust. "When I testify to something I am asking the other to trust that what I am saying is true. To share a testimony is an exchange of trust. Beyond this we cannot go. Most institutions rely fundamentally on the trust they place in the word of the other" (Ricoeur 2004b: 156). In fact, for Ricoeur, testimony is itself an institution because the stability of testimony is reiterated and the trustworthiness attributed to the testifier contributes to the "security of the social bond inasmuch as this rests on confidence in what other people say" (Ricoeur 2004b: 165). This is also the basic premise of the film and what really is absent from the discourse, namely the ability to *hear* the other. In this respect the film's reception in Turkey became an uncanny illustration of what *Ararat* commented on the lack of.

Layers of reception: Beyond *Ararat*

Ararat has been one of the most discussed films in the last few decades in Turkey, yet most of those discussions were conducted without having seen the film. In Turkey, many Turks perceived *Ararat* as a personal attack, mainly due to the dominant prevailing conviction that Armenian claims of genocide are fabricated. In a letter addressed to Egoyan, a young Turkish girl complains upon seeing the film and asks: "Mr. Egoyan, I want to ask you if this event had happened in your history and if you were accused of such a thing what would you do?" (Egoyan 2004a: 897). The film obviously made a mark on this young girl: she found it inaccurate but also personally upsetting. This young woman's reaction on its own could have been insignificant, one among many. However, as I will discuss, it was representative of the general reaction to the film in Turkey, which cannot be seen as merely disagreeing with the film's, or Egoyan's, approach to the subject. Within the context of Turkey such reaction illustrates the result of the ongoing dominant discourse on the subject, which is a denialist one. The Turkish authorities have been denying many of the claims about the genocide. The dominant discourse on the Armenian genocide in Turkey, which is formed around denying accountability, and avoiding the subject when possible, also shaped the film's reception.

The film was received on a canvas that was already painted with Turkish nationalism, which was informed by the official discourse on the Armenian genocide. That is to say the hegemonic nationalist discourse in the country was very much at work and visible in the reception of the film. In Turkey, one of the main concerns of the film, *not* listening to the other, became its own fate. This was the result of two factors. First, most of the analyses of the film in Turkey were produced before anyone had a chance to see the film. From the second half of 2001, when news that *Ararat* was in the production begun disseminating, until May 2002, when the film premiered at the Cannes Film Festival, dozens of news pieces and opinion articles were written about the film in Turkey, all without the writers having seen the film.[15] In other words, the film's "reception" was formed before the film was in actuality received. The second important factor was that the analyses of *Ararat* in the country were limited to a number of controversial scenes taken out of their context, making it easier for such nationalistic discourses to be produced about the film. Hence, the film's reception in Turkey was a complex event, interwoven with, and shaped by, the existing discussions on—and the continuous denial of—the Armenian genocide, which is maintained by the categorical refusal to hear what the other (in this case, the Armenian community) has to say regarding its suffering.

The film provoked reactions in many different spheres of public life in the country. There was also a reactionary campaign before the film's premier, asking the Turkish public to voice their opinion against the film by sending letters to Miramax (the American distributor of the film, not the production company as it was referred to by many in Turkey). The letter urged the company "to carry out proper research on the subject using Ottoman archives" and "not to provoke further antagonisms between two nations." It ended with a warning that if Miramax decided to go ahead with the project, it would become necessary for

Turkish filmgoers to boycott the company.[16] The nature and the intensity of the discussions about the film were also, to a large extent, responsible for Egoyan's decision to screen the film outside the competition at the Cannes Film Festival.[17]

The Turkish authorities also felt obliged to condemn the film and there was discussion about whether or not to allow the film to be screened in Turkey. It was, in the end, given permission, but Belge Film, the company that bought the rights of the film, decided not to screen it since radical nationalist groups "warned" the public that they would "take action" and do whatever necessary to stop the film being shown.[18] In an effort to explain their decision to withdraw the film, Sabahattin Çetin, the owner of Belge Film, said that although they were assured that necessary security measures would be taken in the theaters showing the film, it was simply not acceptable to screen it with heavy police presence and with an audience in fear of an attack.[19] *Ararat* was screened on a national television channel, Kanal Türk, four years after its initial release under the pretext of informing the public, and the argument that any defense strategy could not be successful unless what is being faced is known. The general consensus was that banning the film would not solve the problem, the "problem" being conceived as the film's attitude toward history, rather than Turkey's attitude toward the genocide.

This problematic relation to the film had more to do with the way in which the subject matter, i.e. the Armenian genocide, is perceived in Turkey and less about how *Ararat* deals with it. In fact, to maintain such a problematic relation to the film is possible only by resisting the film's own handling of its subject, which tells a complicated story, one that cannot be reduced to an attack against the Turks. Indeed, the film's reception in Turkey was itself an example of the lack of trust, which the film itself comments on. Even before anyone had the chance to see the film it was generally assumed that if an Armenian made a movie about the massacres of Armenians he/she would, first, represent Turks as less than human, second, provoke hatred, and, finally, be financed by the Armenian lobby.[20] Moreover, the criticism of, as well as the reaction to, the film in Turkey was based largely on the fictional director Edward Saroyan's film (the film-within-the-film) taking it out of its context and treating it as the kernel where the essence of the film is to be found. Such approach either ignored the rest of *Ararat*, which was focusing on the daily encounters of the characters, or accused Egoyan of veiling his "real" intention, that of degrading Turks, by putting the blame on Saroyan.

According to the general public and the opinion leaders in Turkey, Turks do not have any problem with Armenians, and the problem itself is created by these accusations, hence by Armenians themselves. What Gündüz Aktan, a former diplomat, asserts in his article in the *Hürriyet Daily News* is a case in point. According to Aktan, "contrary to the claims of the movie *Ararat*, the Turks never hated Armenians."[21] Aktan's article was written before the film premiered, thus before anyone had a chance to see it. The defensive rhetoric, outlined by Göçek, is embedded even in this short sentence as it reveals the assumption that there is/will be an "attack" on the Turks simply because the film deals with a particularly horrific part of the history of Armenians in Anatolia. In fact, most of these articles are also examples of the republican defensive narrative, as it is still the dominant narrative in Turkey.

In February 2002, journalist Doğan Uluç, referring to the film, wrote that "it seems some Armenian groups, blinded by hatred, will not give up trying to deceive the world with their lies and forged documents."[22] This rhetoric of "invoking hatred amongst two nations" and perceiving the film as part of a larger campaign against Turkey is continuous throughout the film's media coverage. While Tufan Türenç wrote in his column that the film "aimed at creating enemies out of two nations,"[23] Mehmet Ali Kışlalı argued that it was absolutely necessary that Turks see the film since it was a prime example of "how Armenians still see us [the Turks] and how they want to portray us to the world." He concluded that in order to understand the campaign against the Turks in the world (here the author no longer blames Armenians, but the whole world), the Turks must see the film and educate themselves with regard to this rising danger.[24] Similarly, Melih Aşık, columnist for the broadsheet *Milliyet*, argued that *Ararat* was another case of *Midnight Express* (Alan Parker, 1978) and suggested that official bodies and nongovernmental organizations should act "now," rather than later, as the film was still in the process of being made. In line with the rhetoric of liberal nationalism,[25] Aşık recommends that the producers should be reminded that Turkey offers a large market for their business and therefore anything "that might hurt Turkey" should be removed from the film.[26]

The majority of the articles and news pieces about *Ararat* share the supposition that "there is a campaign against Turks and Turkey" and that the Turks are not able to deal effectively with these claims. According to Hasan Pulur, for instance, "it would be a mistake to assume, by looking at the reaction [to the film], that we [the Turks] are attached to our past, to our history and to our values, that is not the case." For Pulur it is precisely because of the existing ignorance about history that "they" [Armenians] are able to turn it against "us" [the Turks].[27]

Another common element shared by many articles written on the film in Turkey was the way they dealt with the past. Best described as disavowal, these articles bring past and present narratives together as it suits their purposes. In the process, discrepancies in their narrative become irrelevant or unimportant. Writing for the newspaper *Sabah*, Erdal Şafak begins his article with an anecdote, which was apparently kept a secret for a long time. He wrote that a French–Armenian professor comes to Turkey with a friend to visit the village his parents originally came from. Upon arrival, they meet the village's imam and, after a lengthy conversation, it is revealed that the imam is in fact the professor's brother: "it turns out that they are part of the same family scattered around by the storm [*kasırga*] in the 1900s," writes Şafak. "While half of the family left, the other half stayed behind and converted to Islam." The imam asks his brother to leave before anyone finds out, as he fears the community will not respect him as a religious leader if they discover that he is in fact a convert [*dönme*], which is also the reason why the story is kept a secret for such a long time. Şafak is writing this article in relation to *Ararat*'s withdrawal from theaters as a result of the radical nationalist threats, and is asking for a calmer response. However, what begins as an article suggesting a less reactionary and more compassionate approach to the subject—and therefore to the film—concludes that the Turks are not "helpless against [genocide] claims" and "are confident and believe that [their] hands are clean."[28] What is noteworthy in this article (and in many others) is the inconsistency latent in its description of the past and the present. Şafak refers to the event as a "storm." Despite his hesitant acknowledgment that "something" happened, he suddenly comes to conclusion that "our hands are clean," which makes one think that the word "storm" was not a metaphor for the catastrophic event that befell Armenians, but rather a term referring to an event that affected everyone, including both Armenians and Turks, as a natural disaster would.

Şafak's article exemplifies a common understanding of the "problem" in Turkey: the problem, according to this understanding, does not arise from the fact that a historical event still awaits recognition, but that people [Armenians, the West, the world] blame Turkey with unacceptable accusations. As Eser Köker and Ülkü Doğanay point out in their report on hate speech in the print media, the way that the problem is defined in the media shows that the "politics of deadlock, which includes the misrecognition of the problem, and the emotional tone that lies behind it, is recruited by media professionals. Just as the way in which the problem is identified involves diverting the focus based on creating false enemies, the solution is also based on ignoring [the real problem] and creating pseudo solutions that are generated by denial strategies" (Köker and Doğanay 2011: 102). In other words, the position adopted by the mainstream media ("we have no problem with Armenians") assumes that history's sheet is clean. As such, the problem comes to be defined as the Armenian demands for recognition of something that did not happen, rather than Turkey's unwillingness to consider what really happened. Such definitions of the problem have also shaped reactions to the film in Turkey, in which it was perceived as part of the problem rather than an articulation of it. The predominant view in Turkey today sees the events as unfortunate, but still refuses to accept accountability, rejecting specifically the accusations regarding genocidal intent, the intention to clear Anatolia of its Armenian population.

Such reactionary approaches to the film were not limited to the newspaper articles, but also shaped the tone of the two books written on the subject by academics. The first book was by Sedat Laçiner and Şenol Kantarcı,[29] neither of whom had seen the film at the time and wrote the book based on the shooting script.[30] In line with the dominant discourse on the subject, and with the aim of discrediting the film, Laçiner and Kantarcı claim that *Ararat* received funding from various Armenian organizations and was made to be a propaganda film. Producing an example of the defensive narrative, the authors argue that the film campaigns against the Turks and predict that it will not only cause problems between the two nations, but also damage Turkey's image in the West. They further question Egoyan's credibility as a director, examining his personal life prior to the film, and suggesting that he is a "radical nationalist" with a certain agenda.[31]

The book includes a section called "scenes depicting Turks as barbaric." According to the authors the film as a whole depicts the Turks as people "who are only capable of doing evil" (Laçiner and Kantarcı 2002: 62). However, their entire argument is based on the scenes that exist in Saroyan's film, which they attribute directly to Egoyan and his intention to depict Turks as inhuman (Laçiner and Kantarcı 2002: 65). Clearly Egoyan is also the creator of the film-within-the-film, but his decision to present those scenes in contrast to the rest of the film cannot be disregarded if the aim is to critically engage with the film. Egoyan's decision to have Saroyan as a character, and his film as the film-within-the film, rather than simply making the film Saroyan makes, is deliberate and crucial. To reiterate the earlier discussion, the film-within-the-film allows Egoyan to create a space for comparison between different representations of the past, and to comment on his own role as a filmmaker as well as on the process of representation. The haste in the manner of writing (based on the screenplay) and publishing Laçiner and Kantarcı's book is a testimony to the aim of the book: to provide a half-baked counter-argument, a common result of the ideological reflex in the country.

The second book published in Turkey, which treats *Ararat* as propaganda, is written by another academic, Birsen Karaca. The book, titled *The Alleged Armenian Genocide Project: Social Memory and Cinema* (2006), includes lengthy discussions of Henri Verneuil's *Mayrig/Mother* (1991) and Sarky Moudrian's *Sons of Sasoun* (1975), in addition to *Ararat*, all of which have some reference to the history of Ottoman Armenians. Karaca, who wrote the book four years after *Ararat*'s release and has actually seen the film, argues that all three of these films are aimed at disseminating a manipulated and one-sided story of the historical events, with an agenda to degrade Turks. Much harsher in tone than its predecessor, the book reproduces the Kemalist nationalist discourse: with a rhetoric against the West (particularly Europe) and Armenians, the author aims to prove that these films are part of a larger agenda intended to damage Turkey's credibility.[32] According to Karaca, Verneuil's *Mayrig* is an open support for the Armenian terror and Moudrian's *Sons of Sasoun* is a musical that makes a legend out of Armenian terror. Her analysis of *Ararat* is also highly deflating as she describes the film as a "documentary on drug smuggling," and provides a highly problematic reading of the film to illustrate her argument (Karaca 2006: 70–115).[33] In addition to her conviction that the film is about drug smuggling, in which the customs officer, David, is involved, the author also thinks that the film is decidedly hostile toward Turks (Karaca 2006: 71) and interested in "creating the worst possible image of Turks for the audiences" (Karaca 2006: 78).

The representation of Turks in the film has indeed been the subject of many of the responses to *Ararat*. The only Turkish character in the film, in addition to the vulgar soldiers in Saroyan's film, who we do not get to know, is the half-Turkish–half-Canadian Ali. His character is important, not only because he is the only Turkish character (albeit half), but also because the exchange between him and Raffi holds a significant place in the narrative. Ali's brief conversation with Saroyan, during which he wants to talk about what he thinks happened to Armenians, disappoints him as Saroyan simply dismisses Ali. Raffi, on the other hand, expresses his disappointment that Saroyan lets Ali go unchallenged. Raffi then, influenced by Ali's moving performance as Cevdet Bey, asks him about this particular incident with Saroyan. During their conversation, Ali repeats the dominant Turkish view on the subject: "It was during the First World War.

People get moved around all the time." Although he does not mean to "deny" but desires to "move on," his answer is, for Raffi, a simple repetition of the denialist rhetoric, which leaves him upset and angry. However, Ali's character does not simply deliver these lines in order to be vilified in the film. On the contrary, Ali himself has to deal with discrimination, particularly by David, his partner Phillip's father. Despite his first-hand experience of not being heard/recognized, he fails to understand the rupture in Raffi's sense of self.[34]

In a lengthy journal article written on the film, Turkish film scholar Aslı Daldal offers a reading of Ali's portrayal as a Muslim gay man, and speculates on Egoyan's intentions for doing so.[35] According to Daldal, "while attempting to present the truth, *Ararat* creates its own 'official history', which is presented as the history," and "the audience is not asked to think about or evaluate the claims of the film, but persuaded in a sense to accept what is presented as absolutely factual" (Daldal 2007: 407–8). She argues that Ali is portrayed as "the other," first as homosexual, second as Muslim, which, according to the author, reflects not only the discrimination that exists in society, but also Egoyan's own manipulative attempt to single Ali out.

> The figure of the Oriental male or female as a gay seducer is a well-known cliché; indeed, the harem and the Turkish bath are the two most popular representations of Ottoman Turkey. [...] Despite the western image of Turkey (especially Istanbul) as the site of a multitude of sexual fantasies, homosexuality is still largely condemned in contemporary Turkey, and Turkish audiences always react when a Turkish character is presented as gay in a foreign movie (as is often the case, especially in anti-Turkish films such as *Midnight Express*). As Ali is the only thoroughly gay character in the film (Phillip previously led a "normal" heterosexual life), his depiction as an isolated man (without any apparent family around him) is the first phase of the marginalization of this fictional Turkish character (Daldal 2007: 414).

Similarly, according to Daldal, Ali is represented as the source of problems and although Egoyan "does not openly condemn Ali's religious 'otherness' [...] he has chosen to depict David's family as devoted Christians," which subjects Ali to discrimination and reminds the audience that "Ali is, after all, not 'one of us', a stranger and, thus, a potential threat" (Daldal 2007: 414–15).

However, what Daldal disregards in her reading of the film is that both Ali's religion and his sexual orientation function to highlight David's character and his uncompromising attitude, rather than Egoyan's. Ali is not treated as the object of desire in the film for the audience or for any other character in the film. He is not lit or dressed differently. He does not even speak English with an accent, which would have been an easier way to highlight his "foreignness," had it been Egoyan's aim to remind the audience that he is a stranger/the other. What Egoyan portrays, I would argue, is not Ali's *difference*, but David's *indifference* to the feelings of those around him. Similarly, Ali's homosexuality functions in the same way as his religion does with regard to David's character: it makes David's rigid and discriminatory attitude visible.

Yet, reactions to *Ararat* were not limited to the world of words. Although not a direct response, *Ararat* also created a response in the form of a film: *120* (2008) directed by Özhan Eren and Murat Saraçoğlu. Often considered as part of the efforts to tell the world the Turkish narrative, *120* claims to be based on a true story that took place during World War I in Van. Özhan Eren, who wrote the script, as well as co-directing the film, says that the project was conceived in his mind when he saw a monument in Van, which was erected in honor of the heroism of 120 children during World War I. Eren, upon becoming aware of this unknown story, decided to make it known to a larger public by making a film about it.

The story takes place in 1915, in the course of a few months following the Balkan War and leading up to the Sarıkamış Battle, in which the Ottoman Army was defeated by the Russians, and for which the commander Enver blamed the Armenians. In the film, after the war breaks out, ammunition left back in a Turkish village near Van needs to be taken to the front. However, because most able men have already joined the army, a group of children volunteer to take the remaining ammunitions from Van to Sarıkamış on foot, which is a couple of days away, and a very dangerous journey due to the severe weather conditions. The children do succeed in delivering the ammunition to the soldiers, but all 120 of them die on their way back due to cold weather.

In many respects *120* is similar to the film Saroyan's makes in *Ararat*, as well as to *The Lark Farm* by the Taviani Brothers. The film aims to publicize a heroic act of ordinary children, who sacrificed their lives for their country: a tale of Turkish nationalism from 1915, told in 2008. Although it does not explicitly deal with the Armenian population in the region, it also does not avoid the subject, passing casual comments on why it was "necessary" to relocate the Armenians. Through the comments made by the characters in passing, the film alleges that it was the Armenians who killed their fellow men and women in order to escalate the problem and thus break free from the Empire. This "fact" is established early in the film when an Armenian doctor is killed, apparently by Armenian revolutionaries, who make it look as though it was done by Turks in order to increase the tension. Armenian families are shown as they leave the region "because they have had enough of the Armenian revolutionaries and their violent ways." In this sense the film is a textbook representation of what Göçek calls "the republican defensive narrative," maintaining the argument that, during World War I, the Armenian population living near the Russian border had to be relocated and that some died along the way because of severe weather conditions.

Moreover, the history of the monument in the city of Van, which is said to have inspired the director to make the film, is interesting. The monument was built in 1976, after being commissioned by the then Mayor Tayyar Dabbaoğlu. Intriguingly, 1976 is also the year ASALA attacked the Turkish consulate in Beirut, the first major attack by them, which brought the organization to the attention of the Turkish public. Their attacks forced Turkey to break its silence on the subject of the Armenian genocide and to find an alternative narrative to the Armenian claims. Therefore, it is not an accident that the sudden emergence of the story of these children in 1976 coincides with ASALA's entry into the public arena.

Furthermore, the narrative surrounding these 120 children is also ambiguous as it is not clear whether they existed in reality, or whether the story was created out of thin air in order to find a binding narrative in retaliation to the accusations of the Armenians, which began systematically at the beginning of the 1970s. According to Dr. Tuncay Öğün from Van Yüzüncü Yıl University, it has not been possible to find satisfying evidence, as yet, to verify the details of the story of these children. However, he adds, this does not mean that they did not exist. On the contrary, he is convinced that they did.[36]

Regardless of whether the event is true, what is important here is how the event is remembered first in 1976 locally (the building of the monument), and later through a film, this time nationally. The creators of the film had no knowledge of the event prior to seeing the monument, and it appears that locals did not know about it either, testifying to the fact that prior to the monument the story was not a local heroic tale. However, after the film's release, and because of the effect it had, the Mayor of Van organized a commemorative walk in the area for the first time and over three million people saw the film in Turkey (in addition to those viewing it on DVD).

Yet, the general response to *Ararat* in Turkey cannot be summarized as dismissive and defensive. The film created, probably, the most intense discussions about a film in the country since Alan Parker's infamous *Midnight Express* (1978). Although the official discourse about the massacres did not change much, public opinion began to change, including a willingness to open the issue to discussion. This is not to say the film on its own triggered such response, but it came at a time at which the Turkish public wanted to discuss its past more, and the political climate supported it to a certain extent. Thus, *Ararat* certainly contributed to the visibility of the issue in Turkey. Recently, a historic Armenian church in Akhtamar island near Van, the church that Raffi visits in *Ararat*, was restored and opened for communion for the first time in ninety-five years. On the surface what appears to be an independent event was, in fact, initiated by Hüseyin Çelik (the deputy leader of the governing party AKP at the time) in 2002. Çelik said that "the best answer to *Ararat* would the restoration of the church" (*Hürriyet*, January 17, 2002). Yet, the rhetoric is still defensive and one that is engaged in finding ways to "answer" *Ararat*.

A few years after the film's release, the first conference, with presentations challenging the official discourse on the Armenian question, took place in Istanbul to discuss the "possibility" of a crime committed by Ottoman author-ities between 1915 and 1918. Despite the protests from radical nationalists and attempts to stop the event (which were successful at first), the conference took place in September 2005. Officially titled "Ottoman Armenians during the Decline of the Empire: Issues of Scientific Responsibility and Democracy," it is also referred to as the "Alternative Armenian Conference."

In 2007, Armenian–Turkish journalist Hrant Dink was killed by a radical nationalist. His murder triggered an unforeseen reaction and thousands attended his funeral. This was followed by an "apology campaign" in 2009, initiated by academics and journalists, and aimed at apologizing to Armenians for the pain they suffered and the insensitivity shown regarding their losses. The campaign was not affiliated with any organization and remained a petition for individuals. However, it created mixed responses, ranging from accusing the people who signed the petition of being traitors, to praising it as a very positive step toward a reconciliation process with Armenia and Armenians. The campaign was also criticized for its "patronizing" attitude, for not involving the Armenian community leaders, and for being dictated to the Turkish public from above, since campaigns such as this require the general public to be involved in order to be meaningful. In this case, no work was done to involve them.[37]

Not surprisingly, the debates *Ararat* has generated have not been limited to Turkey. Because the film refrains from easy conclusions and asks more than it answers, it has created a certain disappointment outside of Turkey. Some critics have complained that it is unnecessarily complicated given its subject matter. One genocide scholar described the film as "too intellectual" and noted that Armenians still lack their own *Schindler's List* (Feinstein unpaginated). Another Armenian–American scholar writes that Egoyan has failed to "fully and conclusively give voice to a true history" and "with the absence of any self-reflexivity, attempts of tackling the effects of the Catastrophe fall short" (Varjabedian 2008: 150–1).[38]

* * *

Ararat deals with a very sensitive issue: the history of the Ottoman Armenians. The film was at the center of many discussions not only because it questions the possibility of representing an event of such a devastating scale, and challenges the traditionally favored approaches to representing traumatic events, but also because its meaning in Turkey is still interwoven with the politics of denial. It is also the only film to date that forced such large-scale discussions on the fate of the Armenians at the beginning of the twentieth century, followed—more than a decade later—by the recent *The Cut* by Fatih Akın.

When read in its entirety *Ararat* appears to have three important, and interwoven, issues at its heart. First is the temporal dislocation occurring as a result of the erasure of memory. The second issue the film tackles is the way humans deal with memory, and the way the needs of present-day conditions shape the narration of the past. Finally, the third fundamental problem explored in *Ararat* concerns the (im)possibility of representing an event that not only devastated the generation who experienced it but that continues to have an effect on the following generations. The director's aesthetic and narrative decisions make use of much of the recurring themes and motifs that this book argues to be inherent in many of the projects dealing with displacement. This includes the director's approach to the concept of time as it moves freely (or perhaps inevitably) between different temporalities, making it a "haunted" narrative. The complexity of the situation, the impossibility of representing the very suffering that is driving the characters' actions as well as the narrative, is presented not through a narrative that assumes a mastery over history but through the admission and addressing of the problems of representation. *Ararat* puts the need, the necessity for recognition, at its center, registering unrecognized pain as an ever-blasting bomb that never ceases to destroy.

Ararat is more about the effects of the event on later generations than about an attempt to represent what "really" happened. More than anything, it is a ghost story. The ghost of Raffi's father, who makes him go to search for "some kind of information" on who he is; the ghost of Celia's father, whose death remains unresolved for Celia and drives her to violent ends to force others to speak out for and about him; looking for something, something to satisfy the ghost, looking for a "shape that is absent."

"*Finding the shape described by* [...] *absence* captures perfectly the paradox of tracking through time and across all those forces that which makes its mark by being there and not there at the same time" (Gordon 2008: 6). Perhaps the most important and powerful example of this search is visible in Gorky's quest to find the shape described by his mother's absence, and Egoyan's aesthetic preferences in representing it. Not only Shushan's ghost is haunting Gorky, but Gorky himself is haunting the narrative space with his silence, with his quest for the shape described by absence. It was perhaps this ghostly presence that gave way both to "exorcise" the film in Turkey in order chase away the ghosts, as well as to grant these ghosts "the right to [...] a hospitable memory" (Derrida 1973: 220).

It should be noted that although there is a tendency to be critically engaged with the past in Turkey, and though there are increasing numbers of films produced on the various "difficult" issues that continue to haunt the present day, the massacre of Armenians is still an underexamined subject. Egoyan's film came at a time when the silence on the subject was already being broken, but created a response that was unforeseen. The film forces the question of absence to the fore, pointing to the absence of the very people it talks about: Armenians in Anatolia, in today's Turkey.

5

The Kurdish Question in Films

In 1999, a famous Kurdish musician/singer, Ahmet Kaya, attended a ceremony at which he was to receive a special award. The guests comprised journalists, actors, actresses, and musicians. In his acceptance speech, he announced that he was working on his new album and that as a Kurdish singer he wanted to sing a Kurdish song, which was going to be included on the forthcoming album. Within minutes, all hell broke loose, apparently to his surprise. He was removed from the venue through the back door as people inside started throwing cutlery at him in protest, shouting there was no such thing as Kurd, and that he was a traitor. A few months after the incident, he left the country, as the media frenzy triggered hostility toward him and his family. He died a year later in his Paris apartment. Ten years after this incident, Turkey started talking about what is referred to by the media as the "Kurdish Extension" (*Kürt Açılımı*): the Turkish government's attempt to start a reconciliation process and improve the situation of Kurds in Turkey.[1] It was in relation to these rapidly changing conditions that the films discussed in this chapter were produced.

In the first half of this chapter, I aim to put the films analyzed in context in order to understand how politics and art have shaped each other. The second half focuses on four films that scrutinize the situation of Kurds in Turkey: *Güneşe Yolculuk/Journey to the Sun* (1999), *Büyük Adam Küçük Aşk/Hejar* (2001), *Gitmek/My Marlon and Brando* (2008), and *Dol/Valley of Tambourines* (2007). All of these films reached a considerable audience both inside and outside of Turkey and, at the time of their release, were considered "novel" in the ways in which they dealt with the Kurdish question, as well as in their representation of Kurds. Although they all differ from one another, they have one thing in common: the theme of displacement. Whether geographical or otherwise, the experience of the displaced is what forms the kernel of these films.

Turkey's "Kurdish question" and film

What is referred to as the "Kurdish question" (or "problem") in Turkey is ongoing, as well as being based in history. Its narration and reception is also constantly changing as the political and social climate evolves. In order to understand the tensions and problems that exist in today's Turkey regarding the Kurds, it is necessary to have a brief overview of the background. The Kurdish question in Turkey broadly refers to issues concerning the cultural rights (or lack of those rights), human rights violations, and the war in Turkey between the state and the PKK (Partiya Karkeren Kurdistan/Kurdistan Workers Party) that lasted more than three decades. According to Mesut Yeğen, a prominent sociologist writing on the Kurdish question, the Kurdish issue in Turkey is not simply a matter of ethnic conflict, but also one of political struggle (Yeğen 2009b: n.p.).

He frames the emergence of the Kurdish question as an issue that is directly related to the modernizing of Turkey, which has consisted of grand projects such as centralizing, nationalizing, and secularizing, and has been spread over the last two hundred years (Yeğen 2009a: 15). The Kurdish question, within the official discourse, was originally described as "political backwardness," "banditry," "feudal resistance," and "foreign provocation," and became a problem of regional backwardness which demanded a solution in the 1950s. Yet, this, according to Yeğen, did not signify an intention to distort reality for ideological purposes on the part of the state, but was rather related to the "discursive formation" within which the official discourse emerged.

The Turkish state referred to the Kurdish question as the "Eastern Issue" for decades, avoiding the use of the word "Kurdish"—thereby ignoring the ethnic side of the problem. Although the Republic recognized the Kurdish identity for a brief period,[2] according to Yeğen "the engagement with a racist version of Turkism in the authoritarianism of the 1930s prompted Turkish nationalism to deny the very existence of ethnic communities other than Turks in Anatolia" (Yeğen 2007: 127). In other words, the changes in Turkish nationalism also altered the perception of the Kurdish question. The 1924 constitution, although acknowledging the existence of different ethnic groups, denied any special rights to those groups. And, as Yeğen notes rather sarcastically, in the 1930s, the state "discovered" that the only ethnic component of Turkey was Turks, and that Kurds were, in fact, "mountain Turks."[3] This was the official state discourse until the beginning of the 1990s (Yeğen 2009a: 126–8).

The process of integrating Kurds into the modern Turkish nation-state was, to a large extent, successful until the beginning of 1980s, but the situation started to change toward the end of that decade. Yeğen connects this change to the newly introduced neo-liberal policies and the effects these policies had on the poorer segments of the society (Yeğen 2006: 15–24). These changes on both a global and local scale, affected the position of the Kurdish question within official and public discourse, as well as changing the Kurdish movement's self-positioning from a local nationalist movement to a more transnational one (Yeğen 2006: 29–45). What is more, the exact same process, neo-liberal globalization, also gave rise to nationalist movements. By the mid-1990s, while extreme nationalism shifted from the discourse of "Kurds are Turks who have forgotten their Turkishness," to "Kurds are untrust-worthy people," mainstream Turkish nationalism "resorted to a selective use of the language it had invented in the early years of the Republic" such as "banditry, foreign incitement and regional underdevelopment" (Yeğen 2007: 137) to characterize the Kurdish question.[4] What is noteworthy about this is that although various causes give rise to nationalism at different times, the language of nationalism remains similar to that of the early years of the Republic.

Today the Kurdish question, and thus Kurdish opposition, cannot be disso-ciated from the process of globalization, as Yeğen notes. He asserts that globalization is the cause of "the increasing significance of human rights discourse in the language of Kurdish resistance, the rising publicity of the Kurdish question after the Gulf War, and the growing impact of the European diaspora on Kurdish mobilization and their impact on the present state of Kurdish unrest is of major importance" (Yeğen 2007: 12). One direct impact of the conflict between Turkish security forces and the Kurdish militants was that it displaced communities in thousands, as ordinary people were forced to abandon their homes in the southeastern and eastern provinces of Turkey. While some of these people stayed within the country's borders, creating a huge population of internally displaced people, others sought refuge abroad, mostly in Europe.

The displacement of Kurds, however, was not an issue that emerged suddenly in the 1980s. Resettlement had been a policy in the early Republic, to create a unified nation and assimilate its minorities, in addition to cultural policies concerning language and education (Yeğen 2006: 49–69). After the 1925 Sheikh Said rebellion (seen as the first significant rebellion by Kurds against the Turkish

Republic), alleged sympathizers, and the families of those who were involved, were resettled to western Turkey. As a continuation of the same policy, the Settlement Legislation (*Sevk ve İskan Kanunu*)[5] of 1934 was introduced, which aimed at spreading out the Kurdish population to break up resistance to the Republic.

Although economic reasons have always caused a continuous migration from villages to nearby cities, the problems of "forced" migration and of internally displaced people became particularly severe after the military coup of 1980, and continued to be until the capture of Abdullah Öcalan, the leader of the PKK, in 1999. The involuntary migration, writes Martin van Bruinessen, "sped up as a result of the military pressure on the region, which impeded normal economic life. The situation further deteriorated with the onset of guerrilla warfare, in which both the PKK and the state demanded that villagers take sides" (van Bruinessen 1995: 7). During the 1990s, many people were forced to move to bigger cities with no prospects for the future and nothing to go back to. Hundreds of villages and hamlets were evacuated, destroying the livelihood of the villagers as a result. For example, according to van Bruinessen the population of Diyarbakir, the major city of southeastern Turkey and, today, the largest Kurdish city, increased "two—or threefold" during this period (van Bruinessen 1995: 10–11) as a result of migration from nearby places. Similarly, a 1998 report from a parliamentary investigation stated that the number of internally displaced people, as a result of the conflict, was 378,335,[6] although human rights organizations have estimated a much higher number. In 2006, an academic survey carried out by Hacettepe University suggested that the number of internally displaced people between 1986 and 2005 was actually around one million (Hacettepe Üniversitesi 2006: 61). Van Bruinessen indicates that despite "restrictions on the flow of information [...] it is clear that forced evictions have been adopted as a deliberate policy at the highest political level" (van Bruinessen 1995: 9).

Although in the early 1990s isolated utterances regarding the Kurdish question were made by senior officials (such as then Prime Minister Süleyman Demirel, who stated that he "recognize[d] Kurdish reality" in 1992), in order for tangible changes to take place, Turkey had to wait several more years. Zeynep Gambetti, writing on the recreation of the public sphere in Diyarbakır, claims that it is now possible to talk about a transition from the "crisis" stage to "redress," the second and third phases of social dramas according to Victor Turner.[7] According to Gambetti there are three main reasons contributing to the passage from "crisis" to "redress": "the unilateral ceasefire declared by the PKK in 1998, the election of HADEP–DEHAP[8] to metropolitan munici-palities in the southeast in March 1999, and the December Helsinki Summit, officially accepting Turkey as a candidate for full European Union Membership" (Gambetti 2005: 51).

In accordance with the European Union's requirements, Turkey introduced new legislation easing the restriction on the use of Kurdish language at the beginning of the 2000s, and in 2008 the state broadcasting corporation TRT launched a new channel to broadcast in Kurdish. The then Prime Minister Recep Tayyip Erdoğan uttered Kurdish words to announce the event during a press conference—a first in the history of Turkish Republic. Although this gesture was welcomed by the Kurdish public, others remained skeptical, especially as the new regulations allowed only the state to broadcast in Kurdish, making it difficult for privately owned media to broadcast in the language. The decision of the Constitutional Court (*Anayasa Mahkemesi*) to ban the pro-Kurdish Democratic Society Party (*Demokratik Toplum Partisi*/DTP) in December 2009 because of its alleged connections to the PKK made the situation more compli-cated, while increasing skepticism among the Kurds. What is more, the Kurds' claim to the right to be educated in Kurdish still remains unviable. And yet, the simple fact that the use of Kurdish in the public sphere is no longer a crime has affected cultural production: not only has the representation of Kurds begun to change as a result, but the use of Kurdish in cinema (and in other areas such as television) has become possible.

The Kurdish question in films

The newly created cultural space has allowed old, but suppressed, issues to be discussed in literature, television programs, music and film, among others. Moreover, existing books, films, and songs that were banned previously in Turkey were allowed into the marketplace. In addition to emerging authors whose novels deal specifically with the effects of the war between the PKK and the Turkish army on both the Turkish and Kurdish populations (such as Murat Uyurkulak's *Har*), the works of Kurdish authors, such as the celebrated Mehmed Uzun, have been translated into Turkish.[9] Musicians who faced prosecution solely because they sang in Kurdish have also been "legalized," and this lift on the ban of speaking or singing in the Kurdish language has helped ease existing tension. Similarly, with regard to film, although new films have been made that deal with aspects of the Kurdish identity (some of which I discuss below), existing films, such as Yılmaz Güney's previously banned work, are now available on DVD in Turkey.

The representation of Kurds in films until the late 1990s follows a similar chronology to the changing discourse summarized above. In line with official policy, until the 1990s Kurds were mostly represented in Turkish cinema without specific reference to their ethnic identity. They appear to be speaking with an accent, obeying different cultural codes, and were called "Easterners" (*Doğulu*)[10] rather than Kurds. With the exception of the work of few directors such as Erden Kıral (*Hakkari'de Bir Mevsim/A Season in Hakkari*, 1983) and Ö. Lütfi Akad (*Düğün/The Wedding*, 1974), the representation of Kurds in films, until the early 1990s, mirrored the official discourse.

The most famous and influential of those few exceptional directors is the aforementioned Yılmaz Güney, himself a politically active Kurd. He started his career as an actor, but is best known for the projects he wrote and directed—some by proxy while he was in prison. Güney's best-known film *Yol/The Way*[11] was directed by Şerif Gören and is based on Güney's detailed descriptions provided while in prison. *Yol*, which won the prestigious Palme d'Or at the 1982 Cannes Film Festival, depicts life under military rule in eastern Turkey, portraying the immediate aftermath of the *coup d'etat* of 1980. The film follows the physical and emotional journeys of five convicts who are released from prison for five days in order to visit their families, on the condition that they return to the prison at the end of that time. However, as they discover during their journey, under military rule the country itself is like prison with a heavy police and army presence on the streets and a strict curfew. The film, like many other films by Güney, was banned in Turkey for a long time, and is the predecessor of films made on the Kurdish issue in successive decades.

The most salient aspect of *The Way* is that of journeying, also a recurring theme in films focusing on Kurds. The repeated occurrence of "journey" as a narrative device is not a coincidence given the Kurds' recent history. According to Asuman Suner, journeying appears to be the leitmotiv of what she loosely defines as the "new political cinema." Putting questions of identity and belonging at the heart of the narrative, these films, Suner points out, "emphasize the subjective experiences", rather than claiming to be objective, and problematize the subject of "national belonging" like never before (Suner 2005: 257). Among these new political films, a large number deal with Kurds, placing journeying at the center of the story: in *Journey to the Sun* (1999), for example, the protagonist Berzan is portrayed as a character who has had to leave his village behind and come to Istanbul, and in *Hejar* (2001), the entire family ends up in Istanbul. In both films the journeys are taken as a direct result of conflict. More recently, a box office hit *Güneşi Gördüm/I Saw the Sun* (2009) tells the story of a family who had to move to Istanbul because their village is evacuated. Aimed at, and seen by, a much larger audience than both *Journey to the Sun* and *Hejar*, *I Saw the Sun*'s popularity can be seen as a sign of the change in the visibility and reception of the problem of internally displaced people, as well as of an ongoing dialogue among these texts.[12]

Journeying inevitably creates a threshold: it creates a liminal place, a passage. Liminality comes after separation, and before aggregation, and together they form the three phases of *rite de passage*, writes Victor Turner. According to Turner, the characteristics of the ritual subject during the liminal period are ambiguous since the subject "passes through a cultural realm that has few or none of the attributes of the past or coming state" (Turner 2008: 94). Displacement, and the type of journeying discussed here, are both conditions requiring liminal existence. "Liminal entities are neither here nor there; they are betwixt and between the positions assigned by law, custom, convention and ceremonial" (Turner 2008: 95).

Journeying in these films is itself a form of existence and most of the time without the subject's knowledge of when and/or where it might end. In this respect, journeying in these stories is very different from travel narratives, in which both the journey itself and its narration happen for different purposes. Travel narratives, more often than not, are a result of voluntary journeys, whereby the traveler knows when and where the journey will end. However, involuntary migration determines a liminal existence as the passage being crossed has "few or none of the attributes of the past or coming state," and the individuals have very limited—or absolutely no—control over their situation.

Another film that tells the story of a journey, as well as that of "disappeared" people, is Tayfun Pirselimoğlu's 2002 *Hiçbiryerde/Innowhereland*. Focusing on a mother (Zuhal Olcay), who travels first to Istanbul and then to Mardin to find her son, who has vanished, the film alludes to the Kurdish conflict and the PKK, as it appears likely that the son has joined the guerilla forces. Similarly, *Işıklar Sönmesin/Let There Be Light* (Reis Çelik, 1996) also deals with the war itself, and is one of the first films to tackle the armed conflict head-on. It tells the story of two men, one of whom fights for the PKK, and the other for the Turkish Army.

The film is also one of the few of its time dealing with the harsh and haunting reality of evacuated villages.

The latter also is dealt with in *Journey to the Sun*, *My Marlon and Brando* and *I Saw the Sun*, which all tackle the problem of displacement. What should be noted here is that all of these films, with the exception of *Let There Be Light*, show real villages that were evacuated. This can be read as a desire to "document" reality, again a common trait in the films dealing with the Kurdish issue. This is partly due to the effects of the armed conflict on civilian populations of the Kurdish region: the need to document stems from the need to prove the authenticity of the wrongdoings, which produces an immaculate attention to detail "to get it right" in recent films. It is perhaps for this reason that emerging Kurdish directors produce an overwhelming number of documentaries each year. For instance, the London Kurdish Film Festival's programme shows a high number of documentaries compared to industry standards. In an interview conducted in 2010, the festival director, Mustafa Gündoğdu, told me that they receive a very large number of films for the festival and usually the 40 percent of the films selected for screening consist of documentaries.

Moreover, the desire to document is not simply limited to the number of documentaries produced. The use of documentary footage also serves to create the chronotope of the homeland in a fiction film. To reiterate the discussion featured in Chapter 2, chronotope in literature is the artistic expression of the "connectedness of temporal and spatial relationships" (Bakhtin 2008: 84) in which time "thickens, takes on flesh, becomes artistically visible; likewise space becomes charged and responsive to the movements of time, plot and history" (Bakhtin 2008: 84). In Robert Stam's words, the chronotope "allows us to historicise the question of space and time in the cinema, […] it reminds us of the life/ world independent of the text and its representation" (Stam 2008: 41).

In keeping with the chronotopic approach, journeying is one of the motifs that not only allows the filmmaker to realistically represent the situation, but also creates a liminal space within the filmic space, where representation of displacement is achieved. In Güney's *Yol*, for instance, it is through the journeys of the inmates that the military regime is represented. Through its specific mode of representation (imprisonment even outside of the prison) the film turns Turkey into "both national panopticon (per Foucault) and a rhizomatic society of control (per Deleuze)" (Naficy 2001: 182). Naficy also makes the point that Güney, by emphasizing the stories of several convicts' wives, "genderizes his claustrophobic chronotopes and emphasizes the double oppression of women"

(Naficy 2001: 183). However, analyzing the film from a feminist perspective, Asuman Suner writes that *The Way* has made its political statement at the expense of women:

> [T]he seemingly uncompromising left-wing critique of the state oppression and feudal culture in *Yol* indeed reflects a tacit masculinist vision in its problematic appropriation of the figure of the victimized Anatolian woman as a metaphor for the "backwardness" of Turkish society. Giving voice to an oppressed ethnic minority, *Yol* makes its radical political statement only by further silencing the subaltern Anatolian woman (Suner 1998: 290).

When we come to the 2000s, the chronotope of the films becomes less claustrophobic. *My Marlon and Brando*, for instance, despite the images of checkpoints, border refusals, and the unhappy ending, is a film dominated by open fields and a sense of liberation when compared to Güney's *The Way*. As its Turkish title suggests ("*gitmek*" means "to go"), the film is about moving toward one's desires, even when it is impossible to arrive at them. In this respect, both *My Marlon and Brando*'s protagonist, Ayça, and the women she encounters during her journey differ from the isolated and oppressed women of *The Way*: it is Ayça's story told through her eyes and her voice. Because what is referred to as the Kurdish question today is not what it was when *The Way* was made, its narration also has changed. Therefore it is important to see these films not as part of the same tradition, but as different approaches to a continuous debate.

The first feature film in Kurdish language, one that also puts journeying at its center, was Nizamettin Arıç's *Klamek jib o Beko/A Song for Beko* (1992). Arıç, who is a Kurdish–Turkish citizen, has been living in Germany since 1983 in political exile and had to complete the scenes that are supposed to take place in Turkey in Armenia, as a result. *A Song for Beko* deals with the eponymous hero's journey after he flees from his village in Turkey to avoid being arrested. He goes first to Syria, then on to northern Iraq, where he stays in a refugee camp with other displaced Kurds, finally ending up in Germany, like the director himself. Arıç's film is also one of the first to deal explicitly with the situation of Kurds, including the 1988 chemical gassing of Kurds in Saddam Hussein's Iraq.

Within the last decade, the number of films coming from Turkey and dealing with Kurdish history and identity, either partly or entirely in Kurdish, has increased dramatically. In 2008, Kazım Öz made his debut with Bahoz/ *Storm* (2008), an attempt to chronicle the Kurdish movement in the 1990s among university students. A popular singer, Mahsun Kırmızıgül, made *Güneşi*

Gördüm/I Saw the Sun in 2009, also the year of Orhan Eskiköy and Özgür Doğan's critically acclaimed documentary *İki Dil Bir Bavul/On the Way to School*, which following its release caused continuous debate on the education system's uncompromising attitude to ethnic identity. Finally, in 2010, the first film made in Turkey that is entirely in the Kurdish language was released. *Min Dit/The Children of Diyarbakir* (Miraz Bezar) subsequently won the best director award in the national competition section of the Istanbul Film Festival.[13] It was followed by another film in Kurdish, *Babamın Sesi/My Father's Voice* (Orhan Eskiköy/Zeynel Doğan, 2012). Before going into detailed analysis of the films, I want to look briefly at *On the Way to School*, *Min Dit*, and *My Father's Voice* in terms of their representation of the Kurdish question, and their use of the Kurdish language.

On the Way to School was made by two young documentary filmmakers, Orhan Eskiköy and Özgür Doğan, and captures the life of a young teacher and his students in a remote town in Urfa, eastern Turkey, populated by Kurds. It tackles the issue of language head-on, dealing directly with the education system in Turkey. The film documents a school year as a young teacher (Emre Aydın) tries to teach the curriculum to his students in Turkish, while the majority of them only speak Kurdish. The idea behind the film originates from the lack of communication between the teachers and the pupils that exists in the current education system, which disregards the Kurdish language. *On the Way to School* successfully captures the situation where the two languages (the official Turkish and the local Kurdish) rub against each other, blocking the possibility of communication, rather than enriching the culture, and, therefore, the lives of these individuals.

The second film, *Min Dit/The Children of Diyarbakir* (Miraz Bezar), on the other hand, is the first film to be made and screened in Turkey that is entirely in Kurdish. The film is based on real events, telling the story of Diyarbakir's orphaned/homeless children. Diyarbakir is not only the biggest Kurdish city in Turkey, but has also received many immigrants from the surrounding villages in the previous years. Set in the 1990s, during which the region underwent a violent period, the film focuses on two young children who witness their parents' murder by JİTEM, an organization that has become the manifestation of the "deep-state", or the state within (*derin devlet*) in Turkey.[14] Following their parents' murder, the children are forced to live on the streets, and through their story the audience is introduced to the larger story of the children of Diyarbakir, a city where homeless children are common.

Both films, as well as *Hejar*, which is analyzed later in this chapter, choose to tell their stories through the eyes of children. The director of *Min Dit* asserts that one of the reasons he used young protagonists is that it is easier for the audience to empathize with children. Bezar, in an interview, explains that he wanted to reach "the people in western Turkey who know nothing about these incidents" (Bezar 2010). However, neither *On the Way to School*, nor *Min Dit,* constructs childhood as a distant place of absolute and unquestionable innocence.

The figure of the child and the depiction of childhood in Turkish cinema have a specific and distinct place. *Yeşilçam* cinema used (and abused to a large extent) the figure of the child as the bearer of innocence, an incorruptible human being, who resists evil but also requires protection from the adults in his/her world. Nurdan Gürbilek reminds us quite rightly of the popularity not only of these films, but of the figure of the crying child, particularly in the late 1970s and early 1980s. Originally a painting by the Italian painter Bruno Amadio, it was mass produced and gained global popularity. This specific image of the boy crying represents not just pain beyond his years, but also a dignity that remains intact despite everything. Unlike the cultural critic Murat Belge, who thinks the image is a manifestation of the guilt the society felt toward its neglected children, Gürbilek writes that the obsession with this image in Turkey in the early 1980s was due to the adults' identification with the innocence of childhood (Gürbilek 2004: 39). However, as Gürbilek points out, the image lost its popularity, or perhaps its credibility, precisely at the moment when the suffering became visible on the faces of real children, when the reality of the homeless children became publicly recognized, and when "the image became face to face with its referent" (Gürbilek 2004: 45).[15]

However, the interest in childhood and the innocence that the figure of the child was assumed to embody did not disappear from the field of the visual completely. Asuman Suner argues that it was at the moment that the figure of the child became associated with fear (in the image of homeless children with their assumed inclination to crime) that society's desire to identify with the mistreated child found its expression in the long gone nostalgic image of childhood (Suner 2005: 83). Suner differentiates between this new image in Turkish cinema and the earlier image of the mistreated child in three distinct areas:

1 The childhood in these new nostalgic films is not individual but collective and inclusive regardless of age, gender, class and political orientation.

2 It is always about the past and never about the present.
3 Unlike its predecessors, it seeks to produce a cultural critique (Suner 2005: 83–4).

Suner indicates that the critique these popular nostalgic films produce is highly problematic as they "try to make sense of the tensions, anxieties and conflicts produced during rapid and complex social change within the simple framework of binary oppositions such as before/after, inside/outside," hence, suggesting that all "evil" comes from "outside," which makes the people unaccountable for any wrongdoings (Suner 2005: 98). The childhood in these films provides a shelter to escape from the realities and responsibilities of the present day.

These three films, *Min Dit*, *Hejar*, and *On the Way to School*, break away from this popular image of the child/childhood, instead seeking to suggest responsibility to their audiences. Hejar's resistance to obey her "savior" in *Hejar*, the children's ease at stealing and accepting abuse as part of normality in *Min Dit*, and the pupils' complete indifference to the teacher's efforts to teach them Turkish in *On the Way to School*, all serve to create an understanding of the world in which the children themselves live. These films, unlike the popular nostalgia films, do not render society as an unaccountable body, but on the contrary as a body that produces these children, as well as the conditions in which they live. In other words, rather than victimizing the children in their representation, and in that way creating a space for the audience to identify with the children as bearers of absolute innocence (hence rendering themselves unaccountable in that identification), these films force identification with the adults.

The third film I want to mention, before going into the detailed analyses of the selected four films, is *My Father's Voice*: a film about an old woman, Base, living on her own in a small town in eastern Turkey. Her younger son, Mehmet, lives in Diyarbakir, but, worried about his mother, comes to visit her. While he is there, he enquires about the voice recordings they used to send to his father, when he was working abroad, in lieu of letters, and starts going through the closets to find the missing ones. Creating an epistolary narrative, the tapes are played in such a way as to form a conversation with not only the present exchanges between the mother and the son, but also between the tapes themselves, which are edited to form an interaction, producing temporal shifts through sound. The audience gradually understands that the father died in a work-related accident, and that the person for whom the mother hopelessly waits is her son, Hasan, who left home to join the guerrilla force. She refuses to go anywhere else in case Hasan returns.

As Mehmet listens to the tapes and takes a journey along memory lane, the film brings the past into the present, highlighting their family life and also the experiences of the Alevi Kurds in the 1970s and 1980s. Through listening to these tapes, Mehmet is reminded of events that he was not able to comprehend as a child, and is now able to ask about them. Along with him, the audience is also forced to confront certain events, one of which is the attacks on Alevi citizens. Mehmet's father had to participate in an organized attack against the Alevis, hiding his own identity in order to protect his family who are Alevi. Once again, making the choice to be visible as who you really are becomes a choice between life and death. Mehmet's access to the full story, however, comes not through the tapes but via an old newspaper that his mother has hidden. It is after finding an old newspaper that he is able to learn the details of the day during which the town turned against the Alevis.

As the film combines past and present through sound, the "now" of the film, the non-diegetic context, also makes itself known through sound, through the use of television that is often playing in the background. The dialogue in *My Father's Voice* is predominantly in Kurdish, and the film repeatedly makes comment on Mehmet's and his brother's difficulties at school because of their native language. As we learn about the problems that the two boys had at school, this functions as a reminder of the current situation, since not much has changed regarding education in the Kurdish language. The television brings the news of Prime Minister Erdoğan's assertion on the *right* to be educated in one's native language. His words, however, were uttered in Germany, regarding the Turkish–German citizens, and were directed at the German government. The film, like many others tackling issues related to Kurds, once again reminds its audience of the pressing question of education in Kurdish, and subtly comments on the discriminatory inconsistency in the official rhetoric on what is and what is not a basic human right.

Güneşe Yolculuk/Journey to the Sun

After debuting with *İz/Trace* (1996), which enjoyed success in many national and international film festivals, director Yeşim Ustaoğlu's second feature film was *Güneşe Yolculuk/Journey to the Sun* (1999). *Journey to the Sun* deals with the "othering" of Kurdish citizens in Turkey, and the identity issues surrounding both the Turkish and Kurdish populations. According to Asuman Suner, the film tells its story "not through identity but through an identity shift," as one of the central characters, Mehmet, is actually not Kurdish, although he is assumed to be, and, as such, is treated as Kurdish by others (Suner 2005: 271).

The central characters are two young men, Berzan (Nazmi Kırık), and Mehmet (Newroz Baz), both of whom experience Istanbul as immigrant workers. Berzan is a Kurd who has escaped to Istanbul from his village, Zorduç, eastern Turkey, after his father is taken by the army from their home, and never returned. Mehmet, on the other hand, is a Turk, who comes to Istanbul from his village, Tire, in western Turkey, in search of a better life. In Istanbul, they both live under very difficult conditions, and share the experience of being lost and displaced in a large city. They meet when ultra-nationalist football fans attack Berzan because he is not celebrating the success of the Turkish football team. Mehmet comes to his rescue and they become friends immediately. Although they are two very different people (Mehmet seems to be less interested in politics, whereas Berzan is politically very active), the violence to which they have been subjected brings them closer.

The first half of the story takes place in Istanbul, in which the city appears as a distant location, a place to which neither Berzan nor Mehmet has direct access. The city, even though it technically includes them in its geographical entity, "happens" elsewhere, for them to watch rather than to be part of. Their lack of a permanent "address" enhances their marginality in relation to the city. In a scene in which Mehmet and Berzan talk about their hometowns in the small room they share, the director cuts to the window, which happens to have bars, and from which the city lights are visible in the distance. The shot configures them "inside," behind the bars. The city imprisons them: it is claustrophobic, and destructive to a degree for all its residents, but specifically for the underclasses. In this respect, Istanbul becomes yet another "small town," with a gigantic population in the way it is experienced by these characters. Once perceived and represented as the city where dreams can come true, Istanbul, in contemporary films, becomes a space of discrimination and poverty.

The marginality of the characters, however, is not limited to their poverty. Later in the film, Mehmet is arrested because a stranger leaves a suspicious bag next to him while he is on the bus. As the police stop the vehicle to search it, they find the bag, which contains a gun. Assuming it belongs to Mehmet, the police take him into custody, and during his interrogation he is constantly accused

Figure 5.1 *Journey to the Sun* (dir. Yeşim Ustaoğlu; from IFR Production; released 1999). Protagonists Berzan and Mehmet together by the Bosporus.

of lying when asked where he is from, because he claims to be from Tire, in western Turkey. According to his interrogators, he appears to be too "dark" to be Turkish. The Kurdish music tape found in his pocket, a present from Berzan, is used against him to prove he is lying. The complexion of his skin determines the limits of his belonging, while being a Kurd becomes an accusation.

Unable to prove his guilt, the police let him go. However, it is now impossible for Mehmet to maintain his old life. He loses his job, and is thrown out of the room he has been sharing with others as a result of the red cross sign that appeared one night on the door. The sign, indicating that he is now a marked man, drives his roommates to evict him in order to stay unmarked, and hence safe. He later sees identical marks on the walls of several houses in an evacuated village, when he travels to some Kurdish towns. Mehmet, in the space of a few days, is left with no job and nowhere to stay. It is Berzan who comes to his rescue, helping him. However, when Berzan dies suspiciously while in police custody, an event that marks Mehmet's psyche, he decides to take Berzan's body back to his homeland, Zorduç. The rest of the film depicts Mehmet's both physical and psychological journey.

Mehmet's struggle with his identity begins with what he sees as the immediate problem: his appearance. Following Berzan's death, Mehmet dyes his hair blond, an act that is suggested partly as a joke by his girlfriend to make him "blend in" more. Yet, although it is an attempt to appear less "dark," and, therefore, more accepted, it underlines Mehmet's darkness by making him even more "visible." Undoubtedly, visibility in general, and Mehmet's visibility in particular, has political connotations.[16] Displacement and discrimination are experiences that will render you visible when you don't want to be, and invisible when your desire is to be seen and recognized. In this sense, Mehmet's story, his body, and, particularly, his skin color, are not only politicized, but also make him unpleasantly visible. His need to feel included determines Mehmet's performance of his identity, and leads him to decide he would be better off with blond hair, with the result that he ends up achieving the opposite of his original intention.

However, Mehmet's most important transformation happens when he journeys to Berzan's village with his friend's body. The journey starts in a stolen car, simply because he cannot afford anything else, and after the car breaks down he uses a number of different vehicles, from buses to trains, finally ending his journey on a horse carriage, carrying his friend's coffin with him. During his journey, Mehmet passes through villages and vast fields in cars, buses, and trains. As Naficy suggests in accented films there is dialectical relation between "the inside closed spaces of the vehicles and the outside open spaces of nature and nation. Inexorably, vehicles provide not only empirical links to geographic places and social groupings but also metaphoric reworkings of notions of travelling, homing and identity" (Naficy 2001: 257). In this respect, while Mehmet's physical journey is represented through these vehicles and, also, through the changing scenery, his inner journey is represented by encounters with strangers, and how each meeting shapes his perception of his own identity.

One such encounter takes place when Mehmet comes across a family whose truck is parked by the side of the road. While a young man changes the tire, Mehmet approaches the old man and, in order to start a conversation, asks where they are going. The old man does not reply but his daughter does: "My father doesn't speak Turkish," she says, "we need to go to Istanbul." The truck, with its load of furniture, indicates that they are moving, and their lack of excitement tells him that it is not a desired journey, but one that they "need to" take. This is the first time that Mehmet encounters the reality of the region. For the rest of his journey, he witnesses children being chased by soldiers because they sell a certain pro-Kurdish newspaper, and evacuated villages with torn-down houses with red crosses on them. Mehmet then reaches a town in which he spends the night. In the morning, however, he witnesses another unusual scene: from the window of his room, he sees that the streets are occupied only by tanks and armed soldiers, scenes reminiscent of a military coup. The shot that follows shows Mehmet's head in water: he washes the dye out of his hair. This is an act that is as symbolic as the original dying of his hair. An act that was triggered by his desire to comply and blend in is now reversed by his anger.

Identity, national or otherwise, is always mediated through the look of the other(s). "To look at ourselves in the mirror is to oversee the reflection of our life in the plane of consciousness of others" writes Stam (Stam 1989: 5). Every time Mehmet meets new eyes he discovers new ways of looking at himself. It is partly due to this new consciousness that he decides to wash the dye out his hair, as the blond man looking back at him in the mirror has become a stranger to him. However, in the act of washing away the dye, he symbolically washes away his old identity as well. Mehmet's departure from "himself" is represented in a scene on a train toward the end of his journey, during which he briefly talks to a fellow traveler who is doing his military service in the region, and who it appears is, in fact, from Mehmet's hometown, Tire. The following conversation takes place between them:

> *Stranger: Where are you going?*
> *Mehmet: Zorduç.*
> *Stranger: Are you from there?*
> *Mehmet: Yes. Where are you from?*
> *Stranger: Tire. Ever heard of it?*
> *Mehmet: Yes. A friend of mine was from Tire. Mehmet. Mehmet Kara. Do you know him?*

This conversation underlines Mehmet's metaphoric reworking of his identity and the notion of home. Rather than revealing his own identity, and possibly forming a bond (since they are both from the same town), Mehmet takes up Berzan's identity, claiming that he is from Zorduç. He then asks the stranger if he knows Mehmet Kara, referring to himself as a friend.[17] The journey becomes a symbolic one, that of "coming home" as he embraces the Kurdish identity that was forced on him prior to his journey. In other words, he becomes Berzan in the Deleuzian sense of the word, as Deleuze sees "becoming" as a process without an end. What was displaced is *replaced*, and will certainly be displaced again.

Mirroring is a significant device in this process as mirrors can function in various ways in films. As the scene in which Mehmet washes the dye from his hair indicates, a mirror image can function to represent a split in identity. However, Ustaoğlu's use of "mirroring" goes beyond the simple use of mirrors. She uses actual mirrors in addition to another reflective surface, one that produces a blurred image: water. The film opens with an ambiguous image, which only makes sense at the end of the film: it is an image of a man carrying a coffin, reflected on the water. The sequence consists of three cuts: in the first two, the camera tracks the young man going in and out of the house, bringing out a coffin, and putting it into a small van (see Figure 5.2). The last shot reveals more of the surroundings, showing the house and the van in the same picture. It ends with the reflected image on the water almost erasing itself through a slight movement on its surface (see Figure 5.3). It is only later on in the film, when we see the actual image again, not the reflection, that we are reminded of the image from the very beginning. In reality, this is Mehmet carrying Berzan's coffin, the image that marks the beginning of his journey. What is interesting here is Ustaoğlu's decision to show the scene reflected on water at the beginning of the film. As well as being an aesthetic choice, it is also a device that works within the entire narrative, since it alludes also to the final sequence of the film, in which water dominates. By displacing certain elements in the narrative by way of introducing them out of context, and later reintroducing them in context, she asks her audience to engage with the story actively, as well as with their own knowledge and memory.

When Mehmet ultimately arrives at Berzan's village with the coffin, he finds a ghost town. The village is now underwater and evacuated. The minaret of the village's mosque, along with the few houses that managed to stay above

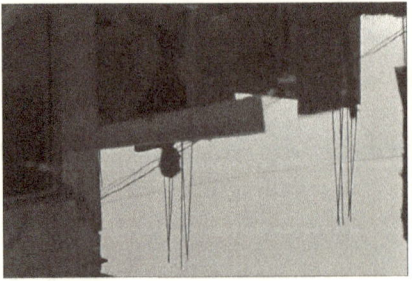
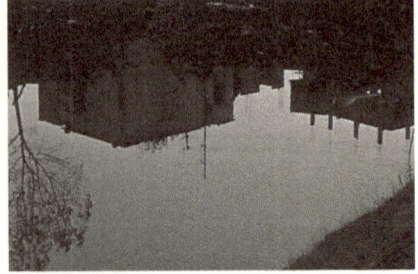

Figure 5.2 *Journey to the Sun* (dir. Yeşim Ustaoğlu; IFR Production, released 1999). Mehmet with the coffin reflected on water.

Figure 5.3 *Journey to the Sun* (dir. Yeşim Ustaoğlu; IFR Production, released 1999). The house reflected on water.

the water level, are the only indicators that there was once a settlement at that specific location. Villages in eastern Turkey, evacuated due to "security" reasons, have been a fact of life since the 1990s, causing thousands of families to leave their homes. However, this image of the village underwater points to another reality, one that has been caused by the project that aimed to help develop the region.[18] For the audience with a little knowledge of the region this image needs no explanation, as it was the fate of many villages. Even though Mehmet fails to deliver his friend's body to his family, he nevertheless decides to "bury" Berzan there, in his hometown; thus, he lets the coffin go into the water.

Ironically, the signboard standing out in the water, reveals the official name of the town: *Susuz*, which means "waterless" in Turkish. This simple revelation not only reminds the audience of the renaming of places engaged by the state (the Kurdish Zorduç is changed to the Turkish *Susuz*), but also tells us about the nature of collective memory. During the film, Berzan does not once refer to his village as *Susuz*; the village is continuously referred as Zorduç in the film. This becomes even more telling considering that the name of the village was most probably changed when Berzan was very young—if not even before he was born. The changed name, signifying the Turkifying attempts of the state, does not, however, resonate in the minds of the individuals, as the village, outside the official space, continues to exist as *Zorduç*.

Finally, the film uses television news to remind the viewer of the political climate of the time, as well as passing important information on to the audience. When, for example, Mehmet sees Berzan being arrested, while watching the news on television, the scene not only serves to forward the narrative by passing the news to Mehmet, but it also reminds the audience of the hunger strikes in protest against solitary confinement that were taking place in various prisons at the time. Berzan is arrested for his participation in the demonstrations, which support the prisoners' demands. In this regard, television news serves are used as a device to create a cinematic chronotope, helping the director to configure spatial and temporal relations, to remind her audience of the world outside the text.

Journey to the Sun was one of the few films made in Turkey during the late 1990s that dealt with the Kurdish issue. The film stood out for its willingness to recognize, not only the existence of Kurdish people in Turkey, but also the reality of life in the region. Its story, at the time, forced a confrontation with the issues surrounding Kurdish existence in the Turkish Republic. Not surprisingly, it also generated discussions about its accuracy. It was suggested that the film does not, in fact, depict the reality, that the events are mostly fictional, and that the representation of the events is one sided. Television critic Yüksel Altuğ, writing for *Sabah*, one of the biggest newspapers in Turkey, criticized the film in his column for failing to show the developed parts of Istanbul, and for suggesting that people can become suspects based only on their skin color. In this respect, the perception of the film was very similar to what Suner calls the "perception of third-world films." According to Suner they are often regarded as "ethnographic sources" which can offer "evidence about the cultures from which they emanate" (Suner 1998: 284). This notion is applicable not just to *Journey to the Sun* but also to most political films from Turkey, as they are often criticized for depicting a depressing picture of the country, and of damaging its image in the West. The film was also a shock to middle-class Turkish viewers as it showed the evacuated villages, and the kind of discrimination that could take place, which was not part of *their* day-to-day reality. This obsession with "reality" partly explains Hüseyin Karabey's approach to the issue, as he prefers to combine documentary with fiction, as seen in his film *My Marlon and Brando* (2008). However, before we look at *My Marlon and Brando*, there was another film that caused intense discussions: Handan İpekçi's *Büyük Adam Küçük Aşk/ Hejar*.

Büyük Adam Küçük Aşk /Hejar

Büyük Adam Küçük Aşk/Hejar (2001) is director Handan İpekçi's second feature film, and caused controversy at the time of its release. *Büyük Adam Küçük Aşk*, which literally translates as "great man little love", was retitled as *Hejar* for international audiences, which means "dispossessed" in Kurdish. It is also the name of the little Kurdish girl whose story is told in the film. Hejar (Dilan Erçetin) is sent to live with her uncle, after her parents are killed in eastern Turkey. Yet, her uncle lives in extreme poverty and unable to look after little Hejar, he leaves her with a distant relative, who is a lawyer in Istanbul. But events take a tragic turn when the police raid the lawyer's flat in order to capture the Kurdish separatist militants who are staying there. Hejar, who ends up seeing the brutal raid from within the wardrobe in which she is hiding, finally takes refuge in the flat next door, where a retired judge, Rıfat (Şükran Güngör), lives. The rest of the film is about the difficult and unlikely relationship that develops between these two characters forced to share the same space.

From this perspective, *Hejar* has a very familiar plot structure with a much-used cliché: two completely opposing characters sharing a small, confined space. There is not only a considerable age and class difference between the two, but they also lack a common language: Hejar does not speak any Turkish, and Rıfat does not speak any Kurdish. Yet, the film's strength comes from the fact that it is a story very close to "home." The tension that exists between the two characters also exists on a macro level and easily translates into real individual experience.

The film was initially accused of creating a one-sided image and portraying the Turkish police force as brutal, and, therefore, was unrealistic. Most of the criticism was about the police raid in which they kill three people. The film was banned after its release, and withdrawn from cinemas. The Turkish Ministry of Culture, which had financially supported the film, demanded the money back, claiming that the submitted script and the finished film were completely different. It went to court, and, in the end, the ban on the film was lifted and it was allowed to be screened publicly.

The allegedly controversial opening sequence shows the police storming the lawyer's flat and opening fire. The two militants, whom the police are after, fire back despite the lawyer's attempts to convince them to surrender, and they are killed immediately. The lawyer, who is initially injured, is also shot dead even though she is not armed and begs for her life. The police's attitude is made even clearer when we hear a policeman, just before the lawyer begs for help, reporting the numbers of dead. Although there are two dead and two injured (the lawyer and a policeman), he announces on his radio that there are *three* dead and one policeman injured, implying that they never had any intention of catching anyone alive. The police search the house while Hejar is hiding. The leader of the group goes to the bathroom and finds a radio. He turns it on to find out about the result of a particular football game, and through the news on the radio the audience finds out that it is the 75th anniversary of the establishment of the Turkish Republic (*Cumhuriyet Bayramı*/Republic Day),[19] which is a significant day for the country, and also a national holiday. The film brings up many of the issues that Turkey at the time was—and to a large extent still is—dealing with: Kurdish identity, the armed conflict with the Kurdish separatists, and Turkey's disposition toward a police state. In fact, at the beginning, immediately after the police raid, the retired judge Rıfat starts writing an article titled: "Police State or Just State?"

The director opens the film with a series of medium close-ups, allowing her to exclude the background and, therefore, delay the orientation for the audience:

Judge Rıfat, his cleaner Sakine (Füsun Demirel), his neighbor Müzeyyen (Yıldız Kenter), little Hejar, Hejar's uncle Evdo (İsmail Hakkı Şen), and the lawyer, are all introduced through fragments of their daily lives. The importance of this sequence, however, lies in the fact that although most of these characters occupy the same building, with the exception of Hejar and her uncle, who are going to the building, they are introduced as though living in completely different locations. It is not until the police raid that we understand Rıfat and the lawyer are next-door neighbors. Similarly, the response to the police raid in her building from the neighbor Müzeyyen is slightly surreal, as she wants to go upstairs with cookies to see Rıfat despite hearing gunfire shortly before. Her reaction can only be perceived "normal" in an environment in which police raids are commonly accepted as part of everyday reality, or as the reaction of a person extremely indifferent to others.

The isolation that exists between the different segments of the society will become even more visible when, later in the film, Rıfat visits Hejar's uncle Evdo, who is living on the outskirts of Istanbul. The difference between the conditions under which these two men are living is astonishing to Rıfat. Evdo lives in a particular neighborhood populated by the poor. This is an image of Istanbul that contradicts with how Rıfat imagined the city (and modern Turkey) would be, and, therefore, it is a great shock to him.

The issue of language is at the center of the film, as it uses characters who are unable to speak to each other: Rıfat and Hejar do not share a common language. Yet, what is important here is the assumed superiority of Turkish. Rıfat, a typical Kemalist republican, is very sensitive about language and has concrete beliefs that are very hard to change. He repeatedly warns his Kurd cleaner, Sakine, not to speak Kurdish with Hejar under any circumstances, and does not want to hear Hejar speak it either, accusing the little girl of intentionally not speaking Turkish, hence rebelling against her savior. Rıfat asserts that she "must speak Turkish in this country" and he is very suspicious of, and hostile toward, those who do not.

There are three very important scenes regarding the use of Kurdish and the depiction of Kurdish identity in the film. The first is when Rıfat takes Hejar to a shop to buy her new clothes. The shopkeeper asks Hejar her name, and Rıfat intervenes, saying that although she is Turkish, she does not speak Turkish as she has been living in Germany. For Rıfat, living in Germany as a Turk is a better excuse for not being able to speak Turkish than living in Turkey as a Kurd. The second scene regarding language signifies a transition in Rıfat's character as he asks Sakine, his cleaner, to teach him certain words in Kurdish so that he can communicate with Hejar. He then takes the little girl fishing, and in the evening, at the dinner table, he speaks to Hejar in Turkish, complaining that this new generation does not appreciate what they have: "They go to private schools, and are educated in English. A nation ought to protect its language." However, immediately after that remark he, for the first time, becomes aware of the injustice. The statement reveals the ambiguity and self-contradicting nature of his position, as well as of that of the state regarding Kurdish identity.

The third scene is when the film reaches its climax with regard to Kurdish identity and language. In a rather modest scene toward the end, Rıfat asks Sakine to run some chores for him. Sakine, for the first time, protests, without being apologetic about her identity. She locks eyes with him and says: "Rojmin! My name is Rojmin, not Sakine." "Rojmin" is a Kurdish name, which she has not been able to use in Rıfat's presence before. This brings the issue of symbolic violence that she (and anyone who cannot speak their own language out of fear) has been subjected to, into visibility.

In his writings on power and symbolic violence, Pierre Bourdieu discusses the ways in which the use of language imposes power over groups who submit without realizing its effects. He asserts that "symbolic power does not reside in 'symbolic systems' in the form of an 'illocutionary force', but that it is defined in and through a given relation between those who exercise power and those who submit to it" (Bourdieu 2005: 170). Sakine's submission to Rıfat's symbolic power is portrayed in her behavior: unlike Hejar's stubborn and rebellious attitude toward Rıfat, Sakine is apologetic every time she is told not to speak Kurdish. Because violence is exercised on the subject when her right to exist as herself within the realm of the visible is taken away, she makes the symbolic violence visible to Rıfat and, thus, asks to be visible as Rojmin.

The tension between the realm of "visible" and "invisible," between the interior and exterior, between what is included and what is excluded is manifested often through the use of space in the film. Hejar's entrance into Rıfat's territory, which can be read as the entrance of the Kurdish language into the space of Turkish, is significant. While Rıfat wants to define what Hejar can and cannot use, she constantly challenges his definitions. She demands a recon-sideration of every single ban imposed on her by breaking every single one. In the end, she leaves Rıfat's territory to live with her uncle, but not before she redefines the space according to the needs of both. This symbolic redefinition takes place when Hejar's uncle comes to visit her and Rıfat reveals his intention to adopt her in order to give her a better life. Hejar, holding her uncle's hand, drags him to Rıfat's study room, a room she has been forbidden to enter, and sits him down on Rıfat's chair, behind his desk. She, then, holds Rıfat's hand and places him in the armchair intended for visitors, an action with which Rıfat complies. This scene shows that the moment Rıfat stops exerting control over the space, it accommodates all three of them equally; thus, the symbolic meaning that was attached to this space by Rıfat has been turned upside down.

A similar tension is also illustrated in the way the film uses Turkish and Kurdish—*Hejar* was one of the first Turkish films to use the Kurdish language. Yet, the film's strength lies not only in the fact that it includes characters who only speak Kurdish, but also in its lack of subtitles. The dialogue between Hejar and Rıfat is not subtitled in Turkish, although Hejar only speaks in Kurdish. The director's decision not to provide subtitles is a statement that forces the Turkish audience to empathize with Hejar (as well as with people whose native language is Kurdish). A simple decision such as this can carry political connotations, or can make a political gesture. Much dismissed, subtitles in fact offer a world of their own to the spectator and İpekçi does make full use of the opportunity that subtitles—or rather the decided lack of them—provides.

Finally, the television news in the film, like in *Journey to the Sun*, is also used here to trigger shared memories of the past for the audience. In *Hejar*, when Rıfat turns the television on out of boredom, and hopelessly changes the channels, all there is to see is news about the war with the Kurdish guerrilla force in eastern Turkey, and reports about the people who died as a result. The third channel he turns to discusses the "*Susurluk* accident." This scandal revealed the relationship between the government and the mafia-like organization known as *Derin Devlet*/Deep State, and was the most important news for months in 1996 Turkey. None of these events are randomly chosen; they have left their mark on Turkish politics and the community, and have the ability to trigger collective memories, which not only situates the story temporally, but also helps the audience to place this specific story within the context of their own stories and imaginations of the past.

However, despite its good intentions, or perhaps *because* of them, the film fails to challenge its audience, as it relies only on emotions induced by one-dimensional characters. It purposefully avoids any complex character representation and uses "common sense" as its main pillar. If meaning can be political "only when it does not let itself be easily stabilized and when it does not rely on any single source of authority, but rather empties it or decentralizes it" (Trinh T. Minh-Ha 1993: 99–100), then *Hejar* fails to do so despite its overtly political outlook. In this sense, a decentralized meaning would arise when the audience becomes aware of the structural injustice regardless of individuals and their behavior, which may or may not be likable. Nevertheless, the film did make a considerable impact at the time, winning several national and international awards, including the "audiences' choice" from the prestigious Istanbul Film Festival. It was also screened on television, and was widely viewed in Turkey. The film certainly has played a role in shifting the perception of Kurdish as the language of the terrorist.

Gitmek/My Marlon and Brando

My Marlon and Brando, director Hüseyin Karabey's first feature film after a number of short films and political documentaries, is based on the true story of a young Turkish woman, Ayça Damgacı, who fell in love with an Iraqi Kurd, Hama Ali, just before the invasion of Iraq in 2003. The film follows Ayça from Istanbul to northern Iraq (the "Autonomous Region of Kurdistan") as she embarks upon a journey, at the end of which she hopes to be reunited with her boyfriend. The screenplay is largely based on the journals that Damgacı kept during her journey, as well as the director's own experiences with Iraqi Kurds in Turkey.

Ayça and Hama Ali both play themselves in the film, and meet and fall in love during a filmshoot in Turkey. After Hama Ali returns to Iraq, their relationship continues over the phone and through the letters that they send to each other. Although Hama Ali promises to come back to Istanbul for her, a year later the Iraq war breaks out, making it impossible to travel to and from the region. As the situation in Iraq deteriorates, even a basic telephone conversation becomes impossible. Ayça runs out of patience and starts looking for ways to travel to northern Iraq herself. The film, to a large extent, is a documentation of her journey as she travels from border to border, trying to meet Hama Ali during the first few weeks of the war.

My Marlon and Brando, shot on location, is an unconventional love story in many ways, not only because a journey from West to East takes place voluntarily, but also because the journey is undertaken by a woman. Karabey, using a very limited number of close-ups, carefully avoids favoring one character's discourse over another, neither victimizing nor heroizing the characters. But this is not to say that the film shies away from making a political statement. On the contrary, by leaving both the story and the characters without stability, the film questions the current political situation. In an interview with me, the director[20] states that the side he himself takes is clear, that of the oppressed, but he also wants his audience to make a decision for themselves, rather than manipulating them into a certain conclusion (i.e. his own). Aware that, as a director, he has already made a choice with regard to what to include and what to exclude in the frame, Karabey instead leaves the audience to scan the screen for clues.

Prior to *My Marlon and Brando*, the director had been making political documentaries but, as he himself wants to underline, he "refute[s] the distinction between documentary and fiction," saying that his films are both at the same time. Karabey's two best-known documentaries, *Boran* (1999) and *Sessiz Ölüm/ Silent Death* (2001), combine both documentary and fiction, continuously crossing between the two. *Boran* is a film inspired by a group of mothers who silently demonstrated every Saturday in Istanbul for three years between 1995 and 1999. Reminiscent of the Mothers of Plaza del Mayo, these women came to be known as the *Cumartesi Anneleri* (Saturday Mothers), meeting each week in one of the busiest districts of Istanbul: Beyoğlu. Their demonstrations were peaceful and had only one aim: to demand information about their children (mostly Kurdish), who had "disappeared" after being taken into custody by the police.[21]

Silent Death, on the other hand, is about the isolation system in prisons. The system, which came to be known as the *F Tipi* (Type F) in Turkey, was put into effect at the end of the 1990s, with the aim of putting inmates into confined spaces. It caused much discussion, along with waves of hunger strikes among the prisoners protesting against it. Karabey combines shots of experts, prison staff, managers, and former inmates talking about the system and solitary confinement in Spain, Italy, Germany, and the United States, in parallel with constructed scenes of a female inmate kept in isolation in Turkey: not only the physical space, but also the mental space shrinks as she is deprived of all communication. Although a documentary, the actual prison-cell scenes in the film are constructed and acted out by a professional actress.

My Marlon and Brando also combines documentary and fiction although, unlike *Boran* and *Silent Death*, it was not classified as a documentary. It is a film that crosses physical borders, as well as breaking textual and formal boundaries, combining documentary with fiction. The film opens with a scene from the making of the film, shot by a hand-held camera in an open field. The director's voice is audible in the background giving orders to the film crew, while Ayça is getting ready for the scene. The actress not only took the journey in real life, but also co-wrote the script with the director. The fact that she repeats the journey later in someone else's work creates complex temporal and spatial relations as three different temporalities are intertwined together: the time of the initial event, the representation of it (making of the film), and the represented event, the work itself. In the opening sequence, where a shot from the "making of" is included, these three temporalities momentarily come together, yet reality and fiction remain intertwined. In the scene Ayça is in the process of making the film that we are watching, and by including this footage at the beginning of the film Karabey twists the distinction between these different chronotopes. He opens the film by making these different temporalities visible to the audience, rather than rendering them invisible.

Karabey's previous engagement in documentary filmmaking influenced *My Marlon and Brando* in a number of ways. He uses archive footage of television news to illustrate the political context as well as to locate the story in time. Television, in the film, is used effectively to remind the audience of the few days before Iraq was invaded by the United States. The most memorable of those images is the moment at which US forces bomb Baghdad, which the world watched on its TV sets as it happend. Similarly, documentary footage in the film also serves to illustrate social conditions.

Writing on the relation between documentary filmmaking and history, Michael Chanan explains that "documentary is related not only to history but often also to memory, and to ask about one is also to raise questions of the other" (Chanan 2007: 257). Although Chanan seems to be assuming a clear distinction between documentary and fictional film, *My Marlon and Brando* is an example of a film that not only combines fiction and documentary, but also occupies a space between the two, as both at the same time without distinction. This is not only an aesthetic choice, but also a choice that is very much determined by the social and political conditions in which these directors live and work. Karabey himself explains that he combines documentary and fiction in order to be as explicit as possible about the reality of the region. During the reconstruction of Ayça's journey, the director decided to film certain events as they happened, such as the Kurdish wedding, and its disruption by the security forces. Similarly, he films Ayça's encounter with the border police and the dialogue between them (as Ayça enquires about the possibility of crossing the border) without intervening, and the evacuated village is filmed without "enhancing" the reality, or changing its "look." Karabey says: "If I were to recon-struct the scene where army officers arrive at the scene of the wedding in order to stop the celebrations that would not change the fact that it happens, but I did not want to allow a space for arguing that it does not happen and that I am misleading the audience." Similarly, Karabey chose to shoot at border crossings, more often than not without applying for the prior permission normally required. He, instead, ordered his crew to continue recording until stopped by the authorities.

One of the differences between documentary and fiction, it seems, is the events' relation to time in terms of immediacy. In documentaries, it is assumed that the consequences of the events (or the content of the interviews) that are unfolding are unknown as they are real and recorded as they take place; in other words, there is little or no screenplay involved. As a result, "real time is thought to be more 'truthful' than 'filmic time'" (Trinh T. Minh-Ha 1993: 94). However, "what is put forth as truth is often nothing more than *a* meaning" (Trinh T. Minh-Ha 1993: 92). In an article which opens with the perhaps contentious sentence "[t]here is no such thing as documentary," Trinh Minh-Ha writes:

> A documentary aware of its own artifice is one that remains sensitive to the flow between fact and fiction. It does not work to conceal or exclude what is normalized as "nonfactual" for it understands the mutual dependence of realism and "artificiality" in the process of filmmaking. [...] Documentary reduced to a mere vehicle of facts may be used to advocate a cause, but it does not constitute one in itself; hence, the perpetuation of the bipartite system of division in the content-versus-form rationale (Trinh T. Minh-Ha 1993: 99).

In this sense, it is possible to talk of *My Marlon and Brando* as a documentary, as it is "aware of its own artifice," and is sensitive to "the flow between fact and fiction." However, this hard and fast classification is of less interest here than the recognition that the film avoids fixed meaning—as do most other films that self-consciously acknowledge what is represented is not *the* meaning but *a* meaning. Its concern is with questioning it, challenging the commonsensical perception that creates *the* meaning.

These films, as Laura Marks asserts, are hybrid in the sense that they "mix documentary, fiction, personal and experimental genres, as well as different media" (Marks 2008: 8). Disregarding limits and conventions, these films cross borders in order to convey their story, and in most cases their stories involve a representation of exclusion due to a "border" whether national, social, personal, or formal. *My Marlon and Brando*, as much as being a story of a journey from Istanbul to northern Iraq, is also a story of illegal immigrants and borders that include some and exclude others. It questions the purpose that these borders (and borders of all kinds) serve, while making those who are otherwise invisible visible, without turning the "violent look" of the dominant culture toward its subjects. The story of the painter Soran is an illustration of this process.

Soran enters the film as Ayça is looking for someone to help her go to northern Iraq. He is an illegal immigrant in Turkey, who has escaped from the war in Iraq. Living in a room with six others under very difficult conditions, he aims to cross the border to Europe. The space people like Soran occupy in a society is always outside of the visibility of daily life and, therefore, they are usually not known to people like Ayça (and for that matter to the majority of the film's audience). This is reflected in Ayça's very naïve, friendly but incredibly unaware attitude. When visiting the building to collect some of Soran's paintings to look after them for him, she asks to use the toilet, which is a communal facility. However, she cannot even enter, revolted by the state of it. Upstairs in Soran's room, still unable to grasp the situation, she assumes that the other people in the room are Soran's guests rather than people he shares the small room with, as it is incomprehensible for her to imagine seven people living in a room so small.

Yet, Karabey does not limit Soran's existence in the story to being an illegal immigrant. He is also a talented painter with a wife and child back in Iraq. This is later contrasted with the representation of Soran (and people like Soran) on the news, when Ayça, who is now on her way to meet Hama Ali, sees him on television. The news announces that the police have arrested thirty illegal immigrants in Istanbul as they were waiting to board a boat to take them to Greece. In terms of aesthetic qualities, the way in which these people are represented in the news is no different from a group of people who carried out a violent attack: they all are engaged in illegal activities. In terms of the news he is disposable, a passerby with no identity other than that of illegal immigrant, and more "illegal" than an "immigrant." Often their moment on television, as part of a news story, is the first and last moment in which such people can become visible, subjecting them, however, to a very violent look.

The television news, with its commitment to concision, favors a type of representation that denies in-depth knowledge to its viewers. However, watching others has to be linked together with "witnessing." Witnesses, writes John Ellis, "have to recognize the other as being like themselves if they are to experience empathic emotions. [...] Empathy requires that the witness acknowledge the status of the other as a person" (Ellis: 73). Inevitably, the image and how it positions the viewer plays a role in whether the viewer is able to develop empathy. Ellis writes, "there is quite literally a world of difference between recognizing individuals as 'just like us' rather than 'like us'. To witness distant individuals and to recognize them as persons is inevitably to see them 'like us'" (Ellis: 75–6). Karabey, acknowledging Soran's existence as a person rather than as a mere "illegal immigrant," allows him to be perceived "like us." Since Soran has been introduced to the story, prior to his capture by the police, he cannot be seen as a mere addition to the statistics of illegal immigration. Through his presence, he makes visible the cultural mechanisms that normally render illegal immigrants invisible. In other words, the director reverses the process, introducing Soran first and foremost as a person, Karabey asks the audience to see Soran as like them and to witness his story.

The category of "illegal immigrant" derives from the absence of a legal right to exist in a certain place, which brings with it the notion of address. This is usually problematized in texts that deal with displacement, voluntary, or involuntary exile. Naficy, in his discussion of "accented cinema," points out that the problem of address, along with territoriality and geography, is emphasized in many of these films. The epistolary form specifically introduces the question of address, which becomes an important narrative device to question the notion in the context of displacement. These films involve "the use of formal properties of letters and telephony to create and exchange meaning. Exile and epistolarity necessitate one another for distance and absence drive them both. However, by addressing someone in an epistle, an illusion of presence is created that hovers in the text's interstices" (Naficy 2001: 5). In *My Marlon and Brando*, director Karabey, relying predominantly on video letters and telephone conversations to narrate the story, creates an epistolary narrative. Throughout the film we watch Hama Ali's video letters to Ayça, and hear Ayça's letters to Hama Ali as diary entries.

There are five video letters in the film and each one, with the exception of the very last letter, contains excerpts from the somewhat absurd films in which Hama Ali acted in Iraq, giving the text a self-reflexive quality. Although the letters help Karabey capture the story, they do not solely function to serve the flow of the plot. As Naficy states, the epistolary form functions as an "expression and inscription of exilic displacement, split subjectivity and multifocalism," and "in the process they raise fascinating questions about the identity of author, addresser, addressee, reader, reciter, and translator of the letters and about their narratological functions and power relations" (Naficy 2001: 103). Karabey plays with the belated nature of letters, and hence, with the notion of linear time, challenging the language of progressive time by means of dislocating it.

The first video letter is sent before the invasion, and Hama Ali speaks of the United States as their potential savior from the oppressive regime of Saddam Hussein. He is willing to fight, he says, by the side of the American forces to be free. However, the tone of the letters gets more pessimistic each time, mentioning the chaos, the fear that people have, and how everybody kills each other. In this sense, these letters have their own narrative development, in addition to the function they serve in the film.

At the beginning, Ayça watches the video letters, then writes her reply, as would be expected within the chronological order of letter communicating. Later in the film, however, Karabey creates a simultaneous dialogue between the characters by using letters and telephone conversations. As the video letter is played, the director cuts to Ayça, who is making a phone call. Although we do not hear Hama Ali's voice (in fact we never hear the other side when Ayça is on the phone), an illusion of conversation is created through editing as the director arranges Ayça's answers in a way to form a meaningful conversation with Hama Ali's video letters. In fact, Hama Ali is never represented in the same temporality as Ayça. His presence in the film is mediated through these video letters. However, not only is the illusion of presence created through epistolary narrative, but also an illusionary bridge is created that overcomes the spatial difference between them, while simultaneously making the separation more obvious.

In his very last video letter, Hama Ali records his attempt to cross the Iraqi border to meet Ayça. As he is speaking to the camera, an unknown source shoots and kills him. This last letter forms the last scene of the film and, within the diegetic time, takes place while Ayça is waiting for Hama Ali. However, this time we "read" the letter before Ayça does. The problem of the belated nature of the letters becomes most visible with this scene, as Hama Ali haunts the narrative with his video letter. His camera, functioning as an extension of his vision, continues recording even after he is dead.

What is more, the letters, already a mediated way of communicating, are in English, which is not the native language of any of the characters in the film. Yet, English is not the only language used in the film. In fact, *My Marlon and Brando* is a film in which subtitles cannot be avoided as four different languages—Turkish, Kurdish, English, and Farsi—are spoken at various times. So much so, that it is one of the films that Naficy calls "calligraphic" as subtitles become inseparable from the image, turning the screen into a calligraphic page. Along with a number of limitations and necessities (such as economic translations), Naficy notes that viewing a calligraphic-accented film can be an "amusing and annoying experience of having to read incorrectly translated and spelled titles" (Naficy 2001: 123). However, subtitles in *My Marlon and Brando* function in the opposite way: the process of translation is so carefully done that some part of the experiences related to speaking a foreign language is lost. When the Iraqi Kurdish immigrant Soran speaks Turkish, he speaks a broken Turkish with an "accent." However, the English translations not only, and inevitably, render his accent invisible, but also create an illusion that he speaks grammatically perfect Turkish, as the translations are perfect. The director told me that this was done on purpose because, if not, "*they* think that it is a mistake created by the inability to correctly translate." Karabey, it seems, made a decision based on the assumed perception of the native English speaker, and provided perfect translations of the dialogue. Although it was acceptable, and normal, for his characters to speak in broken English and with a heavy accent, subtitles are perceived to be outside the filmic space, hence "professionally" done.[22]

A calligraphic film also brings forth the question of power relations and the hierarchal order of languages. Robert Stam, in his application of Bakhtinian concepts to film, points out that "although languages as abstract entities do not exist in hierarchies of value, languages as lived entities operate within hierarchies of power" (Stam 1989: 77). To reiterate the discussion in chapter 2, Bakhtin points out that there are not only different languages or dialects spoken within a given community (polyglossia) but also "social" languages (heteroglossia), the differences in the way language is used between different classes, different professions etc. *My Marlon and Brando* is characterized by the use of not only many languages—English, Kurdish, Farsi, and Turkish (polyglossia)—but also of different social languages: that used among the actors, that between the director and the actor, and those used by people belonging to different social classes and different professions (heteroglossia).

Noticeably, the use of different languages is a key characteristic of films dealing with Kurds. Although it is an aspect of all the films that this project deals with, films about Kurds give special importance to the issue, as one of their most important demands from the Turkish government has been the right to be educated in their native language. However, neither the political and social conditions nor their representation remain the same, and these films reveal the changes in perception and representation of the Kurdish question. While *Hejar* emphasizes the anguish caused by assimilation policies and the ban on language, *My Marlon and Brando* is more concerned to examine and investigate the existence of polyglossia, as well as heteroglossia, that has persisted across both the language ban and assimilation policies.

What differentiates *My Marlon and Brando* from the other films discussed in this section is that while the others bring out the feeling of incarceration and confinement, this film, although acknowledging the confined geographical and discursive space, focuses on the possibility of action, of going away and breaking away. This is due to the discursive space that is created as a result of the political changes that took (and continue to take) place in political, social, and economic life in Turkey. However, it should also be noted here that these films are also the result of changing technological conditions that made the access to the industry relatively easy. *My Marlon and Brando* was shot digitally, making the production process considerably cheaper than using 35mm film, hence, allowing the necessary space and freedom for experimenting with the form.

Dol: The Valley of Tambourines

Dol: The Valley of Tambourines (2007) is a film made by a Kurdish director, Hiner Saleem, which takes place in the border villages in northern Iraq, southeast Turkey and Iran. The central character, Azad (Nazmi Kırık), is a Kurd living in a small Kurdish village, in which the Turkish army has a strong presence. During the wedding celebrations of Azad and his wife-to-be, a quarrel breaks out between the villagers and the army officers after one of them insults the villagers. Azad ends up shooting one of the officers and leaving him wounded. As a result, he flees from his village, journeying between Iraqi Kurdistan and Turkey, illegally crossing borders, and hoping to be reunited with his wife later on. His journey is also a device to set the scene in the region as he witnesses the life in northern Iraq and develops relationships with an organization that appears to be fighting for the rights of Kurds.[23] In his efforts to find a way to rejoin his wife he risks one last visit to his village in the hope of taking his wife away with him, but in an encounter with the army he gets shot.

Dol differs from the rest of the films analyzed in this chapter in the way it uses humor in a subversive manner, despite the darker tones of the story. The film resembles Elia Suleiman's approach to the conflict between Palestine and Israel, as he also tackles the reality of the region in a similar manner, with dark humor. Both directors use absurdity and humor as a way to defy authority and rely on long, idiosyncratic silences rather than meaningful dialogues. In Suleiman's case it is used to decentralize the oppression that the Palestinians are subjected to, as in *Divine Intervention* (2002); in Saleem's case it is the oppression of the Kurds. Laughter in these films is peculiar to the situation and instrumental in portraying the absurdity of the reality.

Carnivalesque laughter, from a Bakhtinian perspective, liberates; it sets free what "common sense" has restrained. Bakhtin describes carnivalesque laughter not as an "individual reaction to some isolated 'comic' event" but as belonging to "all the people"; it "asserts and denies, it buries and revives" (Bakhtin 1984: 11–12). Laughter, then, becomes a weapon that "demolishes fear and piety before an object, before a world, making of it an object of familiar contact and thus clearing the ground for an absolutely free investigation of it" (Bakhtin 2008: 23).

Writing from a similar perspective, Meltem Gürle mentions that texts that use the subversive power of laughter have the potential to "lift the veil of what claims to be the truth," allowing us "a glimpse through the rhetoric of illusion employed by authority" (Gürle: 137). Gürle looks at a novel written by a young novelist Murat Uyurkulak, *Har* (2006), which responds to the political tensions of the last few decades, specifically focusing on the war between the Kurdish guerrillas and the Turkish army.[24] Adopting a similar approach to his subject, Saleem also uses laughter in a subversive manner, mocking an otherwise "serious" set of events. In addition to the absurd situations he creates throughout the film, Saleem also deals with the painful realities of life, such as displacement and death, with laughter; these, in turn, make the seriousness of certain institutions, such as the army, appear "laughable." Yet, Saleem's liberating laughter is not directed at everything that takes itself too seriously. While his dark satire reaches its peak in the scenes that take place in the Kurdish village in Turkey where the army regulates much of the daily life, his approach to his homeland, to Kurdistan, receives a more emotional and nostalgic treatment with idyllic shots of mountains and the surrounding scenery.

Azad's village, a small Kurdish village called Balhova, has a strong and continuous army presence not only because it is a village that is near the border, but also because of the ongoing war against the PKK. The army officers, and specifically their commander-in-chief, assume a visible superiority in the village, and regulate much of life as they wish, which includes policing Turkishness and the Turkish language. The scenes in the village predominantly mock the absurdity of the fact that speaking Kurdish is forbidden. The film opens with a shot of the mountain on which the sentence "how happy is one who says I am a Turk" is written, a well-known sentence from one of Atatürk's speeches (see Figure 5.4). Atatürk uttered the sentence during the construction of the unified Turkish Republic to emphasize that all those who were subject to the Turkish Republic were Turkish, and in the hope that the desired assimilation would take place. However, to have the words written on a mountain's surface, in a village populated by Kurds and visible to the villagers *today*, after eight decades, clearly makes a statement about the fact that any claim to Kurdish identity is unwelcome. In fact to have the words written in public places, in specifically (but not limited to) Kurdish populated areas, has been a common practice in Turkey that emerged after the 1980s, particularly with the rise of the PKK.

Saleem's first comment on the inscription written on the surface of the mountain comes with the opening sequence,as the shot of the inscription is followed by one of a cow, which seems to be looking at the mountain. Saleem cuts to a close-up of the cow, then again to the mountain.[25] The next shot shows the cow dead. It is understood, through Saleem's use of space, that the cow belongs to a person on the other side of the border, which first appeared to be a unified space. We also see a balloon being blown by the soldiers with the same sentence written on it. The balloon will be set free at the very end of the film, much like the balloon that is used in Suleiman's *Divine Intervention* that crosses the Israeli checkpoint with a picture of Arafat on it. Saleem, through his use of space, comments on what that given space constitutes for Kurds (a cultural space called Kurdistan that is spread across Iran, Iraq, and Turkey) and what it means for the Turkish State. For the latter, borders define space and are concrete; illegal passing must not be allowed. However, the borders are concepts, and are constructed as political and geographical entities. Saleem plays with the otherwise established notions about borders through a subversive use of space.

The absurdness of the paranoid attitude toward Kurds and Kurdish culture is also at the center of one of the film's most significant scenes, when Azad is getting married. The wedding, which is very much like a small-scale carnival in the region, is celebrated outdoors and is open to everyone. While the singer (Ciwan Haco)[26] performs Kurdish songs, two high-ranking army officers arrive at the scene. Despite visible discomfort on both sides, the officers are seated with

Figure 5.4 *Dol* (dir. Hiner Saleem; from Hiner Saleem Production Novociné, 2007). Inscription on the mountain ("How happy is one who says I am a Turk").

the fathers of the couple as a sign of respect. However, within a minute of their arrival one of the officers intervenes, saying: "What primitiveness is this? Sing in Turkish!" The singer in return, slightly puzzled, but eager to satisfy the officer, responds: "Could I sing in English my captain?", and without waiting for an answer starts singing: *I just wanna touch you touch you, I just wanna love you love you.* His broken Turkish suggests that he is not a fluent Turkish speaker, hence his choice of English. However, this is not a mere justification for his inability to sing in Turkish: it is a subversive moment in the film, creating a sudden laughter, in which "a new free and critical *historical consciousness*" (Bakhtin 1984: 97, emphasis mine) emerges. Laughter threatens the established, or assumed, power of the authority that wants to be taken as seriously as it takes itself. Its power, and its hierarchical distance, is partly achieved by the complicity of the community. It is laughter that lays down the "prerequisite for fearlessness without which it would be impossible to approach the world realistically" and brings the subject closer because "as distanced image a subject cannot be comical" (Bakhtin 2008: 23).

However, the subject himself, in this case the army officer, realizes the threat posed by the possible comical nature of the situation and is outraged by the singer's unexpected reaction. The singer's failure to understand and acknowledge the intended meaning of the order ("sing in Turkish!") makes the commander want to reestablish the momentarily shaken hierarchical order, hence his degrading comment ("*you fucking people*"). His utterance ends the comical nature of the situation, just as it provokes the father, who is sitting next to him. He punches the commander, and a sudden burst of rage on both sides quickly leads to gunfire. As a result, Azad, the only villager who fires at the army officer, is forced to flee the village.

Saleem's grotesque realism continues throughout the film right up to the very end, where he turns Azad's death into a carnivalesque scene. Azad, after spending a few weeks in the mountains, comes back to fetch his wife. Because of the previous incident he has to be discreet, as he would be arrested immediately if seen. However, his luck fails him; he finds himself in crossfire, receiving a deadly wound. The scene, which builds up in a somewhat conventional way, suddenly changes as soon as Azad is shot. A man with a traditional musical instrument appears, playing a celebratory tune to which Azad starts dancing on the roof of a dwelling, joined by his wife. "The violence is perceived by the audience not as the death or suffering of real people, but in a spirit of carnival and ritual" (Jurij Lotman, quoted in Stam 1989: 116). This is a moment in which the celebration is not about violence but about resistance. While they dance, the balloon (with a message that says "How happy is one who says I am a Turk") is released in the background, slowly disappearing into the skyline, suggesting that resistance will win.

In addition to Azad, there are three other central characters in the film, whose stories intersect: Jekaf, Çeto, and Taman, all of whom are on a journey either voluntary or forced. It is through the intersection of their stories that the director is able to create a unified idea of Kurdistan, which exists as a cultural space as well as a political discourse. Çeto (Abdullah Keskin), who has emigrated to France, travels back to Northern Iraq (Autonomous Region of Kurdistan) to visit his father. Azad and Jekaf (Rojin Ülker) hide in his vehicle while crossing the border from Turkey to Iraq, a scene that introduces both Jekaf and Çeto. Jekaf's family was killed under Saddam Hussein's regime, and she was raped repeatedly by his soldiers. Later, she was sold on to American soldiers, and is now trying to enter northern Iraq with no papers. Her body, the female body as the embodiment of a country, turns into the embodiment of a non-country, and a body onto which the history of Kurds is inscribed. What is more, although the border official Ahmet falls in love with her, his family dismisses her because of her past.

Çeto on the other hand represents the Kurds in Europe, a character who exists in the director's previous work, *Vodka Lemon* (2003), in which his existence in the story is maintained through letters sent to his father from Paris.

We understand that his sister, whose picture on the wall occupies an important space within the film, was killed during Saddam Hussein's regime. Her photograph testifies to her existence, while also reminding us of her absence, as she *has been*, but no longer *is*. The sister's significant absence, her ghostly presence in the film, also alludes to the imaginary land of Kurdistan.

When Çeto's father mentions the discovery of a mass grave near Kirkuk, which includes his daughter's remains, they go to collect her bones, together with many others who come to collect the remains of their families in plastic bags. They come home, sit in the garden before the funeral, before her bones are placed in a coffin. No words are exchanged between them as the director creates this rather uncanny family picture: Çeto, his father, his sister's photograph, and her bones. Saleem often uses past atrocities to bind his narrative together in his attempt to remember the defining moments of the Kurdish identity (see Figure 5.5).

The third character, Taman (Belçim Bilgin), on the other hand, is part of an unnamed political organization that is involved in armed struggle as well as other activities such as schooling children and radio broadcasting. Taman meets Azad in a hospital in which she is receiving treatment, when Azad is visiting Jekaf. Azad asks to go with her to the camp, as he feels he could be of use, and she agrees to take him. She is portrayed as an intelligent and strong woman, but also one without a past. We are given an account of her life at present and her aspirations for the future, but unlike the other characters nothing is known

Figure 5.5 *Dol* (dir. Hiner Saleem; from Hiner Saleem Production Novociné, 2007). Çeto with his sister's picture.

about her past. With Taman, the representation of young Kurdish women, as well as Kurdistan, is complete: the sister who has been murdered and is mourned, the shattered but alive Jekaf and the hopeful, independent, strong and future-looking Taman. What brings these characters together is their Kurdish identity and their intersection in places dominated by Kurds as well as Saleem's treatment of them as a continuation of each other. A comparison between *Dol* and *My Marlon and Brando* also reveals the differences between the chronotope in each film, what and how they remember and relate to Kurdish identity. While *Dol* attempts to create an imaginary unification among the Kurds of Iran, Iraq, and Turkey, *My Marlon and Brando* is more interested in highlighting borders and the limitations they impose rather than suggesting a new, real, or imaginary border.

As well as engaging with the imagined space Kurdistan occupies, Saleem also frequently plays with the space his characters occupy. Saleem's use of space creates a landscape that conforms to the ideal and imagined land of Kurdistan. Moreover, consistent with his subversive treatment of space, he brings inside out, outside in. In *Dol* and in his other films, private and public lose their distinction. These outdoor scenes are not broken up by fences or walls; it becomes normal that a bed, a television, and countless chairs are placed in the idyllic landscape.[27] However, it should be noted that by bringing inside to outside, Saleem subversively reorders the space, mocking the situation by making everywhere and everything habitable, which alludes to the situation of Kurds.

Undoubtedly, *Dol* and its spatio-temporal references cannot be interpreted independently of the creation of the Kurdish region in Iraq, which is an autonomous region with its own parliamentary democracy. Turkey's relation to the region is somewhat ambiguous and cautious as, in addition to political tensions regarding a possibility of a Kurdish nation-state in the region, Turkey took military actions in northern Iraq against the PKK, which heightened tensions there. This finds its way in to the narrative in the form of planes that bomb the guerrilla camp, forcing them to leave for another place yet again.

In addition to his creative use of space, Saleem also uses silence skillfully. In his previous films, as well as in *Dol*, Saleem's characters do not speak very much, hence creating many silent moments. However, Saleem's silences are not only quiet moments in life where words do not mean anything, although there is room for such silence too as exemplified in the scene where Çeto's father collects the bones of his daughter. The director also manufactures silences in scenes, where normally a conversation would take place. In a sequence where a number of villagers visit Çeto's family house, presumably to welcome him, the people do not speak, but stare at each other. Meaningless conversation is replaced by a meaningless silence. These scenes also bring out the other aspects of such gatherings such as bodily gestures which otherwise would go unnoticed.

Saleem himself defines the domination of silences in his films as his particular characteristic, saying that he likes "talking through the pictures, [because] silence can say more than words can" (Saleem: 243). But Saleem's silences are, more often than not, untimely and almost absurd in that they become difficult to understand, to grasp their function within the story. The difficulty to attach an immediate meaning to silences within the plot inevitably makes them visible. Since these silences are not complete silences as the ambient noise continues in these scenes, they become silent moments between individuals, "wordless" exchanges.

As much as silence, Saleem also plays with the words in line with his generally absurd take on the story. Perhaps the most significant sentence uttered in the film is the one by the army second-in command in the village. In contrast to the commander-in-chief, who is rough, intolerant, and violent, the army second-in command does not speak often, except to say the same sentence a few times in the film. He repeatedly, and only during the scenes of violence, says: "This problem will not be solved like this." When the villagers are tortured, and when Azad is shot, he repeatedly utters these very words, while reluctantly taking part in something he does not approve of. His powerless voice makes the absurdity of the situation even more visible.

Saleem's film stands out on two fronts: his particular use of space, and his subversive use of laughter. While his use of space functions to highlight the on-going issues related to the Kurdish situation—the geographical division is contrasted with the cultural continuity—his use of laughter brings out the absurdity of the situation that is often rendered as the reality of the region. As a Kurdish director residing and working in France, Saleem's film illustrates that many of the recurring themes outlined in Chapter 2 stem not from a geographical/cultural positioning but from a political and social one.

* * *

What is referred to as the Kurdish question in Turkey has gained a significant visibility in the public sphere in the last decade. The Kurds' identity, and their demands, are arguably one of the most pressing issues Turkey faces. The difficulties of war, the reality of internally displaced people, and the effects of assimilation policies on the Kurdish citizens are topics constantly scrutinized in the cultural sphere in Turkey.

There has been a significant increase in the number of films dealing with issues surrounding Kurdish identity in Turkey within the past ten years compared to any other single subject. Although they vary in their treatment of the subjects, these films all have one thing in common: displacement and its effects. They not only make certain stories available to the general public, but they also contribute to the discussion of the subject in the public sphere. The most significant example in this respect is the impact *On the Way to School* has made. Since the release of the film, no discussion has taken place on the subject of education in Kurdish, without reference to the film.

As this chapter illustrates, the most salient aspect of these films appears to be their continuous engagement with language, more specifically the use of the Kurdish language in public. The second most important narrative element is their particular use of space as they reorder it to make the power structures that are otherwise rendered invisible, visible. And, finally, the third salient motif, one that is directly related to the use of space, is that in almost all of these films journeying appears to be an important aspect of the narrative, not only as an inevitable part of physical displacement but also as a narrative element that renders the experience of displacement comprehensible on screen.

Coda: *Once Upon a Time in Anatolia*

As I write these words, Nuri Bilge Ceylan's latest film *Kış Uykusu/Winter Sleep* (2014) is being shown in cinemas. It has made Ceylan the first director from Turkey to win the *Palm d'Or* since Yılmaz Güney in 1982. A regular at Cannes, Ceylan's previous film, *Bir Zamanlar Anadolu'da/Once Upon a Time in Anatolia* (2011) was also acknowledged in Cannes, sharing the Grand Prix in 2011 with the Dardenne Brothers' *Le Gamin au Vélo*. *Once Upon a Time in Anatolia* is a poetic film, reflecting on life, death, and everything in between with a peculiar sense of humor. Similar to Ceylan's previous films, it makes generous use of long takes and long shots, combining his signature photographic shots with an immaculate sound design to tell a story that is more than what it seems. By way of concluding this book, but also with an interest in shifting the angle in order to introduce further questions, I would like to read *Once Upon a Time in Anatolia* in relation to the other films that I have examined here, highlighting the aesthetic continuity, and the dialogic relation between this film and the aforementioned ones. Although the film differs from the films analyzed in this study, as it neither explicitly articulates a specific historical wrongdoing nor deals with minorities per se, it—starting with its title—continuously implies what other films openly make their subjects: the past, even buried deep, will not remain in the past.

Throughout this book I have discussed films that scrutinize history and memory, films that deal with past atrocities and that, in doing so, look for ways to translate the experience of displacement into the visual realm. They, I have argued, are decidedly political, consciously looking for novel ways—both narrative and aesthetic—to make connections between the past and present. Hence, it might appear somewhat abrupt to conclude the book with Ceylan's *Once Upon a Time in Anatolia*: a film by a director who is not known for his political filmmaking and a work that does not explicitly focus on a past wrong-doing. Yet, there is an eerie connection between this film and the rest of the films that are openly discussing aspects of facing the past. Starting with its title, the film allows, or perhaps invites, viewers to perform another kind of reading, one that looks into what is buried under the image, under "the skin of the film."

I reference Laura Marks' title of the book, *The Skin of the Film*, for a good reason: not only because the title of the book suggests surface, and, consequently, what that surface conceals underneath, but because the book itself talks about images in relation to excavation, a kind of excavation that wants the truth to surface. According to Marks, "intercultural cinema is in a position to sort through the rubble created by cultural dislocation and read significance in what official history overlooks" (Marks 2000: 28). As discussed throughout the book, what Marks calls "intercultural cinema" does not aim at representing *the* truth, but is interested in exposing what was absent in the narration of it. Hence, both Foucault and Deleuze are important to her discussion, not only with regard to representing experience, but also, inevitably, in relation to producing and representing the truth. Any kind of narration will inevitably operate on selecting elements to form a story.

The answer to the question of how *Once Upon a Time in Anatolia* can be considered to be displaying elements of intercultural cinema, how Ceylan buries the history of the land into his film, will have to lie in his aesthetic preferences, in not only what the film shows and tells, but also in the ways in which it alludes to what it does *not* show and tell: breaking the unity between the sound and the image, between what is said and what is being communicated, between what is heard and what is registered, as well as the specific use of silence, all serve to make the film a text that is aware of absences. The film, in a sense, is reminiscent of the journey taken in it in order to locate the absent body: what is being searched for is not on the surface but buried in the ground. Yet, the film, by consciously framing the narrative as the search for a body in order to shed light on a murder, is then able to halt the expected resolution, that of providing closure with the discovery of the body, in its insistence of higlighting, but not answering, questions in relation to the facts of the matter and the narration of truth. This, then, makes a reading in relation to the history of the land called Anatolia possible. First, the inability to locate the body, then the reluctance to reveal and document the whole truth, make the film not a story of a murder, but rather an allegorical representation of the history of the land, making it a haunting and a haunted narrative.

Loosely based on a true story, *Once Upon a Time in Anatolia* unfolds over a long night in a small town in the Kırıkkale province, and consists of two separate sections. The first part deals with the search for the body, as the murder suspect is expected to show where he buried the body. During the search for the body, the group, consisting of the murder suspects Kenan (Fırat Tanış), his brother, Ramazan (Burhan Yıldız), the prosecutor Nusret (Taner Birsel), the doctor, Cemal (Muhammet Uzuner), the police chief Naci (Yılmaz Erdoğan), the driver, nicknamed "Arab" (Ahmet Mümtaz Taylan), and a few others, visits four potential locations. The first three prove to be wrong, as the accused Kenan fails to locate the body, complaining that "these places all look similar." The group then goes to the house of the mukhtar (the head of the local village)[1] to eat. It is after they depart from the mukhtar's house that they make a final stop at the crack of dawn, and this time Kenan is able to show them where he buried the body. The second part of the film largely takes place at the hospital, concluding with a lengthy on-screen autopsy performed on the deceased.

What stands out throughout the entire film is the constant shift of perspective, both visual and aural, displacing the audience in relation to knowledge (who knows what) and power relations (who gets to decide who knows what). Ceylan's use of space and sound plays a major role in achieving such displacement along with haunting silences that, like many other films in this book, are pregnant with knowledge of the unsaid, the unexposed, the unacknowledged. Starting with its title the film invites questions about the history of the land called Anatolia. Although the title reminds us of Sergio Leone's westerns—*Once Upon a Time in America* (1984), and *Once Upon a Time in the West* (1968)—neither the title nor the film are simple references to Leone. Thinking within the context within which I have been arguing in this book, the context in which slow, but nevertheless growing awareness of the past emerges, *Once Upon a Time in Anatolia* is a haunting title. Because the story does not take place in the undesignated ambiguous "once upon a time," but at present in Anatolia, the knowledge of the land's silenced history lingers over the story, haunting it.

The film opens with three men talking inside a car mechanic's shop. The camera remains outside, where it is dark: the glass between the men and the camera not only makes the image of these men blurry, but also makes the conversation inaudible. Hence, the all-knowing, all-seeing audience does not enter into Ceylan's image, for this is not a film about who knows what, but rather how that knowledge is produced, and what is left out and denied in the process. Such separation of what is visible and what is audible, and the shift in the meaning they carry as a result of that separation, is employed throughout the film. According to Umut Tümay Arslan, the particular use of sound in the film "stains" the continuity and clarity of the image, a stain that disrupts our cognitive process, restricting our confidently subjective distance to the image (Arslan 2012: 198). Ceylan repeatedly reminds his audience of the separation between inside and outside by establishing continuity between the two with imagery, with what is visible, and breaking it with the sound, with what is audible, or vice versa. In Marks' words, "the seeable and the sayable approach each other asymptotically, showing each other to be false even as they require each other to be true" (Marks 2000: 30).

Following the murder, which takes place off-screen, the group makes the first stop to locate the body. On this occasion the camera remains with the accused and the police who are with him, as he looks around trying to understand whether or not this *is* the place. During the following two stops they make, the camera will let them wander into the darkness, at times making them audible but not following them at close proximity, and at times leaving them to completely disappear from both the visual and the audible realm. Instead it will remain with the other men: first the conservation between Arab and the doctor, then the conversation between the doctor and the prosecutor will take place, both of which are filled with silences, both revealing nothing more than the knowledge of the unsaid.

The conversation between the doctor and Arab is triggered by the doctor's encounter with a ghostly image, as he looks for a suitable place to empty his bladder. When he finds a place for the purpose the lightning strikes, rendering the area surrounding him suddenly visible, causing the doctor to jump with fear. What becomes visible in the flash of light are the giant faces carved into the rocky side of the hill, looking down at him: an Anatolian apparition. These carvings appear suddenly, synchronized with the sound of lightning, and haunt him as well as the audience. It is after this incident that the conversation between Arab and the doctor takes place, with displaced sound and image: neither the conversation nor the image seem what they appear to be anymore. The doctor's mention of the carvings with a question mark in his voice fails to enthuse Arab—yes, he says, there are many like those around here. As Arab starts talking about other things, rambling on about his life, Ceylan switches from synchronous sound to non-synchronous, adding more confusion to the image as it becomes less clear how much of what is heard is actually said.

The conversation between the doctor and the prosecutor is also filled with the haunting knowledge of the unsaid. As they talk, a certain discoloration (a stain perhaps) on the prosecutor's face becomes visible as if what is withdrawn from the conversation surfaces on the prosecutor's skin, as if the audience developed another way of seeing which now makes the discoloration visible. He talks about a beautiful pregnant woman, his friend's wife he says, who one day announces that she will die after giving birth to her baby—and she does. The doctor suspects the woman in the story is, in fact, the prosecutor's wife, and that the marks on his face are her revenant. Both the conversation between the doctor and Arab, and the conversation between the doctor and the prosecutor, are filled with moments of silence where the unsaid becomes more important than the said.

This conversation, in addition to being an investigation into how the woman died, also is a conversation about the available evidence. But rather than solving the mystery it becomes a haunting conversation, almost a rehearsal of what is to come in terms of documenting the truth. As the doctor suggests the possibility that certain medicines can cause a heart attack if taken in excess, lack of autopsy makes it impossible to say anything conclusive as to how the woman died. However, although the conversation implies that the lack of autopsy is the reason why the truth is not exposed, this perspective will be shifted at the end: the truth is also what these official documents, such as the autopsy report, continuously fail to register. This will become more evident during the autopsy at the end.

Although most of the characters are haunted by their past, one ghost that achieves what he came for, i.e. justice, is that of the murdered man. During the break at the mukhtar's house, the mukhtar's daughter enters the diegetic space, serving tea for the men, leaving them speechless by the sight of her ethereal beauty. Although her appearance seems to have an impact on everyone, the accused murderer Kenan seems to be the most affected of all, seeing the ghost of the man he murdered. The ghost, appearing only to him, has difficulty breathing. The vision breaks Kenan and leads to his full confession, admitting the reason for the murder was an argument between them as the victim found out that Kenan had a relationship with the man's wife and their child was Kenan's. Yet, although this probably is the only confession in the film (others are reluctant to face their ghosts), and the most important moment in the plot, it, like the murder, takes place off-screen.

When the body is located, following Kenan's confession, the initial examination of the body is carried out without touching it; first the prosecutor then the doctor "looks" at the body dictating what they see for the report. The juridical and the medical gaze, it is assumed, is informed enough to narrate the truth. Representatives of the state apparatus, particularly the police chief, are outraged about how the body is found, hog-tied in order to fit into the car. They feel it is an undignified treatment, but end up doing the same because the ambulance has not been called and the body does not fit into their own car.

Beyond its satirical value, once again the film pitches law and its legitimizing power for its own actions against those who do not possess the right to act on behalf of the law.

The dead body carries the knowledge within, but the power, the producers of knowledge (the law, medicine), has a monopoly over translating and registering it.[2] These two—translating and registering—come together for it is not enough to have the necessary knowledge to translate what may appear as gibberish to the "untrained" eye, one also needs to possess the power to register what has been translated for it to become knowledge. However, even the knowledge the body carries within is at the mercy of the translator, the doctor. As he performs the autopsy by proxy, he does not touch the body instead observes his assistant carrying out the work, he dictates the findings to the officer to be included in the report. Then the knowledge the body carries is noticed by the assistant. He informs the doctor that the victim displays traces of soil in his trachea, suggesting he was buried alive. The doctor, who has the authority to dictate what gets written in the report, pauses momentarily and orders the officer: "Write it down, no abnormalities were found in the trachea area." It is left to us to figure out why the doctor does not allow the official document to state what the body tells him, but the most plausible reason is that he does not wish to further complicate the matter for the law (was he alive when they found him?).

The questions of history and its narration haunt the narrative space, through the story of the dead body: despite the knowledge it carries, it cannot speak it. The system fails to speak for it. The truth becomes not what is documented, but that which is adjacent to what is documented. Similar to the films discussed in the preceding chapters, what is questioned is the truth here: what is put forward as the truth by the official mechanisms. Yet, the truth the body carries with it is not silenced, nor does it disappear as it returns the gaze back to the doctor: blood squirts from it hitting the doctor on the face.

The history and the memory of a place dictate its own way of storytelling, and this is very much visible in Ceylan's film. Anatolia cannot be thought to be without its own murders and massacres in the past, and their denial at present. As Umut Tümay Arslan asserts, the chosen location for this story is Keskin, a small town near the Kırıkkale province, one of the oldest towns in central Anatolia once populated by Armenians and Greeks as well as Muslims (Arslan 2012: 216). Armenians once lived here are mentioned in historian Yusuf Halaçoğlu's book dedicated to prove the Armenian genocide did not happen. According to Halaçoğlu, what happened was a temporary relocation of Armenians due to war conditions. He goes on to explain that although many articles and books are written on the subject of the Armenian genocide in the West "none are based on real and trustworthy documents," and that "Armenians hide behind documents that are fabricated for political and emotional reasons, and deceive the world" (Halaçoğlu 2006: 72).

Yet, even Halaçoğlu admits to the "relocation" of large populations and lists the numbers of people relocated at each location, which according to him proves precision on the part of the Ottoman Empire. According to Halaçoğlu, 1,169 Armenians were "relocated" elsewhere from the small town of Keskin, where Ceylan's film also takes place. Keskin, however, is only a small town, one of many Anatolian towns and villages where Armenians lived for centuries, only to be absent in contemporary Turkey, an absence that needs to be acknowledged.[3] In his efforts to prove not what happened but what did not happen, Halacoğlu lists the number of relocated people in different towns in Anatolia, yet he does not provide any document on whether any of the displaced communities were returned, other than vaguely saying it is not clear. Such narration is also ingrained into popular discussions of the subject. "The archives are open," says the official discourse—although there are restrictions and problems with access. "Leave history to historians" is another utterance often heard in Turkey. However, history is a narration and often narrated by the ones in power. The absence of archives, writes Nichanian, is not an "adjacent fact" but what lies at the core of the will to exterminate. "The true 'fact' here is the destruction of the archive. The ineffectiveness of history is thus an absolutely central phenomenon, constitutive of the facts" (Nichanian 2002: 14).

Ceylan's film, from this perspective, is hard to read without thinking about the history of the region, without making connections to the political rhetoric in circulation today regarding the history of the region. Although the film refrains from openly mentioning Armenians or the history of the region, the haunting title and the haunted characters in denial, as well as the "haunted time" (Berry and Farqhuar 2006), make the film a gesture toward memory and unresolved past; not only on a personal level, but on a larger social level as well. In this sense, *Once Upon a Time in Anatolia* is similar to *Ararat*, since it also uses the personal to hint at the social. What is more, the film haunts the present time, not only by alluding to the absence of people, but also by alluding to unmarked graves, more specifically mass graves, an issue that is still awaiting full confrontation. As was discussed in the previous chapter, actions of the "deep state," particularly in the 1990s in the Kurdish populated areas, are still not fully acknowledged. According to the Human Rights Association's (IHD) interactive map of mass graves in Turkey, there are forty-five known, and a further 303 alleged mass graves in Turkey, the majority of which are in the Kurdish populated cities.[4]

In many respects, I have been arguing that posing the question itself is more important than the answer. The moment the question makes its entry is the moment absences become haunting presences. The silences turn into stains, making themselves known: there is an unquestionable connection between the marks on the prosecutor's face and the bloodstain on the doctor's. But there is also an eerie continuity established throughout the story with the use of space. Starting with the title, Ceylan establishes a sense of space that is vast, that is open and goes beyond the geographic and temporal constraints: it becomes a haunted space. Although the film does not mention the history of the land or the minorities it once was home for, it makes its ghosts inescapable.

If in the future the files about this specific murder are pulled out, the official documented truth will be all there is to know about it. Yet, the film reminds us that archives are full of reports with absences, with omissions and sometimes with total lack of needed documents. Ceylan's cinematic style, his narrative and aesthetic choices constantly remind the audience of the absence, what is not narrated, not seen and not heard: a film about what is lost in the process of translating an event into a document becomes a haunting narrative, a ghostly referral, producing a knowledge of the absences, the absence of the people of Anatolia. Once again the question forces itself into the text: when a tree falls in the forest, and there is no one to hear it, does it make a sound?

* * *

This book looked at the relationship between film and memory, taking memory as a concept and examining how cinema has responded aesthetically to the issues created by the unresolved past, particularly in relation to the concepts of unified citizenship and minorities in Turkey. I have argued that these films contributed to the visibility of different discourses about identity that emerged in the post-1980s context, undermining the general conviction about minorities in Turkey. The films stem from new forms of understanding belonging, and help establish a new discourse, one that is informed by post-national sensibilities. This new understanding, and the ongoing transformation, not only allow a discursive space for these stories to emerge (a space that did not exist in the immediate years following the military coup of 1980), but also demand their own aesthetic. My analysis in this book aims to reveal the particular relation between memory and language, as well as the ways in which the geographies of minority experience affect both narrative and cinematic space. The recurring aesthetic and thematic considerations with which these films engage, are in dialogic relation to the changing social conditions.

I assert, throughout this book, that political and social contexts influence, and, to a certain extent, determine, the aesthetics of the image. In other words, how film deals with its subject matter is not solely dependent on the subject itself. I have illustrated the relevance of this claim in the context of Turkey by looking at three distinct areas of the past, and their representations today: minorities in Turkey and the effects of Turkifying policies; the massacre of Armenians in 1915 and its denial in contemporary Turkey; and, finally, the ongoing struggle of Kurds for the recognition of their rights. The unresolved issues of the past are, by no means, limited to the three areas to which I pay close attention here. As Mithat Sancar writes, Turkey has not yet openly dealt with *any* of the traumatic experiences of its past (Sancar 2007: 259), and the list certainly is long. However, my selection of these themes has depended on their weight on contemporary Turkish politics, as well as their relation to displacement, which, I have argued, is the structuring condition, the "structure of feeling," of these films. What has been displaced and how the consequent problems have been dealt with are two major questions that I have asked of each of the films examined as part of this study. If, as Sancar notes, the process of facing up to the past (on a more official level) depends on a demand coming from society, and that this is only possible by creating a language, a vocabulary, and frame of reference, which addresses the key issues and enables their articulation (Sancar 2007: 260), then these films, regardless of their subject, each contribute to that process.

With the condition of displacement informing these texts, certain stylistic preferences and themes have revealed themselves as recurring throughout my examination. That these categories are not necessarily independent of each other, but are interwoven and dialogic, is particularly important when analyzed in relation to otherwise "unrelated" forms or styles. Hence, one of the aims of the book has been identifying this emergent, and to a large extent unrecognized, continuity among these films. Particularly important in this respect is the attention paid to language. This, as I have demonstrated, has specific political undertones in Turkey and is a recurring motif in films, which has been addressed throughout this book within the context of official language policies, particularly in Chapters 2 and 5. Some of the languages spoken throughout Turkey are now declared at the edge of extinction. Hemshin (Homshetsma) is an example (which is used in *Autumn*), as is Pontus Greek (Ayşe's/Eleni's language in *Waiting for the Clouds*). According to UNESCO's research on the endangered languages of the world, these two languages are in severe danger of extinction along with thirteen other languages still spoken in Turkey (UNESCO, n.d.). In other words these languages are already ghosts themselves: if language *is* the "house of being" (Heidegger) it is also a haunted house in the case of these forgotten/forbidden languages.

Moreover, the entry of these languages into narrative space is also politically charged as a result of linguistic and educational policies. For instance, as discussed in Chapter 5, to make a film in Kurdish in the 1990s was literally impossible in Turkey, and even to use it partly in a film proved problematic. Hence, how language makes its entry into narrative space is highly significant. Similarly, silence offers the possibility, in film, of acknowledging its function to conceal cultural differences. The very existence of silence in film is always already a broken silence and therefore also useful when the overall aim is to arrest the flow of the narrative in order to ask questions. The use of epistolary narrative, or differing but affective uses of space, are also recurring motifs in these films, with each one having roots in the actual experience of displacement: being away from home determines an epistolary relationship to it, and also defines the perception and the use of space of the displaced.

Similarly, as a direct outcome of displacement, the films continuously make use of the ways in which liminality informs both narrative structure and topographic space, as well as the human condition itself. The dialogue between how politics shapes space and in return how cultural products deal with the shift offers a promising area for further research. Especially in the chapter dealing with the Kurds, I have briefly touched on the ways in which certain places are used in films and what they signify; however the subject remains to be investigated in detail. This is not only related to the recurring use of certain spaces but also to how those spaces are represented and what they come to mean in the narrative. This relation also informs how these films deal with other aspects and effects of displacement: the figure of the ghost is an inevitable recurring motif when dealing with an unresolved past, which is linked to both the use of space and the understanding (and structuring) of time in these films.

This book predominantly asked "how" questions: how these films deal with the past and how they respond to their subject aesthetically. However, although not directly addressed, the question of "why these films deal with displacement in the ways identified here" is equally important, and I have made a number of attempts at answering it in various parts of the book. Part of the reason why lies in the fact that these films exist in a world where there is more dialogue than ever before among these texts and their authors. What I have argued in this study is that the dialogic relation between these works and with their surroundings influences and determines the aesthetics of the image. Given that these aesthetic strategies, and recurring motifs, serve toward uncoupling the audience, they all, in their different ways, contribute to the arrest of thoughts in the flow of thinking, giving way to a temporary shock: informed by displacement as the structuring condition, they set out to displace their audiences. In their belated arrival, these films are letters from the past, bringing the ghosts of that past to the "now." How that image develops, and into what, is a potentially fruitful area of examination for the future.

Notes

Introduction

1 This is most visibly the case in the discussions of the Armenian genocide in Turkey, which is discussed at length in Chapter 4. Even when there is agreement on the historical evidence, there is rarely agreement on what the evidence might mean.

2 For an edited collection of articles on the relationship between history, memory, and cinema see Sobchack (1996), Landy (2000), Grainge (2003). For an analysis of history and cinema through the use of flashbacks see Turim (1989). For a comparative study on history and film see Rosenstone (1996).

3 There have been a growing number of publications in recent years on various aspects of the new cinema of Turkey, particularly in relation to identity and memory. In addition to Asuman Suner, Gönül Dönmez-Colin (2008) has written an introductory book on different aspects of identity in Turkish cinema. There have also been two edited collections, with articles looking at various aspects of cinema in Turkey. See Deniz Bayraktar (2009) and Miyase Christen and Nezih Erdogan (2008).

4 See Chapter 2 for a more detailed account of the evacuated villages of Eastern Turkey.

5 See Miyase Christen and Nezih Erdogan (2008); Deniz Bayraktar (2009); Gokcen Karanfil and Serkan Savk (2013); Deniz Bayrakdar and Murat Akser (2014).

6 Practicing mainly in Turkey, Alevis are members of a special sect of Islam incorporating pre-Islamic belief with Shiite Islam.

1. Memory, Identity: The Turkish Context

1 According to Kadıǧolu, the efforts gained momentum in 2001, and important constitutional amendments were made in 2001 and 2004 (Kadıǧolu 2007: 292).

2 For a comprehensive analysis of the history of radio broadcasting in Turkey in relation to nation-building in Turkey, see Ahıska (2010).

3 ROJ TV was not allowed to transmit from within Turkey because it was in Kurdish, hence it broadcast from Denmark. However, Turkey protested to the Danish authorities for allowing it to transmit from Denmark, based on the accusation that it is the mouthpiece of PKK, which Turkey regards as a terrorist organization.

4 I would like to thank Deniz Kandiyoti for suggesting the concept.

5 Unless otherwise stated, all translations from Turkish to English are mine.

6 Although there have been few films on the coup during the 1990s, it seems there has been a particular interest in the subject since the beginning of the 2000s. *Vizontele Tuuba* (Yilmaz Erdogan, 2004), *Babam ve* Oğlum/My *Father and My Son* (Çağan Irmak, 2005), *Beynelmilel/International* (Sırrı Süreyya Önder, 2006), *Eve Dönüş/Return Home* (Ömer Ugur, 2006), *Zincirbozan* (Atil Inanc, 2007), and *O... Çocukları/Sons of B...* (Murat Saracoglu, 2008) were all made between 2004 and 2008.

7 Although they are often used interchangeably with secularism, and even though there are shared traits among them, Taha Parla and Andrew Davison (2004) write that the two are not the same. In Turkey the word *laiklik* is used to describe the relations between the state and the religion; it derives from the French *laicisme*. Parla and Davison note, "Kemalist laicism is most often described throughout the literature as 'secularism', leaving the impressions that Kemalist laicism achieves everything from a radical separation between state and tradition to the privatization or elimination of religion in the conscience." They argue that it is "at odds with these ideals in both concept and practice" (Parla and Davison 2004: 13–14).

8 For a comparative analysis of Greek, Armenian, and Arab nationalisms during the decline of the Ottoman Empire, see Göcek (2002).

9 The idea that the Turkish identity should be protected by the state still continues today. The highly controversial Article 301 makes it possible to prosecute people on the bases of "insulting Turkishness." In 2006, Armenian–Turkish journalist Hrant Dink was prosecuted. Dink was assassinated by a nationalist group in 2007.

10 See *Birinci Türk Tarih Kongresi*, 1932.

11 This hesitant attitude resulted in Turkey waiting twenty-two years, until 1945, for its single-party era to end. Although there was an understanding that transformation was needed, attempts at political pluralism ended in opposition political parties either being closed down, or closing themselves down, because the Republic was "not yet ready." This is usually described as the "tutelary democracy." See Parla and Davison (2004).

12 Kemalism, named after Kemal Atatürk, and based on his ideas and principles, has been the dominant ideology in Turkey. According to Haldun Günalp, Kemalism "was a paradigmatic model of Third World nationalism in that it perceived and defined Westernisation as the attainment of 'universal' civilisation" (Günalp 1997: 61).

13 The politics of creating a unified language is discussed also in Chapter 2 in relation to the films analyzed.

14 Avram Galanti, a Turkish citizen of Jewish origin, wrote a book called *Vatandaş Türkce Konuş!* in order to explain why the transition to Turkish could take time, explaining the situations of the minorities while also trying to convince the minorities to adopt the Turkish language. The book was published in March 1928, two months after the campaign was launched.

15 In their comparative study on nationalism in Turkey and Greece, Umut Özkırımlı and Spyros A. Sofos write that "the Turkish Historical Thesis needs to be understood in the context of the broader Kemalist project which entailed a complete break with the immediate Ottoman Islamic past" (Özkırımlı and Sofos: 96) as its aim was to demonstrate the continuity of the Turks in Anatolia.

16 PKK (Partiya Karkeren Kurdistan) is listed as a terrorist organization by Turkey. Its leader, Abdullah Öcalan, was arrested in 1999, and has been in prison ever since. At the time of writing the Turkish government is engaged in a fragile "peace process" with the Kurdish movement, and Öcalan is participating in discussions with the government through Kurdish MPs. See Chapter 5 for a detailed background.

17 This dilemma is problematized in many recent films by paying exclusive attention to language. Also see Chapter 2.

18 For more on CUP, see Ahmad (2005: 31–51), Zurcher (2004: 93–165).

19 There is also extensive discussion on what happened after the majority of the Armenian population died or was deported, which enhances the accusations against the Turkish state and its complicity. The fate of Armenian properties, many of which were confiscated, forms the major part of these discussions. See Uğur Ümit Üngör and Mehmet Polatel (2011).

20 There have been a number of conferences on the issues of memory and the Armenian genocide in Turkey. The first attempt to discuss the genocide was stopped by a court order. Such attempts also face protests from nationalists. Similarly, historians and other intellectuals who are willing to admit the genocide are called "traitors." Recently, Nobel Prize-winning author Orhan Pamuk faced prosecution and received death threats for a speech he made in Germany, in which he stated, "In Turkey, thirty thousand Kurds and a million Armenians were massacred." See Chapter 4 for a detailed discussion on the existing discourse.

21 Yeşim Ustaoğlu's film *Bulutları Beklerken/Waiting for the Clouds* (2003) deals with this aspect of history from the point of view of a woman who lost her family during the forced migration. The film is discussed in Chapter 3 in detail.

22 Aktar notes that caricatures ridiculing Jews were in circulation from the 1930s, and in 1942 reached their peak, mocking all non-Muslims in the figure of a Jew and picturing them as greedy money grabbers (Aktar 2008: 143).

23 Both the Capital Tax, and the pogrom of September 6 and 7, 1955, were tackled
by the director Tomris Giritlioğlu. Her film on the Capital Tax, *Salkım Hanımın
Taneleri/Mrs. Salkım's Diamonds* (1999), and *Güz Sancısı/Pains of Autumn* (2008),
dealing with the pogrom, are both discussed in Chapter 3.

24 What is referred to as the *1964 İnönü Kararnamesi* (1964 İnönü Enactment) is
one of the least talked about issues in Turkey regarding the minorities. See Aktar
and Demir's (1994) *İstanbul'un Son Sürgünleri* (*The Last Exiles of İstanbul*). See
also Chapter 3, for a discussion of the film *Politiki Kouzina* (Tassos Boulmetis,
2003), which centers around a family who had to leave the country as result of
the enactment. The stories of deported families was also recently the subject of an
exhibition in Istanbul entitled *20 Dollars, 20 Kilos*, as they were only allowed to take
20 dollars and 20 kilos worth of belongings with them.

25 The opening day of the "Grand National Assembly" is celebrated as the "National
Sovereignty and Children's Day" (April 23), the day Atatürk started the War of
Independence is celebrated as "Atatürk's Commemoration, Youth and Sports Day"
(May 19), the establishment of the Republic as the "Republic Day" (October 29), and
the end of the War of Independence is celebrated as the "Victory Day" (August 30).

26 Atatürk's life, including the trivial details of his childhood, is known to anyone
who went to school in Turkey. His picture is still found in every single government
office, as well as in classrooms, and even in some houses. However, although the
fixation with Ataturk, as well as his unquestioned heroic position, is lessening, it
seems that Turkish society is not entirely done with father figures, as the status of
Recep Tayyip Erdoğan seems to indicate.

27 Anıtkabir is a highly charged place in terms of its symbolic value. Protests against
the perceived threat of Islamic fundamentalism always end in Anıtkabir. For a
comparative study on Anıtkabir and the Kocatepe Mosque see Meeker (1997).

28 For an article on the role of the military under the civilian governments since 1980,
see Sakallioğlu (1997).

29 In 2007, a national television channel produced a hugely successful television series
called *Hatırla Sevgili/Remember My Dear* about the events leading up to the military
coup, focusing on the members of the Democratic Party and their families. More
recently another TV series, *Ben Onu Çok Sevdim/I Loved Him Very Much*, although
less successful, focused on Menderes' life. The lack of critical engagement is perhaps
the most common aspect of all these projects, which was particularly salient with
regard to the latter.

30 These changes were given financial infrastructure by the creation of the Armed
Forces Pension Fund in 1961, known as OYAK in Turkey. The special concessions
it enjoys (tax exemption, donations, etc.) made OYAK a very profitable entity
within a few years time, providing extra income for its military investors.

Its investments vary from cement to the automotive industry, from food to finance. According to Taha Parla, the very existence of OYAK can be read in relation to the 1980 coup as telling. According to Parla, OYAK represents a "military capitalist entry into the market," and its sequel TSKGV (Foundation of Strengthening the Turkish Armed Forces), as a "militarizer of the economy" (Parla 1998: 49). Parla reads the existence of OYAK in relation to the 1980 coup and says that by the 1980s the military "had become a big employer of wage labour, in addition to the wage labour employed by its partners as well as other members of its new social class, who had been demanding such measures for some time" (Parla 1998: 43).

31 The Kurdish issue and its representation in film is discussed further in Chapter 5.

32 Originally a term in Islamic art, signifying geometrical shapes and patterns used for ornamental purposes, arabesque music combined different styles in music, from Arabic to Western. According to Meral Özbek, although the term was first used to describe the music itself, "it later came to describe the entire migrant culture formed at the peripheries of Turkish cities" (Özbek 1997: 211). What was considered to be bad taste in music, and therefore banned from the state's broadcasting institution TRT, became a huge phenomenon in Turkey. Özbek argues that although arabesque (culture) was portrayed as a product of a period of transition from traditional to modern society, it was/is in fact "a historical formation of popular culture, constructed and lived through the process of spatial and symbolic migration in the Turkish path through modernity" (Özbek 1997: 211). For a sociological analysis of arabesque music in Turkey, see Meral Özbek, *Popüler Kültür ve Orhan Gencebay Arabeski*, 1991.

33 For a detailed account of Yeşilçam cinema, see Savaş Arslan, *Cinema in Turkey* (2011).

34 For a feminist reading of Güney's *Yol/The Way*, see Suner (1998).

35 In Turkish, the word "inside" (*içerisi*) is also informally used to refer to prison.

36 See Chapter 5.

37 The film *Three Friends* was adapted as a television series in 2014 for the ATV television channel. However, the series removed the Armenian character Artin Dartanyan from the story. For an article on the subject in Turkish, see: http://www.agos.com.tr/tr/yazi/8222/uc-arkadas-in-artin-i-bir-varmis-bir-yokmus (last accessed 29/09/2015).

38 This does not necessarily mean the intent and willingness to represent the Kurdish question existed in the mainstream media, or in popular films, per se. It was, however, never without problems *when* different filmmakers tackled the issue up to, and including, the early 2000s.

2. Recurring Themes and Motifs

1 Verbal hygiene, as defined by Deborah Cameron, refers to the practices "born of an urge to improve or 'clean-up' language" removing unwanted words, expressions, and influences (Cameron: 13).

2 Although the definition of minority was limited to non-Muslims, not all non-Muslim communities enjoyed such rights; smaller Christian groups, such as Assyrians, Caldeans, and Nestorians, were left out (Oran 2006: 67).

3 In both pre- and post-war Europe, specifically in Spain, Germany, and Italy, cinema was used as a tool for propaganda, and the industry was strictly regulated. Martine Danan writes that, "with regard to the foreign movies that were allowed to be imported in to these countries, governments also established guidelines about the versions that could be distributed. Dubbing was often imposed by law. Mussolini prohibited any non-dubbed version from entering his country" (Danan 1991: 611). Franco and Hitler also imposed similar rules, hence dubbing, at least in the early years of the sound film, became a practice imposed by governments in an effort to build and manipulate the nation. Mussolini's decision, in particular, is directly related to the different dialects used in different regions in Italy, and his desire to create a unified language to be used throughout the country.

4 Dubbing has also been the preferred method on state television TRT, the only television broadcaster until the early 1990s. TRT still continues to use dubbing, as opposed to subtitling.

5 Trinh T. Minh-ha claims that subtitles, in general, comply with the ideological apparatus of cinematic reproduction. According to her, "in most translated films, the subtitles usually stay on as long as they technically can—often much longer than the time needed even for a slow reader—it's because translation is conceived here as part of the operation of suture that defines the classical cinematic apparatus and the technological effort it deploys to naturalize a dominant, hierarchically unified worldview" with the aim of "protect[ing] the unity of the subject" (Trinh T. Minh-ha 1992: 208). Nornes, however, writing on different aspects and results of subtitling, partially disagrees with Trinh's analysis and asserts the importance of historical context. For Nornes, Trinh's analysis is weak because "any theorization of subtitles must be considered against its historical moment."

6 *Küba* later travelled within and outside the UK, but the spaces it occupied always resembled the neighborhood itself: an old post office in Preston, a courtroom in Southampton (many of the residents in Küba have their own experiences of courtrooms), and a deserted harbor warehouse in Antwerp. The exhibition can easily be seen as the miniature version of the community, migrating from one place to another. The non-hierarchical disorderly nature of the community can

also be seen as reflected in the layout of both the exhibition space and in the book published by *Artangel* about the exhibition. Inside the exhibition space, the television screens were scattered around the room with no particular order, and were all on at the same time, hence, neither the spatial nor the sonic experience allowed hierarchization of one story over another. Similarly, the book was designed to be an extension of the exhibition with no page numbers and no fixed order: unlike many books, this was ring bound, and the order of its pages could be changed; its size and content could be reduced

7   Liminality is a concept that comes with the baggage of postcolonial theory, as the term was used in a rather positive manner by Homi Bhabha in his *The Location of Culture* (1994). According to a dictionary of the key concepts in postcolonial studies, liminality designates an "in between space in which cultural change may occur" (Ashcroft, Griffits, and Tiffin 2007: 117). Using the stairwell as a metaphor for liminal spaces, Bhabha writes that "the stairwell as a liminal space, in-between the designations of identity, becomes the process of symbolic interaction, the connective tissue that constructs the difference between upper and lower, black and white. The hither and thither of the stairwell, the temporal movement and passage that it allows, prevents identities at either end of it from settling into primordial polarities. This interstitial passage between fixed identifications opens up the possibility of a cultural hybridity that entertains difference without an assumed or imposed hierarchy" (Bhabha 2005: 4). Although it is not my intention, in any form, to provide a critical reading of either the postcolonial theory or Bhabha, it should however be noted that the type of liminality that these films exemplify and the way it is experienced by diegetic characters does not entirely correspond to Bhabha's celebratory perception of the concept and its function in culture. More often than not, what is referred to as a liminal state throughout this study, occurs as a result of polarities rather than preventing them.

8   Although it does not take place in Istanbul, Erdem's *Jin* (2013) also deals with entrapment, this time alluding to the Kurdish armed movement, and focusing on a young woman trying to escape both armed conflict and the army. *Jin* shows a Kurdish guerrilla woman in the mountains in Eastern Turkey, almost equating her with other animals in terms of her adapting to the space around her. However, the situation changes once she is in the city, where her entrapment, both inside and outside, begins.

9   For an analysis of German/Turkish director Fatih Akın's films and his relation to *Heimat* as a "structuring absence," see Berghahn (2006).

10 See E. P. Thompson (1967) for a detailed comparison between task-oriented and industrial time.

11 This complicated relation will be discussed in more detail in relation to Egoyan's *Ararat* in Chapter 4.

12 For a detailed analysis of Frampton's (*nostalgia*) in relation to Benjamin's "dialectical image," see Rachel Moore 2006: 53–61.

3. Covering and Discovering: Non-Muslim Minorities and Film

1 For a comparative study on Turkish and Greek history textbooks see Millas (1991).

2 "Population Exchange Museum" was opened in 2011. For detailed information see: http://www.mubadelemuzesi.net/default.aspx (accessed 29/08/2015).

3 Aslı Iğsız, for example, shows that the experience of the Greek–Turkish population exchange of 1923 is rediscovered and represented in 1990s music and literature, through a close analysis of two cultural organizations: Belge Publishing and Kalan Music Productions (Iğsız 2007).

4 See Ayhan Aktar (2008).

5 Çicek Taksi/Flower Taxi (1995–2003, Erler Film), Ikinci Bahar/Second Spring (1998–2001, Erler Film and Most Production), Süper Baba/Super Dad (1993–1997, Kare Ajans Production), Ekmek Teknesi/Bread and Butter (2002–2005, Sinegraf and Pana Film production) are some of the examples.

6 *Hurdacı* is someone who sells various recycled bits and pieces on a cart; *zerzevatçı* is a mobile grocery, and *simitçi* is a street vendor selling bagel-like breads. They, along with other vendors, go around the neighborhoods, and make themselves known to the people by shouting, announcing what they sell. These vendors used to be a daily part of life, creating one of the most distinct sounds of the city. However, they have slowly started to disappear in recent years.

7 In the region, inhabitants of these mountain villages move higher up with the arrival of summer, many of them with their livestock. They then return with the arrival of autumn. Ustaoğlu also made a documentary about this seasonal migration called *Sırtlarındaki Hayat/Life on Their Shoulder* during her stay in the region.

8 For an article that compares and contrasts *Waiting for the Clouds* to *Offside*, particularly in relation to the representation of minorities and the silence surrounding their identity, see Suner (2009).

9 Adam Lowenstein makes a similar comparison in an essay in which he investigates allegory in relation to the representation of traumatic events, specifically the representation of Hiroshima in Japanese cinema. See Lowenstein (2004).

4. Representing the Armenian Genocide: *Ararat* and Beyond

1   A shorter version of this chapter was published in the *Cinema Journal*. See "Past Not-So-Perfect: *Ararat* and Its Reception in Turkey," *Cinema Journal* 54 (1) (2014): 45–64.

2   Akçam writes that although these two events appear to be local and hence differ from the massacres of 1915, they in fact served to legitimize the hatred and violence against the Armenian population. According to Akçam, "with the establishment of the Hamidiye Regiments, [...] the 'reward' mechanism for dealing with Armenians began to gain a more systematic character" (Akçam 2007: 35). Hovanissian, on the other hand, points out the differences between the massacres up to and after 1915. According to him, although there appears to be a continuum of violence against Armenians in the Ottoman Empire, "the objectives of Abdül Hamid in the 1890s were quite different from those of Young Turks in 1915." While Abdül Hamid "resorted to massacres in his futile efforts to maintain the old order," the Young Turks "perpetrated genocide to overturn the status quo and create a new order and a new frame of reference in which there was no place at all for Armenians" (Hovanissian 2004: 226).

3   According to this argument, these events are not within the limits of language and, therefore, any attempt to represent them will inevitably fail. The argument usually is put forward in relation to the representation of The Holocaust, but is also extended to traumatic experiences in general. See Cathy Caruth (1995, 1996).

4   For detailed information on the film, see Anthony Slide (2014).

5   Akın, Q&A, London Film Festival 2014.

6   Turkish–Armenian film critic Alin Tasçıyan, for instance, writes that the film shows what it really means to be deported (*tehcir*), a word preferred within the official discourse in Turkey regarding the event, hence in a sense refraining from calling it a genocide. See http://haber.star.com.tr/yazar/tehcir-kavraminin-altini-dolduran--bir-film/yazi-934458 (accessed 29/08/2015).

7   Similar to *Ararat*'s reception, the talk of Akın's "genocide" movie started prior to the film's release. However, having learned from previous cases, Akın was very careful about what was available about the film in the media; hence, even the official trailer was released only shortly before the film's première at the Venice Film Festival at the end of August. Akın gave his first interview in Turkey about the film to the Armenian newspaper *Agos* (http://www.agos.com.tr/tr/yazi/7726/otuken-dergisi-nden-agos-a-acik-tehdit) (accessed 29/08/2015). Following the interview, the ultra-nationalist publication *Ötüken* threatened both the newspaper and the director, declaring that they would permit absolutely no theater to screen the film, and noting that "they are following the situation closely with their white berets," an open threat, as the white beret has become a highly controversial

symbol in Turkey since the assassination of Hrant Dink. It is even more controversial when used to threaten *Agos*, since Dink was the editor-in-chief of the newspaper prior to his murder. He was shot dead right outside of the *Agos* building in Istanbul, in broad daylight. His killer was wearing a white beret at the time, which was later appropriated by ultra-nationalists as a symbol.

8   The term "prosthetic memory" has been coined by Alison Landsberg to describe cultural memory generated through mass culture (Landsberg 2004).

9   Egoyan explores this tension in a short film based on Samuel Beckett's *Krapp's Last Tape*. As Krapp (John Hurt) listens to his past from voice recordings, and finds a moment in which he takes refuge (the memory of a lover), he tenderly embraces the tape recorder. The tape itself provides a tactile experience and, for a moment, substitutes the loss, which is more difficult with a digital recording.

10 Clarence Ussher's book, *An American Physician in Turkey*, was first published in 1917.

11 The book, *Black Angel: The Life of Arshile Gorky*, written by Nouritza Matossian, is used in the film as the book Ani wrote.

12 I borrow this wordplay from Jale Parla (2003).

13 Marks' haptical images are different than Deleuze's haptic images. Marks' use corresponds to Deleuze's optical images and, therefore, to his "time-image": images that break sensory–motor connections, and lack causality between them.

14 According to Marc Nichanian, the airport serves as the gate of the civilized world and David as the guardian of that gate. The encounter, writes Nichanian, is "exactly like in Kafka's brief text 'Before the Law', [Raffi] encounters the guardian of the law, the civilized world. [...] Egoyan, for the first time ever, organises an encounter with the civilised world" (Nichanian 2004: 152), and it is during this encounter that the relation between truth and testimony is challenged.

15 Here my use of the word "reception" also includes the responses and reactions to the film prior to its release. Hence, I talk about the film's reception as an idea, as well as a text.

16 "Ararat Savaşı," *Milliyet*, February 27, 2002.

17 Egoyan, it is reported, did not want to screen his film as part of the competition "in order to assuage the intense controversy it was expected to arouse." See: http://tiff.net/CANADIANFILMENCYCLOPEDIA/content/films/ararat (accessed 29/08/2015). However, in Turkey it was reported that the film was rejected as part of the competition by the festival committee itself (http://www.milliyet.com.tr/ararat-cannesda-yarisma-disi-kaldi/guncel/haberdetayarsiv/25.04.2002/246207/default.htm) (accessed 29/08/2015).

18 In a press release, Alişan Satılmış, the president of the youth wing (*Ülkü Ocakları*) of the Nationalist Action Party (*Milliyetçi Hareket Partisi*), stated that "those who show the courage to screen the film should also remember that there is a price to pay for

such hostility against Turks." To read the press release in Turkish, see http://www. bozkurt.net/modules.php?name=News&file=print&sid=1905 (accessed 29/08/2015).

19 "Ararat'ın Gösterimi İptal Edildi," *Milliyet,* January 9, 2004, http://www.milliyet.com. tr/2004/01/09/guncel/gun01.html (accessed 29/08/2015).

20 In Turkey, within the dominant discourse on the subject of the Armenian genocide, the term "Armenian Lobby" is used to refer to the Armenian Diaspora, and the presumed propaganda activities by this group, which is imagined to be a homogenous entity.

21 Gündüz Aktan, "Why Cannot it Be?" *Hürriyet Daily News,* January 9, 2002. http:// www.hurriyetdailynews.com/why-can-not-it-be.aspx?pageID=438&n=why-can-not-it-be-2002-01-09 (accessed 29/08/2015). Aktan is known for his engagement with the subject. As well as his writing on the Armenian issue (most of which in line with the Republican defensive narrative per Göcek) he was the former president of ASAM (Avrasya Stratejik Araştırmalar Merkezi/Center for Eurasian Strategic Studies). Please also see endnote 29.

22 Doğan Uluç, "Ararat'a Karşı Büyük Hile," *Hürriyet,* February 24, 2002. http://www. hurriyet.com.tr/index/ArsivNews.aspx?id=56157 (accessed 29/08/2015).

23 Tufan Türenç, "Aynı Yanlışı *Ararat* İçin de Yapmayalım," *Hürriyet,* December, 29, 2001. http://webarsiv.hurriyet.com.tr/2001/12/29/68902.asp (accessed 29/08/2015).

24 Mehmet Ali Kışlalı, "*Ararat* Seyredilmeli," *Radikal,* March 7, 2002. http://www.radikal.com.tr/haber.php?haberno=31207 (accessed 29/08/2015).

25 Writing on Turkish nationalism, Tanıl Bora argues that from the 1990s onward two dynamics were at play in the shaping of Turkish nationalism in a rapidly globalizing world: "reactionary nationalistic movement," which use the "theme of national survival"; and "pro-Western nationalistic movement." Influenced by these two dynamics, Bora defines five main nationalist languages in Turkey: official nationalism (Atatürk Nationalism), Kemalist Nationalism (Ulusçuluk), liberal nationalism, Turkist radical nationalism and the recently rising nationalism in Islamism. However, rather than being mutually exclusive these five categories are interfused, "which ultimately reinforces the hegemony of nationalism." See: Tanıl Bora, (2003, 436).

26 Melih Aşık, "*Ararat* Yolda," *Milliyet,* June 23, 2001, http://www.milliyet.com.tr /2001/06/23/yazar/asik.html (accessed 29/08/2015).

27 Hasan Pulur, "*Ararat* Filmi ve Şehit Tıbbiyeliler," *Milliyet,* May 24, 2002. http://www.milliyet.com.tr/2002/05/24/yazar/pulur.html (accessed 29/08/2015).

28 Erdal Şafak, "*Ararat* Kavgası," *Sabah,* January 11, 2004. http://arsiv.sabah.com.tr/2004/01/11/yaz08-10-110-20040105.html (accessed 29/08/2015).

29 The book was published by the research centre, ASAM–ERAREN (Avrasya Stratejik Araştırmalar Merkezi-Ermeni Arastirmalari Enstitüsü/Center for Eurasian Strategic

Studies-Institute for Armenian Research). Taner Akçam describes ASAM as the propaganda center of the Turkish government, used to disseminate the official ideology of the state on the Armenian problem. ASAM changed its name in 2005 to the Centre for Research on Crimes Against Humanity (Akçam 2008: 168).

30 According to Egoyan, the shooting script was not publicly available at the time the book was written, but "somehow found its way to Turkey" (Egoyan 2004a: 898).

31 In addition to the general tone of the book that argues for Egoyan's nationalist views, the authors also explicitly state that Egoyan was "radicalized" during and after his university years, particularly after meeting his wife, Arsine Khanjian. See Laçiner and Kantarcı (2002: 51).

32 The author is so determined to prove her point that she goes as far as claiming that ASALA was active even in 2004 and killed five Turkish officers in Iraq (Karaca 2006: 30). However, the organization ceased to be active from the late 1980s.

33 Karaca does not provide any rationale for her analysis in order to prove that the film is about drug smuggling more than anything else. It is unclear how this conviction ties into her general argument, that the film is a propaganda film hostile toward Turks.

34 As I will discuss later, Ali is not the only character in the film who suffers from not being heard, but still fails to "listen." Ani, who has dedicated her life to raising awareness on the Armenian genocide, fails to hear Celia's pain, even though she is the only person who can provide closure to the issue of Celia's father's suicide.

35 Unlike the two books mentioned here, Daldal's article was published in a peer-reviewed academic journal, and provides a comprehensive and balanced discussion of the film. See Daldal (2007).

36 Öğün, Tuncay. "Tarihçiler 120 Kahraman Çocuğu Araştırıyor" *MyNet Haber*, January 23, 2008, http://www.mynet.com/haber/guncel/tarihciler-120-kahraman-cocugu-arastiriyor-386088-1 (accessed 29/08/2015).

37 This was the core of the discussion in a panel in May 2010 in Istanbul, which was organized as part of the Hrant Dink memorial workshop. Contrary to the general and self-celebratory feeling among intellectuals toward a reconciliation process, panelists argued that the liberal discourse also embeds itself as a version of the official discourse, that visibility is still a very fragile issue for Armenians. Ayda Erbal particularly criticized the apology campaign, saying that it does not qualify as an apology, since the offender does not identify himself/herself as the offender. (Erbal here is referring to the text written for the campaign.) The campaign was called "I apologise to Armenians." See http://www.ermenilerdenozurdiliyorum.com/ (accessed 29/08/2015). For a report on this particular panel discussion see http://www.armenianweekly.com/2010/08/03/gunaysu-silenced-but-resilient-a-groundbreaking-panel-discussion-in-istanbul/ (accessed 29/08/2015). For Erbal's article on the campaign see Erbal 2012.

38 Varjabedian is not referring to the text when he is talking about self-reflexivity. He is asking Egoyan himself to be self-reflexive as the "author–historian," and include his own "experiences." The film, according to Varjabedian, "does not give the viewer even a glimpse of the personal and lived experiences [of Egoyan]," and it fails to portray "the interpretation of [Egoyan's] personal experiences and autobiography with the collective memory of his communal group," i.e. diaspora Armenians.

5. The Kurdish Question in Films

1 In 2010, a year after it was mentioned by Prime Minister Recep Tayyip Erdogan, the "Kurdish extension" failed to achieve any of its main goals, since it turned a blind eye to some of the most fundamental demands from the Kurds in Turkey, such as the right to be educated in their native language. Perhaps realizing that the process cannot be one-way, the AKP government had a second attempt in 2012, this time naming it "peace process" (*barış süreci*) or "solution process" (çözüm süreci).

2 According to Mesut Yeğen, "*Amasya Protokolü*, a document signed in 1919 between the Ottoman government, in occupied Istanbul, and the representatives of ARMHC [*Anadolu ve Rumeli Mudafai Hukuk Cemiyeti*/Societies for the Defense of Rights of Anatolia and Rumelia], recognized Turks and Kurds as the two major Muslim communities living in the Ottoman land. The recognition of this 'objective fact' was supported by the acknowledgment of the Ottoman territory as the home of both Turks and Kurds. Defining Kurds as an inseparable element of the Ottoman nation, the document reiterated that the ethnic and social (cultural) rights of Kurds were to be recognized" (Yeğen 2007: 127).

3 Kurds were referred to as "mountain Turks," and there were efforts to prove that the language they spoke was in fact a version of Turkish. As late as 1980s, state-funded projects were still trying to prove the non-existence of Kurds. In 1983, a book titled *Kurmanci ve Zaza Türkçeleri Üzerine Bir Araştırma* (A Reserach on Kurmanci and Zaza Dialects of Turkish Language), was written by Professor Tuncer Gülensoy, and published by the Research Institute of Turkish Culture. The book tries to prove that *Kurmanci* and *Zaza* (two different dialects of Kurdish that are spoken by Kurds in Turkey) are in fact a variation of Turkish, without making any reference to Kurdish or Kurds.

4 Yeğen notes that until the 1960s, the preeminent other of both extreme and mainstream Turkish nationalism was non-Muslimhood (Yeğen 2007: 146).

5 Kurds organized a number of uprisings against the Turkish state until the 1930s. The state managed to keep control of the situation, although with some brutal actions taken against those who revolted. In 1934, the government introduced

"*Sevk İskan Kanunu*" (Settlement Legislation) targeted particularly at the organized Kurds, wanting to spread them all over Turkey and, therefore, break their resistance. The legislation aimed at relocating Kurds in areas populated by Turks, and Turks in areas populated by Kurds. According to Mesut Yeğen, the primary aim of the legislation was to "reshuffle the demographic composition of Anatolia according to ethnic measurements" (Yeğen 2009a: 92).

6 The report is available from: http://www.tbmm.gov.tr/develop/owa/Tutanak_B_ SD.birlesim_ baslangic?P4=377&P5=B&PAGE1=1&PAGE2=102 (accessed 29/08/2015). This report is important because it also signifies a change in attitude toward the reality of the internally displaced people in Turkey. Although there are a number of reports by human rights organizations on people who were forced to leave their villages, as well as villages that were burned down in order to deprive PKK of the logistic support that these villagers allegedly provided to PKK, the reality of internally displaced people was denied to a large extent by the official discourse prior to this report.

7 Turner defines social dramas as "units of a harmonic or disharmonic process, arising in conflict situations" (Turner 1974: 37). Conflict, according to Turner, brings "fundamental aspects of society" into prominence, causing individuals to take sides "in terms of deeply entrenched moral imperatives and constraints" (Turner 1974: 35). He identifies four main phases of social dramas. The first phase is the "breach of regular, norm governed social relations," followed by the "crisis," which creates conflicting or antagonistic parties. Each public crisis has "liminal characteristics, since it is a threshold between more or less stable phases of the social process" (Turner 1974: 39). Crisis is followed by the third phase, "redressive action," where redressive mechanisms are brought into operation. "When redress fails there is usually regression to crisis" (Turner 1974: 41); if it succeeds, it is followed by the "reintegration" phase.

8 The history of Kurdish political parties in Turkey is a complicated one, with continual bans and reformations with different names. DEHAP (*Demokratik Halk Partisi*/Democratic People's Party) was a pro-Kurdish political party formed as a continuation of HADEP (*Halkın Demokrasi Partisi*/People's Democratic Party) after it was banned. DTO (Democratic Society Party) was formed later, only to be banned from political life in December 2009. The decision to ban this party from political life is based on a variation of the same fundamental objection: its relations to the PKK. The party continued its political life as BDP (*Barış ve Demokrasi Partisi*/Peace and Democracy Party), and, in 2012, formed HDP (*Halkların Demokratik Partisi*/People's Democratic Party).

9 Mehmet Uzun, probably the most prominent literary figure in the Kurdish language, lived in exile for twenty years, finally returning to Turkey in 2007. He died in Diyarbakır in 2008.

10 The term "easterner" is loaded with meaning, not only referring to eastern Turkey, where the Kurdish population lived for centuries, but also marking the rest of the country as western, hence modern, while also denying the Kurds their identity.

11 Although *Yol* is translated as *The Way*, in Turkish the word "yol" is used interchangeably to mean both "the way"/"the road" and "the journey" itself.

12 *Güneşi Gördüm/I Saw the Sun* was the fourth most successful film of 2009, and one of the most successful films of all time in Turkey based on box-office returns.

13 This on its own implies a significant attitude change in Turkey: Bezar was born in Turkey, but grew up in Germany, and his film is entirely in Kurdish. Nevertheless, it was selected to compete in the "national competition." Similarly, in 2010, Mustafa Gündoğan, the director of the Kurdish Film Festival in London, was invited by the curators of *If Istanbul* (a festival aimed at showcasing independent films) to put together a selection of Kurdish films. The special screenings were called "The Opening," referring to the government's *Kürt Açılımı* (Kurdish Opening).

14 JİTEM stands for *Jandarma İstihbarat ve Terörle Mücadele* (Gendarmerie Intelligence and Counter-Terror Service). Between 1990 and 1994, a large number of Kurdish opinion leaders were assassinated by "unknown actors" (*faili meçhul*), and according to Martin van Bruinessen, many of these killings were carried out by "persons acting on the instructions of or in cooperation with the police, or in particular, the intelligence service of the gendarmerie, JITEM" (van Bruinessen, 1996: 21).

15 Growing up in Turkey in the 1980s, I remember being exposed to this image often as it was framed and hung in many places, including my grandparents' house. It remains a mystery to me why a crying child became a poster boy for people in Turkey, hence both Belge's and Gürbilek's analysis provide a plausible explanation.

16 In this sense, the scene is reminiscent of the 2001 art installation for the Venice Biennale by Santiago Sierra, who dyed 133 dark-haired immigrants' hair to blond. Normally rendered invisible on the streets, Sierra makes them uncomfortably visible in this otherwise "glamorous" city, Venice. I bring in Sierra here as an example to highlight the similar experiences shared by otherwise unrelated communities.

17 Mehmet's surname "Kara" means "black" in Turkish.

18 As part of the *South-Eastern Anatolia Project*'s water resources programme (which came to be known as GAP in Turkey), it was intended to help improve the socio-economic conditions of the region. Twenty-two dams were to be built in the region, some of which resulted in scenes similar to that in the final scene of the film, flooding the villages nearby. The project has been criticized for reducing the issue to a socio-economic problem, and disregarding its ethno-political nature. A similar image (a village underwater) is also used by one of the most celebrated films in the

history of cinema in Turkey, *Eşkıya/Bandit* (Yavuz Turgul, 1996). The film, which is usually regarded as the first of the new Turkish cinema, begins with the protagonist (Şener Şen) being released from prison after thirty years, and finding his entire village underwater.

19 Although it was made in 2001, the film informs the audience through radio news that the story takes place in 1998 as the 75th anniversary of the republic indicates. The date is significant because it suggests that the war is still ongoing and that the legislation that lifts the ban on speaking Kurdish is not in place yet.

20 Unless noted otherwise, statements made by the director himself are quoted from the interview that I conducted with the director in March 2009, in Istanbul.

21 Saturday Mothers' weekly sit-ins stopped due to continuous police intimidation. They resumed their meetings in 2009.

22 Most of these directors are involved partly or entirely in the translation process, specifically with the English translations. The director of *Min Dit*, Miraz Bezar, also told me that he was involved in the translation process. However, Bezar himself thinks that it is an unnecessary involvement, and he prefers not to be involved.

23 Although the name of the organization is never disclosed, it is highly likely that Salem had the PKK in mind.

24 Focusing on the chapter of the book called "Cinema Grande," in which the characters create a world of their own in an abandoned cinema, Gürle claims that cinema is an ideal place "for creating replicas that shatter the ground of what claims to be the original" (Gürle 2007: 136). For her, the use of cinema as a locus for illusion in the book may be read as the author's way of saying that "the only way to deal with the rhetoric of illusion generated and disseminated by the totalizing system is to create a counter-illusion, which manifests itself in the form of art" (Gürle 2007: 136).

25 Although not as a device to create laughter, Karabey in *Gitmek* also briefly shows a similar inscription, this time on the wall facing the Iranian border which reads "Turkish Republic is a secular state."

26 Ciwan Haco is a well-known Kurdish singer.

27 Yılmaz Özdil reads this as an attempt to invent a mixed cultural space by juxtaposing the rural and the domestic (Özdil: 230).

Coda: *Once Upon a Time in Anatolia*

1 A mukhtar is the elected head of a village or a neighborhood.

2 For an engaging article written in Turkish on autopsy as spectacle and its use in films, as well as an analysis of the autopsy sequence in this film see Erdem (2012).

3 Halaçoğlu also mentions the Decree of December 1918, which allowed Armenians who wished to come back and reclaim their properties to return. According to Halaçoğlu, this is yet more proof that the aim was never to clear Anatolia of Armenians, but rather to temporarily relocate them. Yet, this on its own does not say anything about the initial act.

4 I would like to thank Professor Chris Berry for pointing out the possible connection to the mass graves in Turkey. The interactive map is avaliable on IHD's website: http://www.ihddiyarbakir.org/Map.aspx (accessed 29/08/2015).

Bibliography

Abisel, Nilgün. *Türk Sineması Üzerine Yazılar* [*Writings on Turkish Cinema*]. Ankara: Phoenix, 2005.

Ahıska, Meltem. "Occidentalism: The Historical Fantasy of the Modern." *South Atlantic Quarterly*, 102: 2–3 (2003): 351–79.

Ahıska, Meltem. *Radyonun Sihirli Kapısı: Garbiyatçılık ve Politik Öznellik* [*Occidentalism in Turkey: Questions of Modernity and National Identity in Turkish Radio Broadcasting*]. İstanbul: Metis, 2005.

Ahıska, Meltem. *Occidentalism in Turkey: Questions of Modernity and National Identity in Turkish Radio Broadcasting*. London: I. B Tauris, 2010.

Ahmad, Feroz. *The Making of Modern Turkey*. London: Routledge, 2005.

Akçam, Taner. "Türk Ulusal Kimliği Üzerine Bazı Tezler" ["Some Theses on Turkish National Identity"]. In *Milliyetçilik* [*Nationalism*]. Edited by Tanil Bora and Murat Gultekingil. İstanbul: İletisim, 2003: 53–62.

Akçam, Taner. *A Shameful Act: The Armenian Genocide and the Question of Turkish Responsibility*. Translated by Paul Bessemer. London: Constable, 2007.

Akçam, Taner. *Ermeni Meselesi Hallolunmuştur: Osmanlı Belgelerine Göre Savaş Yıllarında Ermenilere Yönelik Politikalar*. Istanbul: İletişim Yayınları, 2008.

Aktar, Ayhan. *Varlık Vergisi ve Türkleştirme Politikaları* [*The Capital Tax and the Turkifikation Policies*]. İstanbul: İletişim, 2008.

Aktar, Rıdvan, and Hülya Demir. *İstanbul'un Son Sürgünleri* [*The Last Exiles of Istanbul*]. İstanbul: İletişim, 1994.

Alper, Özcan. "Bu Film Benim Vicdan Borcumdu" ["I Owed This Film to My Conscience"]. Interview by Gülşen Işeri. *Birgün*, June 11, 2008.

Altınay, Ayşe Gül. "In Search of Silenced Grandparents: Ottoman Armenian Survivors and their (Muslim) Grandchildren." In *The Armenian Genocide, Turkey and Europe*, edited by Hans-Lukas Kieser and Elmar Plozza. Zürich: Chronos, November 2006: 117–32.

Altman, Janet Gurkin. *Epistolary Approaches to a Form*. Columbus: Ohio State University Press, 1982.

Appadurai, Arjun. *Modernity at Large: Cultural Dimensions of Globalization*. Minneapolis: University of Minnesota Press, 1996.

Appadurai, Arjun. *Fear of Small Numbers*. Durham, NC: Duke University Press, 2006.

Arslan, Savaş. *Cinema in Turkey: A New Critical History*. Oxford: Oxford University Press, 2011.

Arslan, Umut Tümay. *Mazi Kabrinin Hortlakları* [*Specters of Grave Called Past*]. İstanbul: Metis, 2010.

Arslan, Umut Tümay. "Bozkirdaki Labirent" ["The Labyrinth in the Steppes"]. In *Bir Kapidan Gireceksin* [*You'll Be Entering Through a Door*]. Edited by Umut T. Arslan. İstanbul: Metis, 2012: 193–218.

Aslan, Senem. "Citizen Speak Turkish!: A Nation in the Making." *Nationalism and Ethnic Politics*, 13, no. 2 (2007): 245–72.

Ashcroft, Bill, Garret Griffiths, and Helen Tiffin. *Post-Colonial Studies: The Key Concepts*. New York: Routledge, 2007.

Atakav, Eyem. *Women and Turkish Cinema: Gender Politics, Cultural Identity, and Representation*. New York: Routledge, 2013.

Aytuğ, Yüksel. "Gel de Elin Alman'ına Anlat" ["Explain this to a Foreigner"]. *Sabah*, October 23, 2004. http://www.sabah.com.tr/yazarlar/gunaydin/aytug/2004/10/23/gel_de_elin_alman_ina_anlat (accessed 29/08/2015).

Aytürk, İlker. "Turkish Linguists Against the West: The Origins of Linguistic Nationalism in Atatürk's Turkey." *Middle Eastern Studies*, 40, no. 6 (2004): 1–25.

Bachelard, Gaston. *The Poetics of Space*. Translated by Maria Jolas. Boston: Beacon Press, 1994.

Bakhtin, Mikhail. *Rabelais and His World*. Translated by Hélène Iswolsky. Bloomington: Indiana University Press, 1984.

Bakhtin, Mikhail. *The Dialogic Imagination: Four Essays*. Translated by Caryl Emerson and Michael Holquist. Texas: University of Texas Press, 2008 [1981]: 3–40.

Bakhtin, Mikhail, and V. N. Voloshinov. *Marxism and the Philosophy of Language*. Translated by Ladislav Metejka and I. R. Titunik. Cambridge, MA: Harvard University Press, 1986.

Bal, Mieke. *Travelling Concepts in the Humanities*. Toronto: University of Toronto Press, 2002.

Bali, N. Rıfat. "Foreword: *Vatandaş Türkçe Konuş!*" In *Vatandaş Türkçe Konuş* [*Citizen Speak Turkish*] by Avram Galanti. Ankara: Kebikeç, 2000.

Bali, N. Rıfat. *The "Varlık Vergisi" Affair: A Study of its Legacy*. İstanbul: İsis Press, 2005.

Barthes, Roland. "Rhetoric of the Image." In *Image, Music, Text*. Edited and Translated by Stephen Heath. London: Fontana Press, 1977: 32–51.

Barthes, Roland. *Camera Lucida*. Translated by Richard Howard. London: Vintage, 2000.

Bayraktar, Deniz, ed. *Cinema and Politics: Turkish Cinema and The New Europe*. Newcastle: Cambridge Scholars Publishing, 2009.

Bayraktar, Deniz, and Murat Akser, eds. *New Cinema, New Media: Reinventing Turkish Cinema*. Newcastle: Cambridge Scholars Publishing, 2014.

Bazin, Andre. "The Ontology of the Photographic Image." In *What is Cinema: Volume I*. Edited and Translated by Hugh Gray. California: University of California Press, 1967: 9–16.

Bellour, Raymond. "The Pensive Spectator." *The Cinematic*. Edited by David Campany, 119–23. Translated by Lynne Kirby. London: Whitechapel and MIT Press, 2007.

Benjamin, Walter. "Little History of Photography." In *Selected Writings 2, Part 2 1931–1933*. Edited by Michael W. Jennings et. al. Translated by Emund Jephcott and Kingsles Shorter et. al. Cambridge: Harvard University Press, 1999: 507–30.

Benjamin, Walter. *The Arcades Project*. Translated by H. Eiland and K. McLaughlin. Cambridge, MA: Harvard University Press, 2002.

Benjamin, Walter. *Illuminations*. Translated by Harry Zohn. London: Pimlico, 2007.

Berghahn, Daniela. "No Place Like Home?: Or Impossible Homecomings in the Films of Fatih Akin." *New Cinemas*, 4, no. 3 (2006): 141–57.

Berghahn, Daniela. "From Turkish Greengrocer to Drag Queen: Reassessing Patriarchy in Recent Turkish German Coming-of-age Films." *New Cinemas*, 7, no. 1 (2009): 55–69.

Berghahn, Daniela, and Claudia Sternberg. "Locating Migrant and Diasporic Cinema in Contemporary Europe." In *European Cinema in Motion: Migrant and Diasporic Film in Contemporary Europe*. Edited by Daniela Berghahn and Claudia Sternberg. London: Palgrave Macmillan, 2010: 12–49.

Berry, Chris, and Mary Farquhar. *China on Screen*. New York: Columbia University Press, 2006.

Bezar, Miraz. "Director Miraz Bezar Wants to Restrain Violence With His Film." Interview by N. Özbudak and M. Gökçe. *Today's Zaman*, April 11, 2010.

Bezar, Miraz. E-mail interview. April 2010.

Bhabha, Homi. *Location of Culture*. New York: Routledge, 2005.

Birinci Türk Tarih Kongresi [*The First Turkish History Conference*] Ankara: T. C. Maarif Vekaleti, 1933.

Bora, Tanıl. "Nationalist Discourses in Turkey." *South Atlantic Quarterly*, 102: 2/3 (2003): 433–51.

Bourdieu, Pierre. *Language and Symbolic Power*. Translated by G. Raymond and M. Adamson. Cambridge: Polity Press, 2005.

Boym, Svetlana. *The Future of Nostalgia*. New York: Basic Books, 2001.

Brown, Wendy. *Edgework*, New Jersey: Princeton: 2005.

Bruinessen, Martin van. "Forced Evacuations and Destruction of Villages in Dersim (Tunceli) and Western Bingol" (1995). http://www.let.uu.nl/~martin.vanbruinessen/personal /publications/Forced_evacuations.pdf (accessed 29/08/2015).

Bruinessen, Martin van. "Turkey's Death Squads." *Middle East Report*, 199 (1996): 20–3.

Cameron, Deborah. *Verbal Hygiene*. London: Routledge, 2003.

Caruth, Cathy, ed. *Trauma: Explorations in Memory*. Baltimore: The Johns Hopkins University Press, 1995.

Caruth, Cathy. *Unclaimed Experience: Trauma, Narrative, and History*. Baltimore: The Johns Hopkins University Press, 1996.

Çelik, Hüseyin. "Kilisenin Onarımı Ararat'a En Güzel Yanıt Olur" ["The Best Answer to *Ararat* is to Repair the Church"]. *Hürriyet*, January 17, 2002. http://hurarsiv. hurriyet.com.tr/goster/haber.aspx?id=48880 (accessed 29/08/2015).

Chanan, Michael. *The Politics of Documentary*. London: BFI Publishing, 2007.

Daldal, Aslı. "*Ararat* and the Politics of 'Preserving' Denial." *Patterns of Prejudice*, 41, no. 5 (2007): 407–34.

Danan, Matine. "Dubbing as an Expression of Nationalism." *Meta: Translator's Journal*, 36, no. 4 (1991): 606–14.

Deleuze, Gilles. *Cinema 2: The Time-Image*. Translated by Hugh Tomlinson and Robert Galeta. London: The Athlone Press, 2000.

Derrida, Jacques. *Speech and Phenomena and Other Essays on Husserl's Theory of Signs*. Translated by Newton Garver. Evanston: Northwestern University Press, 1973.

Derrida, Jacques. *Spectres of Marx: The State of the Debt, the Work of Mourning and the New International*. Translated by Peggy Kamuf. London: Routledge, 1994.

Dink, Hrant. *İki Yakın Halk, İki Uzak Komşu* [*Two Close People, Two Far Neighbours*]. İstanbul: Uluslararası Hant Dink Vakfı Yayınları, 2008.

Doanne, Mary Ann. *The Emergence of Cinematic Time*. Cambridge, MA: Harvard University Press, 2002.

Dönmez-Colin, Gönül. *Turkish Cinema: Identity, Distance and Belonging*. London: Reaktion, 2008.

Dönmez-Colin, Gönül. *The Routledge Dictionary of Turkish Cinema*. New York: Routledge, 2013.

Ellis, John. "What Are We Expected to Feel? Witness, Textuality and the Audiovisual." *Screen*, 50, no. 1 (2009): 67–76.

Egoyan, Atom. "The Accented Style of the Independent Transnational Cinema: A Conversation with Atom Egoyan" (interview by Hamid Naficy). In *Cultural Producers in Perilous States: Editing Events, Documenting Change*. Edited by George E. Marcus. Chicago: University of Chicago Press, 1997: 179–231.

Egoyan, Atom. "In Other Words: Poetic Licence and the Incarnation of History." *University of Toronto Quarterly*, 73, no. 3 (2004a): 886–905.

Egoyan, Atom. "Interview with Peter Harcourt." In *Film Voices*. Edited by Gerald Duchovnay. New York: State University of New York Press, 2004b: 215–24.

Egoyan, Atom. "Ripple Effects: Atom Egoyan Speaks with Monique Tschofen." In *Image and Territory: Essays on Atom Egoyan*. Edited by Monique Tschofen and Jenifer Burwell, 343–57. Ontario: Wilfrid Laurier University Press, 2007.

Egoyan, Atom. "The Senses and Substitution: A Conversation with Atom Egoyan" (interview with Emma Wilson). In *Paragraph*, 31, no. 2 (2008): 252–62.

Erbal, Ayda. "Mea Cuplas, Negotiations, Apologias" in *Reconciliation, Civil Society, and the Politics of Memory: Transnational Initiatives in the 20th and 21st Century*. Edited by Birgit Schewelling, 51–97. Bielefeld: Transcript Verlag, 2013.

Erdem, Tuna. "Anatomi Tiyatrolarından Sinemaya Bir Seyirlik Olarak Otopsi" ["From Anatomical Theatre to Cinema: Autopsy as a Spectacle"]. In *Ölüm Sana Mekan* [*Death, Art, Space*]. Edited by Gevher Gökçe Acar, 313–148. Istanbul: DAKAM, 2012.

Erdoğan, Nezih. "*Eşkıya/The Bandit, The Cinema of North Africa and the Middle East.* Edited by Gönül Dönmez-Colin. London: Wallflower, 2007: 181–90.

Erdoğan, Nezih, and Deniz Göktürk. "Turkish Cinema." In *Companion Encyclopedia of Middle Eastern and North African Film*. Edited by Oliver Leaman: London: Routledge, 2001: 553–73.

Ezra, Elizabeth, and Terry Rowden. "General Introduction: What is Transnational Cinema?" In *Transnational Cinema: The Film Reader*. Edited by E. Elizabeth and T. Rowden. London: Routledge, 2006: 1–12.

Feinstein, Stephen. "Art, Memory and the Armenian Genocide." http://www.chgs.umn.edu/histories/turkishArmenian/atrpArtMemory.pdf (accessed 29/08/2015).

Galanti Avram. *Vatandaş Türkçe Konuş!* [*Citizen Speak Turkish*]. Ankara: Kebikeç, 2000.

Gambetti, Zeynep. "The Conflictual (Trans)formation of the Public Sphere in Urban Space: The Case of Diyarbakir." *New Perspectives on Turkey*, Spring 32, (2005): 43–71.

Gennep, Arnold van. *The Rites of Passage*. Translated by Monika B. Vizedom and Gabrielle L. Caffe. London: Routledge, 1960.

Göçek, Fatma Müge. "Reconstructing the Turkish Historiography on the Armenian Massacres and Deaths of 1915." In *Confronting the Armenian Genocide: Looking Backward, Moving Forward*. Edited by Richard G. Hovannisian. New Jersey: Transaction Publishers, 2003: 209–30.

Gordon, F. Avery. *Ghostly Matters: Haunting and the Sociological Imagination*. Minneapolis: University of Minnesota Press, 2008.

Grainge, Paul., ed. *Memory and Popular Film*. Manchester: Manchester University Press, 2003.

Gülensoy, Tuncer. *Kurmanci ve Zaza Türkçeleri Üzerine Bir İnceleme* [*An Analysis of Kurmanci and Zaza Turkish*]. Ankara: Türk Kültürünü Araştırma Enstitüsü, 1983.

Günalp, Haldun. "Modernization Policies and Islamist Politics in Turkey." In *Rethinking Modernity and National Identity in Turkey*. Edited by Sibel Bozdoğan and Reşat Kasaba. Seattle: University of Washington Press, 1997: 52–63.

Gündoğdu, Mustafa. Personal Interview. February 2010.

Gunning, Tom. "What Is the Point of an Index? Or Faking Photographs." *Nordicom Review*, 1–2 (2004): 39–49.

Gürata, Ahmet. "Imitation of Life: Cross-Cultural Reception and Remakes in Turkish Cinema." Unpublished Dissertation. University Of London, 2002.

Gürbilek, Nurdan. *Kötü Çocuk Türk* [*Turk the Naughty Child*], İstanbul: Metis, 2004.

Gürbilek, Nurdan. *Vitrinde Yaşamak: 1980' lerin Kültürel İklimi* [*Living in a Window Display: Cultural Climate in the 1980s*]. İstanbul: Metis, 2007.

Gürle, Meltem. "Cinema Grande and the Rhetoric of Illusion in Uyurkulak's Har." *New Perspectives on Turkey*, 36 (2007): 125–44.

Guttstadt, Corry. *Turkey, the Jews and the Holocaust*. Cambridge: Cambridge University Press, 2009.

Hacettepe Üniversitesi, Nüfus Etüdleri Enstitüsü. *Türkiye Göç ve Yerinden Olmuş Nüfus Araştırması* [*Immigration and Displaced Populations in Turkey*]. Ankara: 2006.

Halacoğlu, Yusuf. *Sürgünden Soykırıma Ermeni İddiaları* [*Armenian Claims From Exile to Genocide*]. İstanbul: Babiali Kültür Yayıncılığı, 2006.

Higson, Andrew. "The Concept of National Cinema." *Screen*, 30, no. 4. (1989): 36–46.

Higson, Andrew. "The Limiting Imagination of National Cinema." In *Cinema and Nation*. Edited by Mete Hjort and Scott Mackenzie. London: Routledge, 2000.

Hirsch, Joshua. *After Image: Film, Trauma, and the Holocaust*. Philadelphia: Temple University Press, 2004.

Hirschon, Renée. "Unmixing Peoples in the Aegean Region." In *Crossing the Aegean: an Appraisal of the 1923 Compulsory Population Exchange*. Edited by Renée Hirschon. New York: Berghahn Books, 2006: 3–12.

Hodgkin, Katharine, and Susannah Radstone. "Introduction: Contested Pasts." In *Contested Pasts: The Politics of Memory*. Edited by Katharine Hodgkin and Susannah Radstone. New York: Routledge, 2003: 1–21.

Hovanissian, Richard, ed. "The Armenian Question in the Ottoman Empire 1876 to 1914." In *The Armenian People from Ancient to Modern Times Vol II*. New York: St. Martin's Press, 2004.

Huyssen, Andreas. *Twilight Memories: Marking Time in a Culture of Amnesia*. London: Routledge, 1995.

Huyssen, Andreas. *Present Pasts: Urban Palimpsests and the Politics of Memory*. Stanford: Stanford University Press, 2003.

Huyssen, Andreas. "Nostalgia for Ruins." *Grey Room*. Spring, no. 23 (2006): 6–21.

Jones, Jonathan. "The Artist and His Mother, Arshile Gorky." http://www.guardian.co.uk/culture/2002/mar/30/art (accessed 29/08/2015).

Iğsız, Aslı. "Polyphony and Geographic Kinship in Anatolia: Framing the Turkish–Greek Compulsory Population Exchange." In *The Politics of Public Memory in Turkey*. Edited by Esra Özyürek. New York: Syracuse University Press, 2007: 162–87.

Kadıoğlu, Ayşe. "Denationalisation of Citizenship? The Turkish Experience." *Citizenship Studies*, 1, no. 3 (2007): 283–99.

Karabey, Hüseyin. Personal Interview. March 2009

Karaca, Birsen. *Sozde Ermeni Soykirimi Projesi: Toplumsal Bellek ve Sinema* [*Alleged Armenian Genocide Project: Social Memory and Cinema*]. İstanbul: Say, 2006.

Karanfil, Gokcen, and Serkan Savk, eds. *Imaginaries Out of Place: Cinema, Transnationalities and Turkey*. Newcastle: Cambridge Scholars Publishing, 2013.

Kasaba, Reşat. "Kemalist Certainties and Modern Ambiguities." In *Rethinking Modernity and National Identity in Turkey*. Edited by Sibel Bozdoğan and Reşat Kasaba. Seattle: University of Washington Press, 1997: 15–36.

Kentel, Ferhat, Ahıska, Meltem; Genç, Fırat, et. al. *Milletin Bölünmez Bütünlüğü: Demokratikleşme Sürecinde Parçalayan Milliyetcilik(ler)*. İstanbul: TESEV Yayınlari, 2007.

Keyder, Çağlar. "Whither the Project of Modernity?" In *Rethinking Modernity and National Identity in Turkey*. Edited by Sibel Bozdoğan and Reşat Kasaba. Seattle: University of Washington Press, 1997: 37–51.

Keyder, Çağlar. "The Setting." In *Istanbul: Between the Global and the Local*. Edited by Çaglar Keyder. İstanbul: Rowman & Littlefield, 1999: 3–28.

Keyder, Çağlar. "The Consequences of the Exchange of Populations for Turkey." In *Crossing the Aegean: An Appraisal of the 1923 Compulsory Population Exchange*. Edited by Renée Hirschon. New York: Berghahn Books, 2006: 39–52.

Köker, Eser, and Ülkü Doğanay. *Irkçı Değilim Ama: Yazılı Basında Irkçı-Ayrımcı Söylemler [I'm Not Racist But: Racist Discourse in the Print Media]*. Ankara: IHOP Yayınları, 2011.

Kolluoğlu-Kırlı, Biray. "The Play of Memory, Counter-Memory: Building Izmir on Smyrna's Ashes." *New Perspectives on Turkey* 26, (2002): 1–28.

Kolluoğlu-Kırlı, Biray. "Forgetting the Smyrna Fire." *History Workshop Journal*, 60 (2005): 25–44.

Konstantarakos, Myrto. "Introduction." In *Spaces in European Cinema*. Edited by Konstantarakos, Myrto. London: Intellect, 2000: 1–7.

Kristen, Miyase, and Nezih Erdogan, eds. *Shifting Landscapes: Film and Media in European Context*. Newcastle: Cambridge Scholars Publishing, 2008.

Lacan, Jacques. *The Four Fundamental Concepts of Psychoanalysis*. Edited by Jacques-Alain Miller. Translated by Alan Sheridan. New York: Norton, 1977.

Laciner, Sedat, and Kantarci Senol. *Ararat: Sanatsal Ermeni Propagandasi [Ararat: An Artistic Armenian Propaganda]*. Ankara: ASAM, 2002.

Landsberg, Alison. *Prosthetic Memory: The Transformation of American Culture in the Age of Mass Culture*. New York: Columbia University Press, 2004.

Landy, Marcia, ed. *The Historical Film: History and Memory in Media*. New Brunswick: Rutgers University Press. 2000.

Lowenstein, Adam. "Allegorising Hiroshima: Shindo Kaneto's Onibaba as Trauma Text." In *Trauma and Cinema: Cross-Cultural Explorations*. Edited by E. Ann Kaplan and Ban Wang. Hong Kong: Hong Kong University Press, 2004: 145–61.

Mahçupyan, Etyen. "*Güz Sancısı* Casts Light on Dark Chapter of Turkish Past." *Today's Zaman*, February 21, 2009.

Markovitz, Jonathan. "*Ararat* and Collective Memories of the Armenian Genocide." *Holocaust and Genocide Studies*, 20, no. 2 (2006): 235–55.

Marks, Laura. *The Skin of the Film: Intercultural Cinema, Embodiment and the Senses.* Durham, NC: Duke University Press, 2000.

Meeker, E. Michael. "Once There Was, Once There Wasn't: National Monuments and Interpersonal Exchange." In *Rethinking Modernity and National Identity in Turkey.* Edited by Sibel Bozdogan and Resat Kasaba. Seattle: University of Washington Press, 1997, 157–91.

Millas, Hercules. "History Textbooks in Greece and Turkey." *History Workshop Journal,* 31 (1991): 21–33.

Millas, Hercules. "The Exchange of Populations in Turkish Literature: Undertone of Texts." In *Crossing the Aegean: an Appraisal of the 1923 Compulsory Population Exchange.* Edited by Renée Hirschon. New York: Berghahn Books, 2006: 221–33.

Moore, Rachel. *Hollis Frampton (Nostalgia).* London: Afterall Books, 2006.

Mulvey, Laura. *Death 24x a Second: Stillness and the Moving Image.* London: Reaktion Books, 2006.

Mutlu, Dilek Kaya. "The Russian Monument at Ayastefanos (San Stefano): Between Defeat and Revenge, Remembering and Forgetting." *Middle Eastern Studies,* 43, no. 1 (2007): 75–86.

Mutlu, Dilek Kaya. "Between Tradition and Modernity: Yeşilcam Melodrama, its Stars and Their Audiences." *Middle Eastern Studies,* 46, no. 3 (2010): 417–31.

Naficy, Hamid. *An Accented Cinema: Exilic and Diasporic Filmmaking.* Princeton: Princeton University Press, 2001.

Neyzi, Leyla. "Gülümser's Story: Life History Narratives, Memory and Belonging in Turkey." *New Perspectives on Turkey,* 20 (1999): 1–26.

Neyzi, Leyla. *Ben Kimim: Türkiye'de Sözlü Tarih, Kimlik ve Öznellik.* İstanbul: İletisim, 2007.

Neyzi, Leyla. "Remembering Smyrna/Izmir Shared History Shared Trauma." *History and Memory,* 20: 2 (2008): 106–27.

Nichanian, Marc. "Representation and Historicity." *Armenian Review,* 49, no. 1–4 (2004): 149–61.

Nora, Pierre. *Realms of Memory: The Construction of the French Past.* New York: Columbia University Press, 1996.

Nornes, Abé Mark. "For an Abusive Subtitling." *Film Quarterly,* 52, no. 3 (1999): 17–34.

Ökte, Faik. *The Tragedy of the Turkish Capital Tax.* Translated by Geoffrey Cox. London: Croom Helm, 1987.

Ökten, Nazlı. "An Endless Death and an Eternal Mourning." In *The Politics of Public Memory in Turkey.* Edited by Esra Özyürek. New York: Syracuse University Press, 2007: 95–113.

Olick, K. Jeffrey. "Memory and the Nation: Continuities, Conflicts, and Transformations." *Social Science History,* Winter, vol. 22, no. 4. (1998): 377–87.

Olick, K. Jeffrey. *The Politics of Regret: On Collective Memory and Historical Responsibility.* New York: Routledge, 2007.

Oran, Baskın. *Türkiye'de Azınlıklar: Kavramlar, Teori, Lozan, İç Mevzuat, İçtihat Uygulama* [*Minorities in Turkey: Concepts, Theory, Lausanne, Regulation and Jurisprudence*]. İstanbul: İletisim, 2006.

Oran, Baskın. "The Minority Concept and Rights in Turkey: The Lausanne Peace Treaty and Current Issues." In *Human Rights in Turkey*. Edited by Zehra Kabasakal Arat. Philadelphia: University of Pennsylvania, 2007: 35–56.

Özbek, Meral. "Arabesk Culture: A Case of Modernization and Popular Identity." In *Rethinking Modernity and National Identity in Turkey*. Edited by Sibel Bozdoğan and Reşat Kasaba. Seattle: University of Washington Press, 1997: 211–32.

Özdil, Yilmaz. "Kürt Sinemasında Kürdistan Manzarasının İnşaası: *Dol* Filmi" ["Kurdish Cinema and Construction of Kurdish Scenery: *Dol*," *Kürt Sineması: Yurtsuzluk, Sınır ve Ölüm* [*Kurdish Cinema: Displacement, Border and Death*]. Edited by Müjde Arslan. İstanbul: Agora Kitaplığı, 2009: 215–40.

Özkırımlı, Umut, and A. Spyros Sofos. *Tormented by History*. London: Hurst and Company, 2008.

Özyürek, Esra. "Introduction." In *The Politics of Public Memory in Turkey*. Edited by Esra Özyürek. New York: Syracuse University Press, 2007: 1–15.

Parla, Jale. "Car Narratives: A Subgenre in Turkish Novel Writing." *South Atlantic Quarterly*, 102, (2/3) (2003): 535–50.

Parla, Taha. "Mercantile Militarism." *New Perspectives on Turkey*, Fall 19 (1998): 29–52.

Parla, Taha, and Andrew Davison. *Corporatist Ideology in Kemalist Turkey*. New York: Syracuse University Press, 2004.

Pasolini, Pier Paolo. "The Cinema of Poetry." In *Movies and Methods Vol. 1*. Edited by Bill Nichols. Translated by Marianne de Vettimo and Jacques Bontemps. Berkeley: University of California Press, 1976: 542–58.

Pence, Jeffrey. "Postcinema/Postmemory." In *Memory and Popular Film*. Edited by Paul Grainge. Manchester: Manchester University Press, 2003: 237–55.

Ricoeur, Paul. *Memory, History, Forgetting*. Translated by Kathleen Blamey and David Pellauer. Chicago: The University of Chicago Press, 2004a.

Ricoeur, Paul. "Imagination, Testimony and Trust." In *On Paul Ricoeur: The Owl of Minerva*. Edited by Richard Kearney. Aldershot: Ashgate Publishing, 2004b: 151–6.

Ritivoi, Andreea Deciu. *Yesterday's Self: Nostalgia and the Immigrant Identity*. Oxford: Rowman and Littlefield Publishers, 2002.

Rodowick, N. David. *Gilles Deleuze's Time Machine*. Durham, NC: Duke University Press, 2003.

Rollet, Sylvia. "Discontinuous Transmission." *Armenian Review*, 49 (1–4) (2004): 61–83.

Rosenstone, Robert. *Visions of the Past: The Challenge of Film to Our Idea of History*. Cambridge, MA: Harvard University Press, 1996.

Sakallioğlu, Ümit Cizre. "The Anatomy of Turkish Military's Political Autonomy." *Comparative Politics*, 29 (1997): 151–66.

Saleem, Hiner. "Sessizlik Kelimelerden Çok Daha Fazlasını Anlatır." In *Kürt Sinemasi: Yurtsuzluk, Sınır ve Ölüm*. Edited by Müjde Arslan. İstanbul: Agora, 2009: 241–44.

Sancar, Mithat. *Geçmişle Hesaplaşma: Unutma Kültüründen Hatırlama Kültürüne* [*Facing the Past: From Culture of Amnesia to Culture of Memory*]. İstanbul: İletisim, 2007.

Sassen, Saskia. "Towards Post-National and Denationalized Citizenship." In *Handbook of Citizenship Studies*. Edited by Engin Isin and Bryan Turner. London: 2002: 277–91.

Schwartz, Barry. *Abraham Lincoln and the Forge of National Memory*. Chicago: University of Chicago Press, 2000.

Schwarz, Bill. "Memory, Temporality, Modernity: Les Lieux de Memoires." In *Memory: Histories, Theories, Debates*. Edited by Susannah Radstone and Bill Schwarz. New York: Fordham University Press, 2010: 41–58.

Scognamillo, Giovanni. *Türk Sinema Tarihi*. İstanbul: Metis, 2003.

Slide, Anthony. *Ravished Armenia and the Story of Aurora Mardiganian*. Jackson: The University Press of Mississippi, 2014.

Sobchack, Vivian, ed. *The Persistence of History: Cinema, Television and the Modern Event*. New York: Routledge, 1996.

Stam, Robert. *Subversive Pleasures: Bakhtin, Cultural Criticism and Film*. Baltimore: The Johns Hopkins University Press, 1989.

Suner, Asuman. "Speaking the Experience of Political Oppression with a Masculine Voice: Making Feminist Sense of Yılmaz Güney's *Yol*." *Social Identities*, 4, (2), (1998): 283–300.

Suner, Asuman. "Nostalgia for an Imaginary Home: Memory, Space, and Identity in the New Turkish Cinema." *New Perspectives on Turkey*, Autumn 27 (2002): 61–76.

Suner, Asuman. *Hayalet Ev: Yeni Türk Sinemasinda Aidiyet, Kimlik ve Bellek* [*Haunted House: Belonging, Identity and Memory in New Turkish Cinema*]. İstanbul: Metis, 2005.

Suner, Asuman. "Silenced Memories: Notes on Remembering in New Turkish Cinema." *New Cinemas: Journal of Contemporary Film*, 7, (1) (2009): 71–81.

Suner, Asuman. *New Turkish Cinema*. London: I. B. Tauris, 2010.

Thompson, E. Palmer. "Time Work-Discipline and Industrial Capitalism." *Past and Present*, 38 (1967): 56–97.

Tikveş, Özkan. *Mukayeseli Hukukta ve Türk Hukukunda Sinema Filmlerinin Sansürü* [*Film Censorship in Comparative Law and Turkish Law*]. Istanbul: İstanbul Üniversitesi Yayınları, 1968.

Trinh T. Minh-Ha. "Who Is Speaking?: Of Nation Community and First Person Interviews (with Isaac Julien and Laura Mulvey)." In *Framer Framed*. London: Routledge, 1992: 191–210.

Trinh T. Minh-Ha. "The Totalizing Quest of Meaning." In *Theorising Documentary*. Edited by Mihael Renov. New York: Routledge, 1993: 90–107.

Turim, Maureen. *Flashbacks in Film: Memory and History*. New York: Routledge, 1989.

Turner, Victor. *Dramas, Fields and Metaphors: Symbolic Action in Human Society*. Ithaca: Cornell University Press, 1974.

Turner, Victor. *The Ritual Process: Structure and Anti-Structure*. New Brunswick: Aldine Transaction Press, 2008.

Ünal, Ümit. Interview. "Dokuz Kere Turkiye [Nine Times Turkey]." *Radikal*, November 15, 2002.

Ünal, Ümit. E-mail Interview. March 2010.

UNESCO. *Atlas of the World's Languages in Danger*. http://www.unesco.org/culture/languages-atlas/index.php (accessed 29/08/2015).

Üngör, Uğur Ümit, and Mehmet Polatel. *Confiscation and Destruction: The Young Turk Seizure of Armenian Property*. London: Bloomsbury, 2011.

Usher, D. Clarence. *An American Physician in Turkey: A Narrative of Adventures in Peace and in War*. New York: Houghton Mifflin Co., 1917.

Ustaoğlu, Yeşim. "Press Kit: Waiting for the Clouds." Silkroad Productions. http://www.silkroadproduction.com/pdfs/presskit.pdf (accessed 29/08/2015).

Varjabedian, Hrag. "Historicization of the Armenian Catastrophe: From Concrete to the mythical." In *The Armenian Genocide: Cultural and Ethical Legacies*. Edited by Richard Hovannisian. New Brunswick: Transaction Publishers, 2008.

Williams, Raymond. *Marxism and Literature*. Oxford: Oxford University Press, 1977.

White, Hayden. "Historical Emplotment and the Problem of Truth." In *Probing the Limits of Representation: Nazism and the Final Solution*. Edited by Saul Friedlander. Cambridge, MA: Harvard University Press, 1992: 37–53.

White, Hayden. "The Modernist Event." In *The Persistence of History: Cinema, Television and the Modern Event*. Edited by Vivian Sobchack. New York: Routledge, 1996: 17–38.

Wollen, Peter. "Fire and Ice." In *The Cinematic*. Edited by David Campany. London: Whitechapel and MIT Press, 2007: 108–13.

Yeğen, Mesut. *Müstakbel Türk'ten Sözde Vatandaşa* [*From Prospective Turk to Alleged Citizen*]. İstanbul: Metis, 2006.

Yeğen, Mesut. "Turkish Nationalism and the Kurdish Question." *Ethnic and Racial Studies*, 30, no.1 (2007): 119–51.

Yeğen, Mesut. *Devlet Söyleminde Kürt Sorunu* [*Kurdish Issue in State Discourse*]. İstanbul: Metis, 2009a.

Yeğen, Mesut. "İyi Çocuk Kürt" ["The Good Kid Kurd"]. *Radikal 2*, December 22, 2009b.

Yeğen, Mesut. "İki Dil Bir Cumhuriyet" ["Two Languages on Republic"]. *Radikal 2*, October 25, 2009c.

Zurcher, Erik Jan. *Turkey a Modern History*. London: I. B. Tauris, 2004.

Index

Index